Frank Hayward Severance

Old Trails on the Niagara Frontier

Frank Hayward Severance

Old Trails on the Niagara Frontier

ISBN/EAN: 9783743340305

Manufactured in Europe, USA, Canada, Australia, Japa

Cover: Foto ©ninafisch / pixelio.de

Manufactured and distributed by brebook publishing software (www.brebook.com)

Frank Hayward Severance

Old Trails on the Niagara Frontier

Old Trails

on the

Niagara Frontier

By Frank H. Severance

BUFFALO N Y

MDCCCXCIX

TO THE

Young People of the Schools

OF BUFFALO,

Many of whom, on sundry pleasant occasions, have accompanied me, in school-room talks, over some of the Old Trails which run in and out of our home region, these studies of Niagara Frontier History are cordially inscribed.

F. H. S.

CONTENTS.

DEDICATION,	v
PREFACE,	ix
THE CROSS BEARERS,	1
THE PASCHAL OF THE GREAT PINCH,	43
WITH BOLTON AT FORT NIAGARA,	63
WHAT BEFEL DAVID OGDEN,	107
A FORT NIAGARA CENTENNIAL,	141
THE JOURNALS AND JOURNEYS OF AN EARLY BUFFALO MERCHANT,	163
MISADVENTURES OF ROBERT MARSH,	195
UNDERGROUND TRAILS,	227
NIAGARA AND THE POETS,	275

PREFACE.

THE essays herein contained have been written at "odd moments," and for divers purposes. Their chief value lies in the fact that they illustrate, several of them by means of individual experiences, certain typical and well-defined periods in the history of the Niagara region. By "Niagara region," a phrase which no doubt occurs pretty often in the following pages, I mean to designate in a historic, not a scenic, sense the frontier territory of the Niagara from Lake Erie to Lake Ontario. It is a region which has a concrete but as yet for the most part unwritten history of its own. The value of its past to the student, as is ever the case with "local history" in its worthy aspect, depends upon the importance of its relation to the general history of our country. That the Niagara region has played an important part in that history, is an assurance wholly superfluous for even the most casual student of American development. All that the following studies undertake is to give a glimpse, with such fidelity as may be, of events and conditions hereabouts existing, at periods which may fairly be termed typical.

"The Cross Bearers," a paper originally prepared as a lecture for a class that was studying the history of the Catholic Church in America, is, so far as I am aware, the first attempt to review in a single narrative all of the French missions in this immediate vicinity, and the work of the English-speaking missionary priests who said mass in the Niagara region prior to its full organization under ecclesiastical jurisdiction. The data are drawn from the original sources — the Jesuit Relations, Champlain, Le Clercq, Hennepin, Charlevoix, Crespel and other early writers whose works, in any edition, are often inaccessible to the student. For data relating to Bishop Burke, and for other valuable assistance, I am indebted to my friend the Very Rev. Wm. R. Harris, Dean of St. Catharines.

Preface.

"The Paschal of the Great Pinch" is an attempt to picture, in narrative form, conditions conceived to exist at Fort Niagara in 1687–'8, when the Marquis de Denonville made his abortive attempt to occupy that point. Lest any reader shall be in doubt as to the genuineness of the memoirs of the Chevalier De Tregay, I beg to assure him that Lieut. De Tregay is no myth. His name, and practically all the facts on which my sketch is based, will be found in the Paris Documents (IV.), "Documentary History of the State of New York," Vol. I. This paper stands for the French period on the Niagara; the two next following, for the British period.

"With Bolton at Fort Niagara" is almost wholly drawn from unpublished records, chiefly the Haldimand Papers, the originals of which are in the British Museum, but certified copies of which are readily accessible to the student in the Archives at Ottawa. I have made but a slight study of the great mass of material from which practically the history of the Niagara region during the Revolution is to be written; yet it is probable that this slight study makes known for the first time, to students of our home history, such facts as the employment of Hessians on the Niagara during the Revolution, the first bringing hither of the American flag, possibly even the work and fate of Lieut. Col. Bolton himself.

The next paper, "What Befel David Ogden," is drawn from a widely different, though scarcely less known source. The personal narrative is based on an obscure pamphlet by Josiah Priest, published at Lansingburgh, N. Y., in 1840. I am aware that Priest is not altogether trustworthy as a historian. Dr. Thos. W. Field calls him a "prolific, needy and unscrupulous author" [*See* "An Essay Toward an Indian Bibliography"]; yet he concedes to his works "a large amount of historic material obtained at some pains from sources more or less authentic." My judgment is, that Priest is least trustworthy in his more ambitious work; whereas his unpretentious pamphlets, wretchedly printed at a country press sixty years ago, contain true narratives of individual undertakings in the Revolution, Indian captivities and other pioneer experiences, gathered by the writer direct from the hero whose adventures he wrote down, without literary skill it is true, but also without apparent perversion or exaggeration. The very circumstantiality with which David Ogden's experiences are narrated is evidence of their genuineness. Corroborative evidence is also furnished by the lately-published muster-rolls of New York regiments during the Revolution. In the Third Regiment of Tryon County militia, among the enlisted men, appears the name of David Ogden ["New York in the Revolution," 2d ed., p. 181], and there was but one David Ogden, not merely in the Tryon County militia, but so far as these records show, in the entire soldiery of New York State. In the same regiment there was also a "Daniel" Ogden, Sr., possibly David's father. The name Daniel Ogden also occurs in the list of Tryon County Rangers ["New York in the Revolution," 2d ed., p. 186], a service in which we would naturally expect to find one whom the Indian Brant called "the beaver hunter, that old scouter." In short, I think we may accept David as altogether genuine, and in his adventures — never told before, I believe, as a part of Niagara history — may find an example of patriotic suffering and endurance wholly typical of what many another underwent at that time and in this region.

The "Fort Niagara Centennial Address" is here included because its most important part relates to that period in our history immediately following the Revolution, the "hold-over period," during which, for thirteen years after the Treaty of 1783, the British continued to occupy Fort Niagara and other lake posts. What I say on the negotiations leading to the final relinquishment of Fort Niagara is based on information gleaned from the manuscript records in London and Ottawa.

"The Journals and Journeys of an Early Buffalo Merchant" is also a contribution to local annals from an unpublished source, being drawn from the MS. journals of John Lay, very kindly placed in my hands by members of his family. They afford a picture of conditions hereabouts and elsewhere, during the years 1810–'23, which I have thought worthy of preservation.

Preface.

In the "Misadventures of Robert Marsh" I have endeavored by means of a personal narrative to illustrate another period in our history. The misguided Marsh fairly stands for many of the so-called Patriots whose uprising on this border is known as Mackenzie's Rebellion of 1837–'8. The considerable literature on this subject includes a number of personal narratives, for the most part published in small editions and now hard to find; but the scarcest of all, so far as my experience has discovered, is that from which I have drawn the story of Robert Marsh: "Seven Years of My Life, or Narrative of a Patriot Exile, who together with eighty-two American Citizens were illegally tried for rebellion in Upper Canada and transported to Van Dieman's Land," etc., etc. It is an exceedingly prolix and pretentious title, after the fashion of the time, prefacing a badly-written, poorly-printed volume of 207 pages, turned out by the press of Faxon & Stevens, Buffalo, 1848. In view of the fact that neither in Sabin nor any other bibliography have I found any mention of this book, and the further fact that in fifteen years of somewhat diligent book-hunting I have discovered but one copy, it is no exaggeration to call Marsh's "Narrative" "scarce," if not "rare."

The incidents related in "Underground Trails" are illustrative of many an episode at the eastern end of Lake Erie in the days preceding the Civil War. I had the facts of the principal adventures some years ago from the late Mr. Frank Henry of Erie, Pa., who had himself been a participant in more than one worthy enterprise of the Underground Railroad. Sketches based on information supplied by Mr. Henry, and originally written out for the Erie Gazette, are the latter part of the paper as it now stands.

The last essay, "Niagara and the Poets," is a following of "Old Trails" chiefly in a literary sense, but it is thought its inclusion here will not be found inappropriate to the general character of the collection.

I must add a word of grateful acknowledgment for help received from Douglas Brymner, Dominion Archivist, at Ottawa; from the Hon. Peter A. Porter of Niagara Falls, N. Y., Charles W. Dobbins of New York City, and John Miller, Erie, Pa.   F. H. S.

The Cross Bearers.

THE CROSS BEARERS.

I INVITE YOU to consider briefly with me the beginnings of known history in our home region. Of the general character of that history, as a part of the exploration and settlement of the lake region, you are already familiar. What I undertake is to direct special attention to a few of the individuals who made that history — for history, in the ultimate analysis, is merely the record of the result of personal character and influence; and it is striking to note how relatively few and individual are the dominating minds.

Remembering this, when we turn to trace the story of the Niagara, we find the initial impulses strikingly different from those which lie at the base of history in many places. Often the first chapter in the story is a record of war for war's sake — the aim being conquest, acquisition of territory, or the search for gold. Not so here. The first invasion of white men in this mid-lake region was a mission of peace and good will. Our history begins in a sweet and heroic obedience to commands passed down direct from the Founder of Christianity Himself. Into these wilds, long before the banner of any earthly kingdom was planted here, was borne the cross of Christ. Here the crucifix preceded the sword; the altar was built before the hearth.

Now, I care not what the faith of the student be, he cannot escape the facts. The cross is stamped upon the first page of our home history — of this Buffalo and the banks of the Niagara; and whoever would know something of that history must follow the footsteps of those who first brought the cross to these shores. It is, therefore, a brief following of the personal experiences of these early cross bearers that we undertake; but first, a word may be permitted by way of reminder as to the conditions here existing when our recorded history begins.

From remote days unrecorded, the territory bordering the Niagara, between Lakes Erie and Ontario, was occupied by a nation of Indians called the Neuters. A few of their villages were on the east side of the river, the easternmost being supposed to have stood near the present site of Lockport. The greater part of the Niagara peninsula of Ontario and the north shore of Lake Erie was their territory. To the east of them, in the Genesee valley and beyond, dwelt the Senecas, the westernmost of the Iroquois tribes. To the north of them, on Lake Huron and the Georgian Bay, dwelt the Hurons. About 1650 the Iroquois overran the Neuter territory, destroyed the nation and made the region east of the Niagara a part of their own territory; though more than a century elapsed, after their conquest of the Neuters, before the Senecas made permanent villages on Buffalo Creek and near the Niagara. It is necessary to bear this fact in mind, in considering the visits of white men to this region during that period; it had become territory of the Senecas, but they only occupied it at intervals, on hunting or fishing expeditions.

During the latter years of Neuter possession of our region, missionaries began to approach the Niagara from two directions; but long before any brave soul had neared it through what is now New York State,— then the heart of the fierce Iroquois country,— others, more successful, had come down from the early-established missions among the Hurons, had sojourned among the Neuters and had offered Christian prayers among the savages east of the Niagara.

Note, therefore, that the first white man known to have visited the Niagara region was a Catholic priest. Moreover, so far as is ascertained, he was the first man, coming from what is now Canada, to bring the Christian faith into the present territory of the United States. This man was Joseph de la Roche Dallion.[1] The date of his visit is 1626.

Father Dallion was a Franciscan of the Recollect reform, who had been for a time at the mission among the Hurons, then carried on jointly by priests and lay brothers of the Recollects and also by Fathers of the

---

[1] Often spelled "Daillon" or "d'Allion," the latter form suggesting origin from the name of a place, as is common in the French. Charlevoix sometimes wrongly has it "de Dallion." I follow the spelling as given in the priest's own signature to a letter to a friend in Paris, dated at "Tonachain [Toanchain], Huron village, this 18th July, 1627," and signed "Joseph De La Roche Dallion." The student of seventeenth-century history need not be reminded that little uniformity in the spelling of proper names can be looked for, either in printed books or manuscripts. In French, as in English, men spelled their names in different ways — Shakespeare, it is said, achieving thirty-nine variations. The matter bears on our present study because the diversity of spelling may involve the young student in perplexity. Thus, the name of the priests Lalemant (there were three of them) is given by Le Clercq as "Lallemant," by Charlevoix

Society of Jesus. On October 18th of this year (1626), he left his companions, resolved to carry the cross among the people of the Neuter nation. An interpreter, Bruslé, had "told wonders" of these people. Bruslé, it would seem, therefore, had been among them; and although, as I have said, Father Dallion was the first white man known to have reached the Niagara, yet it is just to consider the probabilities in the case of this all but unknown interpreter. There are plausible grounds for belief, but no proof, that Étienne Bruslé was the first white man who ever saw Niagara Falls. No adventurer in our region had a more remarkable career than his, yet but little of it is known to us. He was with Champlain on his journey to the Huron country. He left that explorer in September, 1615, at the outlet of Lake Simcoe, and went on a most perilous mission into the country of the Andastes, allies of the Hurons, to enlist them against the Iroquois. The Andastes lived on the head-waters of the Susquehanna, and along the south shore of Lake Erie, the present site of Buffalo being generally included within the bounds of their territory. Champlain saw nothing

---

(a much later historian) as "Lallemant" or "Lalemant," but in the contemporary "Relations" of 1641-'42 as "Lallemant," "Lalemant" or "L'allemant." Many other names are equally variable, changes due to elision being sometimes, but not always, indicated by accents, as "Bruslé," "Brûlé." Thus we have "Jolliet" or "Joliet," "De Gallinée" or "De Galinée," "Du Lu," "Du Luth," "Duluth," etc. When we turn to modern English, the confusion is much — and needlessly — increased. Dr. Shea, the learned translator and editor of Le Clercq, apparently aimed to put all the names into English, without accents. Parkman, or his publishers, have been guilty of many inconsistencies, now speaking of "Brébeuf," now of "Brebeuf," and changing "Le Clercq" to "Le Clerc." The "Historical Writings" of Buffalo's pre-eminent student in this field, Orsamus H. Marshall, share with many less valuable works — the present, no doubt, among them — these inconsistencies of style in the use of proper names.

more of Bruslé for three years, but in the summer of 1618 met him at Saut St. Louis. Bruslé had had wonderful adventures, had even been bound to the stake and burned so severely that he must have been frightfully scarred. The name by which we know him may have been given him on this account. He was saved from death by what the Indians regarded as an exhibition of wrath on the part of the Great Spirit. I find no trace of him between 1618 and 1626, when Father Dallion appears to have taken counsel of him regarding the Neuters. Bruslé was murdered by the Hurons near Penetanguishene in 1632. What is known of him is learned from Champlain's narrative of the voyage of 1618 (edition of 1627). Sagard also speaks of him, and says he made an exploration of the upper lakes—a claim not generally credited. Parkman, drawing from these sources and the "Relations," tells his story in "The Pioneers of France in the New World," admiringly calls him "That Pioneer of Pioneers," and says that he seems to have visited the Eries in 1615.

The interesting thing about him in connection with our present study is the fact that he appears to have been the forerunner of Dallion among the savages of the Niagara. There is no white man named in history who may be even conjectured, with any plausibility, to have visited the Niagara earlier than Bruslé.[1]

---

[1] Mr. Consul W. Butterfield, whose "History of Brûlé's Discoveries and Explorations, 1610-1626," has appeared since the above was written, is of opinion that Brûlé did not visit the falls, nor gain any particular knowledge of Lake Erie, as that lake is not shown on Champlain's map of 1632; but that he and his Indian escort crossed the Niagara near Lake Ontario, "into what is now Western New York, in the present county of Niagara,"

Stimulated by this interpreter's reports, by the encouragement of his companions and the promptings of his own zeal, Father Dallion set out for the unknown regions. Two Frenchmen, Grenole and Lavallée, accompanied him. They tramped the trail for six days through the woods, apparently rounding the western end of Lake Ontario, and coming eastward through the Niagara Peninsula. They were well received at the villages, given venison, squashes and parched corn to eat, and were shown no sign of hostility. "All were astonished to see me dressed as I was," writes the father, "and to see that I desired nothing of theirs, except that I invited them by signs to lift their eyes to heaven, make the sign of the cross and receive the faith of Jesus Christ." The good priest, however, had another object, somewhat unusual to the men of his calling. At the sixth village, where he had been advised to remain, a council was held. "There I told them, as well as I could, that I came on behalf of the French to contract alliance and friendship with them, and to invite them to come to trade. I also begged them to allow me to remain in their country, to be able to instruct them in the law of our God, which is the only means of going to paradise." The

---

and that "the journey was doubtless pursued through what are now the counties of Erie, Genesee, Wyoming, Livingston, Steuben and Chemung into Tioga," and thence down the Susquehanna. It is probable that Brûlé's party would follow existing trails, and one of the best defined trails, at a later period when the Senecas occupied the country as far west as the Niagara, followed this easterly course; but there were other trails, one of which lay along the east bank of the Niagara. So long as we have no other original source of information except Champlain, Sagard and Le Caron, none of whom has left any explicit record of Brûlé's journeyings hereabouts, so long must his exact path in the Niagara region remain untraced.

Neuters accepted the priest's offers, and the first recorded trade in the Niagara region was made when he presented them "little knives and other trifles." They adopted him into the tribe, and gave him a father, the chief Souharissen.

After this cordial welcome, Grenole and Lavallée returned to the Hurons, leaving Father Joseph "the happiest man in the world, hoping to do something there to advance God's glory, or at least to discover the means, which would be no small thing, and to endeavor to discover the mouth of the river of Hiroquois, in order to bring them to trade." After speaking of the people and his efforts to teach them, he continues: "I have always seen them constant in their resolution to go with at least four canoes to the trade, if I would guide them, the whole difficulty being that we did not know the way. Yroquet, an Indian known in those countries, who had come there with twenty of his men hunting for beaver, and who took fully 500, would never give us any mark to know the mouth of the river. He and several Hurons assured us that it was only ten days' journey to the trading place; but we were afraid of taking one river for another, and losing our way or dying of hunger on the land." So excellent an authority as Dr. John Gilmary Shea says: "This was evidently the Niagara River, and the route through Lake Ontario. He (Dallion) apparently crossed the river, as he was on the Iroquois frontier." The great conquest of the Neuters by the Iroquois was not until 1648 or 1650. Just what the "Iroquois frontier" was in 1627 is uncertain. It appears to have been about midway between the Niagara and the Genesee, the easternmost Neuter village being some thirty miles east of the Niagara. The Recollect appears therefore as the first man to write of the Niagara, from personal knowledge, and of its mouth as a place of trade. The above quotations are from the letter Father Dallion wrote to one of his friends in France July 18, 1627, he having then returned to Toanchain, a Huron village. I have followed the text as given by Sagard. It is significant that Le Clercq, in his "Premier Établissement de la Foy," etc., gives a portion of Dallion's account of his visit to the Neuters, but omits nearly everything he says about trade.

Father Dallion sojourned three winter months with the Neuters, but the latter part of the stay was far from agreeable. The Hurons, he says, having discovered that he talked of leading the Neuters to trade, at once spread false and evil reports of him. They said he was a great magician; that he was a poisoner, that he tainted the air of the country where he tarried, and that if the Neuters did not kill him, he would burn their villages and kill their children. The priest was at a disadvantage in not having much command of the Neuter dialect, and it is not strange, after the evil report had once been started, that he should have seemed to engage in some devilish incantation whenever he held the cross before them or sought to baptize the children. When one reflects upon the dense wall of ignorance and superstition against which his every effort at moral or spiritual teaching was impotent, the admiration for the martyr spirit which animated the effort is tempered by amazement that an acute and sagacious man should have thought it well to "labor" in such an obviously ineffective way. But history is full of instances of ardent devotion to aims which the "practical" man would denounce at once as unattainable. That Father Dallion was animated by the spirit of the martyrs is attested in his own account of what befel him. A treacherous band of ten came to him and tried to pick a quarrel. "One knocked me down with a blow of his fist, another took an ax and tried to split my head. God averted his hand; the blow fell on a post near me. I also received much other ill-treatment; but that is what we came to seek in this country." His assailants robbed him of many of his possessions, including his breviary and compass. These precious things, which were no doubt "big medicine" in the eyes of his ungracious hosts, were afterwards returned. The news of his maltreatment reached the ears of Fathers Brébeuf and De la Nouë at the Huron mission. They sent the messenger, Grenole, to bring him back, if found alive. Father Dallion returned with Grenole early in the year 1627; and so ended the first recorded visit of white man to the Niagara region.

For fourteen years succeeding, I find no allusion to our district. Then comes an episode which is so adventurous and so heroic, so endowed with beauty and devotion, that it should be familiar to all who give any heed to what has happened in the vicinity of the Niagara.

Jean de Brébeuf was a missionary priest of the Jesuits. That implies much; but in his case even such a general imputation of exalted qualities falls short of justice. His is a superb figure, a splendid acquisition to the line of heroic figures that pass in shadowy procession along the horizon of our home history. Trace the narrative of his life as sedulously as we may, examine his character and conduct in whatever critical light we may choose to study them, and still the noble figure of Father Brébeuf is seen without a flaw. There were those of his order whose acts were at times open to two constructions. Some of them were charged, by men of other faith and hostile allegiance, with using their priestly privileges as a cloak for worldly objects. No such charge was ever brought against Father Brébeuf. The guilelessness and heroism of his life are unassailable.

He was of a noble Normandy family, and when he comes upon the scene, on the banks of the Niagara, he was forty-seven years old. He had come out to Quebec fifteen years before and had been assigned to the Huron mission. In 1628 he was called back to Quebec, but five years later he was allowed to return to his charge in the remote wilderness. The record of his work and sufferings there is not a part of our present story. Those who seek a marvelous exemplification of human endurance and devotion, may find it in the ancient Relations of the order. He lived amid threats and plots against his life, he endured what seems unendurable, and his zeal throve on the experience. In November, 1640, he and a companion, the priest Joseph Chaumonot, resolved to carry the cross to the Neuter nation. They no doubt knew of Father Dallion's dismal experience; and were spurred on thereby. Like him, they sought martyrdom. Their route from the Huron country to the Niagara has been traced with skill and probable accuracy by the Very Rev. Wm. R. Harris, Dean of St. Catharines. At this time the Neuter nation lived to the north of Lake Erie throughout what we know as the Niagara Peninsula, and on both sides of the Niagara, their most eastern village being near the present site of Lockport. From an uncertain boundary, thereabouts, they confronted the possessions of the Senecas, who a few years later were to wipe them off the face of the earth and occupy all their territory east of the lake and river.

Fathers Brébeuf and Chaumonot set out on their hazardous mission November 2d, in the year named, from a Huron town in the present township of Medonte, Ontario. (Near Penetanguishene, on Georgian Bay.) Their probable path was through the present towns of Beeton, Orangeville, Georgetown, Hamilton and St. Catharines. They came out upon the Niagara just north of the Queenston escarpment. The journey thus far had been a succession of hardships. The interpreters whom they had engaged to act as guides deserted them at the outset. Ahead of them went the reputation which the Hurons spread abroad, that they were magicians and carried all manner of evils with them. Father Brébeuf was a man of extraordinary physical strength. Many a time, in years gone by, he had astonished the Indians by his endurance at the paddle, and in carrying great loads over the portages. His companion, Chaumonot, was smaller and weaker, but was equally sustained by faith in Divine guidance. On their way through the forests, Father Brébeuf was cheered by a vision of angels, beckoning him on; but when he and his companion finally stood on the banks of the Niagara, under the leaden sky of late November, there was little of the beatific in the prospect. They crossed the swirling stream — by what means must be left to conjecture, the probability being in favor of a light bark canoe — and on the eastern bank found themselves in the hostile village of Onguiara — the first-mentioned settlement on the banks of our river.

Here the half-famished priests were charged with having come to ruin the people. They were refused shelter and food, but finally found opportunity to step into a wigwam, where Indian custom, augmented by fear, permitted them to remain. The braves gathered around, and proposed to put them to death. "I am tired," cried one, "eating the dark flesh of our enemies, and I want to taste the white flesh of the Frenchman." So at least is the record in the Relation. Another drew bow to pierce the heart of Chaumonot; but all fell back in awe when the stalwart Brébeuf stepped forth into their midst, without weapon and without fear, and raising his hand exclaimed: "We have not come here for any other purpose than to do you a friendly service. We wish to teach you to worship the Master of Life, so that you may be happy in this world and in the other."

Whether or not any of the spiritual import of his speech was comprehended cannot be said; but the temper of the crowd changed, so that, instead of threatening immediate death, they began to take a curious, childish interest in the two "black-gowns"; examining the priests' clothes, and appropriating their hats and other loose articles. The travelers completely mystified them by reading a written message, and thus getting at another's thoughts without a spoken word. The Relation is rich in details of this sort, and of the wretchedness of the life which the missionaries led. They visited other "towns," as the collections of bark wigwams are called; but everywhere they were looked upon as necromancers, and their lives were spared only through fear.

Far into the winter the priests endured all manner of hardship. Food was sometimes thrown to them as to a worthless dog, sometimes denied altogether, and then they had to make shift with such roots and barks or chance game as their poor woodcraft enabled them to procure, or the meager winter woods afforded. On one occasion, when a chief frankly told them that his people would have killed them long before, but for fear that the spirits of the priests would in vengeance destroy them, Brébeuf began to assure him that his mission was only to do good; whereupon the savage replied by spitting in the priest's face; and the priest thanked God that he was worthy of the same indignity which had been put upon Jesus Christ. When one faces his foes in such a spirit, there is absolutely nothing to fear. And yet, after four months of these experiences, there seems not to have been the slightest sign of any good result. The savages were as invulnerable to any moral or spiritual teachings as the chill earth itself. Dumb brutes would have shown more return for kindness than they. The saying of Chateaubriand, that man without religion is the most dangerous animal that walks the earth, found full justification in these savages. Finally, Brébeuf and his associate determined to withdraw from the absolutely fruitless field, and began to retrace their steps towards Huronia.

It was near the middle of February, 1641, when they began their retreat from the land of the Neuters. The story of that retreat, as indeed of the whole mission, has been most beautifully told, with a sympathetic fervency impossible for one not richly endowed with faith to simulate, by Dean Harris. Let his account of what happened stand here:

"The snow was falling when they left the village Onguiara, crossed the Niagara River near Queenston, ascended its banks and disappeared in the shadowy forest. The path, which led through an unbroken wilderness, lay buried in snow. The cold pierced them through and through. The cords on Fr. Chaumonot's snow-shoe broke, and his stiffened fingers could scarcely tie the knot. Innumerable flakes of snow were falling from innumerable branches. Their only food was a pittance of Indian corn mixed with melted snow; their only guide, a compass. Worn and spent with hardships, these saintly men, carrying in sacks their portable altar, were returning to announce to their priestly companions on the Wye the dismal news of their melancholy failure and defeat. There was not a hungry wolf that passed them but looked back and half forgave their being human. There was not a tree but looked down upon them with pity and commiseration. Night was closing in when, spent with fatigue, they saw smoke rising at a distance. Soon they reached a clearing and descried before them a cluster of bark lodges. Here these Christian soldiers of the cross bivouacked for the night.

"Early that evening while Chaumonot, worn with traveling and overcome with sleep, threw himself to rest on a bed that was not made up since the creation of the world, Father Brébeuf, to escape for a time the acrid and pungent smoke that filled the cabin, went out to commune with God alone in prayer. . . . He moved toward the margin of the woods, when presently he stopped as if transfixed. Far away to the southeast, high in the air and boldly outlined, a huge cross floated suspended in mid-heaven. Was it stationary? No, it moved toward him from the land of the Iroquois. The saintly face lighted with unwonted splendor, for he saw in the vision the presage of the martyr's crown. Tree and hillside, lodge and village, faded away, and while the cross was still slowly approaching, the soul of the great priest went out in ecstasy, in loving adoration to his Lord and his God. . . . Overcome with emotion, he exclaimed, 'Who will separate me from the love of my Lord? Shall tribulation, nakedness, peril, distress, or famine, or the sword?' Emparadised in ecstatic vision, he again cries out with enthusiastic loyalty, '*Sentio me vehementer impelli ad moriendum pro Christo*'—'I feel within me a mighty impulse to die for Christ'—and flinging himself upon his knees as a victim for the sacrifice or a holocaust for sin, he registered his wondrous vow to meet martyrdom, when it came to him, with the joy and resignation befitting a disciple of his Lord.

"When he returned to himself the cross had faded away, innumerable stars were brightly shining, the cold was wrapping him in icy mantle, and he retraced his footsteps to the smoky cabin. He flung himself beside his weary brother and laid him down to rest. When morning broke they began anew their toilsome journey, holding friendly converse.

"'Was the cross large?' asked Father Chaumonot.

"'Large,' spoke back the other, 'yes, large enough to crucify us all.'"

It is idle to insist on judgments by the ordinary standards in a case like this. As Parkman says, it belongs not to history, but to psychology. Brébeuf saw the luminous cross in the heavens above the

Niagara; not the material, out-reaching arms of Niagara's spray, rising columnar from the chasm, then resting, with crosslike extensions on the quiet air, white and pallid under the winter moon. Such phenomena are not unusual above the cataract, but may not be offered in explanation of the priest's vision. He was in the neighborhood of Grimsby, full twenty miles from the falls, when he saw the cross; much too far away to catch the gleam of frosted spray. Nor is it a gracious spirit which seeks a material explanation for his vision. The cross truly presaged his martyrdom; and although the feet of Father Brébeuf never again sought the ungrateful land of the Neuters, yet his visit and his vision were not wholly without fruit. They endow local history with an example of pure devotion to the betterment of others, unsurpassed in all the annals of the holy orders. To Brébeuf the miraculous cross foretold martyrdom, and thereby was it a sign of conquest and of victory to this heroic Constantine of the Niagara.

After Brébeuf and Chaumonot had turned their backs on the Neuters, the Niagara region was apparently unvisited by white men for more than a quarter of a century. These were not, however, years of peaceful hunting and still more placid corn and pumpkin-growing, such as some romantic writers have been fond of ascribing to the red men when they were unmolested by the whites. As a matter of fact, and as Fathers Dallion, Brébeuf and Chaumonot had discovered, the people who claimed the banks of the lower reaches of the Niagara as within their territory, were the embodiment of all that was vile and barbarous. There is no record that they had a village at the angle of lake and river, where now stands old Fort Niagara. It would have been strange, however, if they did not occasionally occupy that sightly plateau with their wigwams or huts, while they were laying in a supply of fish. If trees ever covered the spot they were killed by early camp-fires, probably long before the coming of the whites. Among the earliest allusions to the point is one which speaks of the difficulty of getting wood there; and such a treeless tract, in this part of the country, could usually be attributed to the denudation consequent on Indian occupancy.

A decade or so after the retreat of the missionaries came that fierce Indian strife which annihilated the Neuters and gave Niagara's banks into the keeping of the fiercer but somewhat nobler Iroquois. The story of this Indian war has been told with all possible illumination from the few meager records that are known; and it only concerns the present chronicle to note that about 1650 the site of Fort Niagara passed under Seneca domination. The Senecas had no permanent town in the vicinity, but undoubtedly made it a rendezvous for war parties, and for hunting and fishing expeditions.

Meanwhile, the Jesuits in their Relations, and after them the cartographers in Europe, were making hearsay allusions to the Niagara or locating it, with much

The Cross Bearers.

inaccuracy, on their now grotesque maps. In 1648 the Jesuit Ragueneau, writing to the Superior at Paris, mentions Niagara, which he had never seen or approached, as "a cataract of frightful height." L'Allemant in the Relation published in 1642, had alluded to the river, but not to the fall. Sanson, in 1656, put "Ongiara" on his famous map; and four years later the map of Creuxius, published with his great "Historiæ Canadensis," gave our river and fall the Latin dignity of "Ongiara Catarractes." One map-maker copied from another, so that even by the middle of the seventeenth century, the reading and student world — small and ecclesiastical as it mostly was — began to have some inkling of the main features and continental position of the mid-lake region for the possession of which, a little later, several Forts Niagara were to be projected. It is not, however, until 1669 that we come to another definite episode in the history of the region.

In that year came hither the Sulpitian missionaries, François Dollier de Casson and René de Bréhant[1] de Galinée. They were bent on carrying the cross to nations hitherto unreached, on Western rivers. With them was the young Robert Cavelier, known as La Salle, who was less interested in carrying the cross than in exploring the country. Their expedition left Montreal July 6th, nine canoes in all. They made their way up the St. Lawrence, skirted the south shore of Lake Ontario, and on Aug. 10th were at Irondequoit Bay.

---

[1] "Brehan de Gallinée," in Margry. Shea has it "Brehaut de Galinée."

They made a most eventful visit to the Seneca villages south of the bay. Thence they continued westward, apparently by Indian trails overland, and not by canoe. De Galinée, who was the historian of the expedition, says that they came to a river "one eighth of a league broad and extremely rapid, forming the outlet or communication from Lake Erie to Lake Ontario," and he continues with a somewhat detailed account of Niagara Falls, which, although he passed near them, he did not turn aside to see. The Sulpitians and La Salle crossed the river, apparently below Lewiston. They may indeed have come to the river at its mouth, skirting the lake shore. One may infer either course from the narrative of de Galinée, which goes on to say that five days after passing the river they "arrived at the extremity of Lake Ontario, where there is a fine, large sandy bay . . . and where we unloaded our canoes."

Pushing on westward, late in September, on the trail between Burlington Bay and the Grand River, they met Joliet, returning from his expedition in search of copper mines on Lake Superior. This meeting in the wilderness is a suggestive and picturesque subject, but we may not dwell on it here. Joliet, though he had thus preceded La Salle and the Sulpitians in the exploration of the lakes, had gone west by the old northern route along the Ottawa, Lake Nipissing and the French River. He was never on the Niagara, for after his meeting with La Salle, he continued eastward by way of the Grand River valley and Lake Ontario. Fear of the savages deterred him from coming by way of the

The Cross Bearers.

Niagara, and thereby, it is not unlikely, becoming the white discoverer of Niagara Falls.[1] He was the first white man, so far as records relate, to come eastward through the Detroit River and Lake Erie. Our lake was therefore "discovered" from the west—a fact perhaps without parallel in the history of American exploration.

After the meeting with Joliet, La Salle left the missionaries, who, taking advantage of information had from Joliet, followed the Grand River down to Lake Erie. Subsequently they passed through Lake Erie to the westward, the first of white men to explore the lake in that direction. De Galinée's map (1669) is the first that gives us the north shore of Lake Erie with approximate

---

[1] Why Joliet left the Lake Erie route on his way east, for one much more difficult, has been a matter of some discussion. According to the Abbé Galinée, he was induced to turn aside by an Iroquois Indian who had been a prisoner among the Ottawas. Joliet persuaded the Ottawas to let this prisoner return with him. As they drew near the Niagara the Iroquois became afraid lest he should fall into the hands of the ancient enemies of the Iroquois, the Andastes, although the habitat of that people is usually given as from about the site of Buffalo to the west and southwest. At any rate it was the representations of this Iroquois prisoner and guide which apparently turned Joliet into the Grand River and kept him away from the Niagara. The paragraph in de Galinée bearing on the matter is as follows:

" Ce fut cet Iroquois qui montra à M. Jolliet un nouveau chemin que les François n'avoient point sceu jusques alors pour revenir des Outaouacs dans le pays des Iroquois. Cependant la crainte que ce sauvage eut de retomber entre les mains des Antastoes luy fit dire à M. Jolliet qu'il falloit qu'il quittast son canot et marchast par terre plustost qu'il n'eust fallu, et mesme sans cette terreur du sauvage, M. Jolliet eust pu venir par eau jusques dans le lac Ontario, en faisant un portage de demi-lieue pour éviter le grand sault dont j'ay déjà parlé, mais enfin il fut obligé par son guide de faire cinquante lieues par terre, et abandonner son canot sur le bord du lac Erié."

It is singular that so important a relation in the history of our region has never been published in English. De Galinée's original MS. Journal is preserved in the Bibliothèque Nationale, in Paris. It was first printed in French by M. Pierre Margry in 1879; but five years prior to that date Mr. O. H. Marshall of Buffalo, having been granted access to M. Margry's MS. copy, made extracts, which were printed in English in 1874. These were only a small portion of the Abbé's valuable record. The Ontario Historical Society has for some time contemplated the translation and publication of the complete Journal—a work which students of the early history of the lake region will hope soon to see accomplished.

accuracy. On October 15th this devout man and his companion reached Lake Erie, which they described as "a vast sea, tossed by tempestuous winds." Deterred by the lateness of the season from attempting further travel by this course, they determined to winter where they were, and built a cabin for their shelter.

Occasionally they were visited in their hut by Iroquois beaver hunters. For five months and eleven days they remained in their winter quarters and on the 23d of March, 1670, being Passion Sunday, they erected a cross as a memorial of their long sojourn. The official record of the act is as follows :

"We the undersigned certify that we have seen affixed on the lands of the lake called Erié the arms of the King of France with this inscription : 'The year of salvation 1669, Clement IX. being seated in St. Peter's chair, Louis XIV. reigning in France, M. de Courcelle being Governor of New France, and M. Talon being intendant therein for the King, there arrived in this place two missionaries from Montreal accompanied by seven other Frenchmen, who, the first of all European peoples, have wintered on this lake, of which, as of a territory not occupied, they have taken possession in the name of their King by the apposition of his arms, which they have attached to the foot of this cross. In witness whereof we have signed the present certificate.'

"FRANÇOIS DOLLIER,
"Priest of the Diocese of Nantes in Brittany.
"DE GALINÉE,
"Deacon of the Diocese of Rennes in Brittany."

The winter was exceedingly mild, but the stream[1] was still frozen on the 26th of March, when they portaged their canoes and goods to the lake to resume

---
[1] Probably that now known as Patterson's Creek.

their westward journey. Unfortunately losing one of their canoes in a gale they were obliged to divide their party, four men with the luggage going in the two remaining canoes; while the rest, including the missionaries, undertook the wearisome journey on foot all the way from Long Point to the mouth of the Kettle Creek. De Galinée grows enthusiastic in his admiration for the immense quantities of game and fruits opposite Long Point and calls the country the terrestrial Paradise of Canada. "The grapes were as large and as sweet as the finest in France. The wine made from them was as good as *vin de Grave.*" He admires the profusion of walnuts, chestnuts, wild apples and plums. Bears were fatter and better to the palate than the most "savory" pigs in France. Deer wandered in herds of fifty to an hundred. Sometimes even two hundred would be seen feeding together. Before arriving at the sand beach which then connected Long Point with the mainland they had to cross two streams. To cross the first stream they were forced to walk four leagues inland before they found a satisfactory place to cross. One whole day was spent in constructing a raft to cross Big Creek, and after another delay caused by a severe snow-storm, they successfully effected a crossing and found on the west side a marshy meadow two hundred paces wide into which they sank to their girdles in mud and slush. Beset by dangers and retarded by inclement weather, they at last arrived at Kettle Creek, where they expected to find the canoe in which Joliet had come down Lake Huron and the

Detroit and which he had told them was hidden there. Great was their disappointment to find that the Indians had taken it. However, later in the day, while gathering some wood for a fire, they found the canoe between two logs and joyfully bore it to the lake. In the vicinity of their encampment the hunters failed to secure any game, and for four or five days the party subsisted on boiled maize. The whole party then paddled up the lake to a place where game was plentiful and the hunters saw more than two hundred deer in one herd, but missed their aim. Disheartened at their failure and craving meat, they shot and skinned a miserable wolf and had it ready for the kettle when one of the men saw some thirty deer on the other side of the small lake they were on. The party succeeded in surrounding the deer and, forcing them into the water, killed ten of them. Now well supplied with both fresh and smoked meat, they continued their journey, traveled nearly fifty miles in one day and came to a beautiful sand beach (Point Pelée), where they drew up their canoes and camped for the night. During the night a terrific gale came up from the northeast. Awakened by the storm they made all shift to save their canoes and cargoes. Dollier's and de Galinée's canoes were saved, but the other one was swept away with its contents of provisions, goods for barter, ammunition, and, worst of all, the altar service, with which they intended establishing their mission among the Pottawatamies.

The loss of their altar service caused them to aban-

The Cross Bearers. 25

don the mission and they set out to return to Montreal, but strangely enough chose the long, roundabout journey by way of the Detroit, Lake Huron and the French River, in preference to the route by which they had come, or by the outlet of Lake Erie, which they had crossed the autumn before. Thus de Galinée and Dollier de Casson, like Joliet,— not to revert to Champlain half a century earlier,— missed the opportunity, which seemed to wait for them, of exploring the eastern end of Lake Erie, of correctly mapping the Niagara and observing and describing its incomparable cataract. Obviously the Niagara region was shunned less on account of its real difficulties, which were not then known, than through terror of the Iroquois. Our two Sulpitians reached Montreal June 18, 1670, which date marks the close of the third missionary visitation in the history of the Niagara.

And now I approach the point at which many writers of our local history have chosen to begin their story— the famous expedition of La Salle and his companions in 1678-'79. For the purpose of the present study we may omit the more familiar aspects of that adventure, and limit our regard to the acts of the holy men who continue the interrupted chain of missionary work on the Niagara. On December 6th, St. Nicholas Day, 1678, with an advance party under La Motte de Lussiére, came the Flemish Recollect, Louis Hennepin. As the bark in which they had crossed stormy Lake Ontario at length entered the Niagara, they chanted the Ambrosian hymn, "Te Deum Laudamus," and there is no gainsaying the sincerity of that thank-offering for perils escaped. Five days later, being encamped on the present site of Niagara, Ont., Father Hennepin celebrated the first mass ever said in the vicinity. A few days later, on the site of Lewiston, he had completed a bark chapel, in which was held the first Christian service which had been held on the eastern side of the Niagara since the visit of Brébeuf thirty-eight years before. Father Hennepin has left abundant chronicles of his activities on the Niagara. As soon as the construction of the Griffon was begun above the falls a chapel was established there, near the mouth of Cayuga Creek. Having blessed this pioneer vessel of the upper lakes, when she was launched, he set out for Fort Frontenac in the interests of the enterprise, and was accompanied to the Niagara, on his return, by the Superior of the mission, Father Gabriel de la Ribourde, and Fathers Zénobius Membré and Melithon Watteaux. All through that summer these devoted priests shared the varied labors of the camp. Hennepin tells us how he and his companions toiled back and forth over the portage around the falls, sometimes with their portable altar, sometimes with provisions, rigging or other equipment for the ship. "Father Gabriel," he says, "though of sixty-five years of age, bore with great vigor the fatigue of that journey, and went thrice up and down those three mountains, which are pretty high and steep." This glimpse of the saintly old priest is a reminiscence to cherish in our local annals. He was

The Cross Bearers. 27

the last of a noble family in Burgundy who gave up worldly wealth and station to enter the Order of St. Francis. He came to Canada in 1670, and was the first Superior of the restored Recollect mission in that country. There is a discrepancy between Hennepin and Le Clercq as to his age; the former says he was sixty-five years old in 1679, when he was on the Niagara; the later speaks of him as being in his seventieth year in 1680. Of the three missionaries who with La Salle sailed up the Niagara in August, 1679, and with prayers and hymns boldly faced the dangers of the unknown lake, the venerable Father Gabriel was first of all to receive the martyr's crown. A year later, September 9, 1680, while engaged at his devotions, he was basely murdered by three Indians. To Father Membré there were allotted five years of missionary labor before he, too, was to fall a victim to the savage. Father Hennepin lived many years, and his chronicles stand to-day as in some respects the foundation of our local history. But cherish as we may the memory of this trio of missionaries, the imagination turns with a yet fonder regard back to the devoted priest who was not permitted to voyage westward from the Niagara with the gallant La Salle. When the Griffon sailed, Father Melithon Watteaux was left behind in the little palisaded house at Niagara as chaplain. He takes his place in our history as the first Catholic priest appointed to minister to whites in New York State. On May 27, 1679, La Salle had made a grant of land at Niagara to these Recollect Fathers, for a residence and cemetery, and this was the first property in the present State of New York to which the Catholic Church held title. Who can say what were the experiences of the priest during the succeeding winter in the loneliness and dangers of the savage-infested wilderness? Nowhere have I as yet found any detailed account of his sojourn. We know, however, that it was not long. During the succeeding years there was some passing to and fro. In 1680 La Salle, returning east, passed the site of his ruined and abandoned fort. He was again on the Niagara in 1681 with a considerable party bound for the Miami. Father Membré, who was with him, returned east in October, 1682, by the Niagara route; and La Salle himself passed down the river again in 1683 — his last visit to the Niagara. His blockhouse, within which was Father Melithon's chapel, had been burned by the Senecas.

From this time on for over half a century the missionary work in our region centered at Fort Niagara, which still stands, a manifold reminder of the romantic past, at the mouth of the river. Four years after La Salle's last passage through the Niagara — in 1687 — the Marquis de Denonville led his famous expedition against the Senecas. With him in this campaign was a band of Western Indians, who were attended by the Jesuit Father Enjalran. He was wounded in the battle with the Senecas near Boughton Hill, but appears to have accompanied de Denonville to his rendezvous on the site of Fort Niagara. Here he undoubtedly exercised his sacred office; and since the construction of Fort Niagara began at this time his name may head the list of priests officiating at that stronghold. He was soon after dispatched on a peace mission to the West, which was the special scene of his labors. His part, for some years to come, was to be an important one as Superior of the Jesuit Mission at Michillimackinac.

As soon as Fort Niagara was garrisoned, Father Jean de Lamberville was sent thither as chaplain. For the student, it would be profitable to dwell at length upon the ministrations of this devoted priest. He was of the Society of Jesus, had come out to Canada in 1668, and labored in the Onondaga mission from 1671 to 1687. His work is indelibly written on the history of missions in our State. He was the innocent cause of a party of Iroquois falling into the hands of the French, who sent them to France, where they toiled in the king's galleys. When de Denonville, in 1687, left at Fort Niagara a garrison of one hundred men under the Chevalier de la Mothe, Father Lamberville came to minister to them. The hostile Iroquois had been dealt a heavy blow, but a more insidious and dreadful enemy soon appeared within the gates. The provisions which had been left for the men proved utterly unfit for food, so that disease, with astounding swiftness, swept away most of the garrison, including the commander. Father Lamberville, himself, was soon stricken down with the scurvy. Every man in the fort would no doubt have perished but for the timely arrival of a party of friendly Miami Indians, through whose good offices the few survivors, Father Lamberville among them, were enabled to make their way to Catarouquoi — now Kingston, Ont. There he recovered; and he continued in the Canadian missions until 1698, when he returned to France.

Not willing to see his ambitious fort on the Niagara so soon abandoned, de Denonville sent out a new garrison and with them came Father Pierre Milet. He had labored, with rich results, among the Onondagas and Oneidas. No sooner was he among his countrymen, in this remote and forlorn corner of the earth, than he took up his spiritual work with characteristic zeal. On Good Friday of that year, 1688, in the center of the square within the palisades, he caused to be erected a great cross. It was of wood, eighteen feet high, hewn from the forest trees and neatly framed. On the arms of it was carved in abbreviated words the sacred legend, "*Regnat, Vincit, Imperat Christus,*" and in the midst of it was engraven the Sacred Heart. Surrounded by the officers of the garrison, — gallant men of France, with shining records, some of them were, — by the soldiers, laborers and friendly Indians, Father Milet solemnly blessed it. Can you not see the little band, kneeling about that symbol of conquest? Around them were the humble cabins and quarters of the soldiers. One of them, holding the altar, was consecrated to worship. Beyond ran the palisades and earthworks — feeble fortifications between the feeble garrison and the limitless, foe-infested wilderness. On one hand smiled the blue Ontario, and at their feet ran the gleaming Niagara, already a synonym of hardship and suffering in the annals of three of the religious orders. What wonder that the sense of isolation and feebleness was borne in upon the little band, or that they devoutly bowed before the cross which was the visible emblem of their strength and consolation in the wilderness. Where is the artist who shall paint us this scene, unique in the annals of any people?

And yet, but a few months later — September 15th of that year — the garrison was recalled, the post abandoned, the palisades broken down, the cabins left rifled and empty; and when priest and soldiers had sailed away, and only the prowling wolf or the stealthy Indian ventured near the spot, Father Milet's great cross still loomed amid the solitude, a silent witness of the faith which knows no vanquishing.

There followed an interim in the occupancy of the Niagara when neither sword nor altar held sway here; nor was the altar reëstablished in our region until the permanent rebuilding of Fort Niagara in 1726. True, Father Charlevoix passed up the river in 1721, and has left an interesting account of his journey, his view of the falls, and his brief tarrying at the carrying-place — now Lewiston. This spot was the principal rendezvous of the region for many years; and here, at the cabin of the interpreter Joncaire, where Father Charlevoix was received, we may be sure that spiritual ministrations were not omitted. A somewhat similar incident, twenty-eight years later, was the coming to these shores of the Jesuit Father Bonnecamps. He was not only the spiritual leader but appears to have acted as pilot and guide to De Céloron's expedition — an abortive attempt on the part of Louis XV. to reëstablish the claims of France to the inland regions of America. The expedition came up the St. Lawrence and through Lake Ontario, reaching Fort Niagara on July 6, 1749. It passed up the river, across to the south shore of Lake Erie and by way of Chautauqua Lake and the Allegheny down the Ohio. Returning from its utterly futile adventure, we find the party resting at Fort Niagara for three days, October 19–21. Who the resident chaplain was at the post at that date I have not been able to ascertain; but we may be sure that he had a glad greeting for Father Bonnecamps. From 1726, when, as already mentioned, the fort was rebuilt, until its surrender to Sir Wm. Johnson in 1759, a garrison was continually maintained, and without doubt was constantly attended by a chaplain. The register of the post during these years has never been found — the presumption being that it was destroyed by the English — so that the complete list of priests who ministered there is not known.

Only here and there from other sources do we glean a name by which to continue the succession. Father Crespel was stationed at Fort Niagara for about three years from 1729, interrupting his ministrations there with a journey to Detroit, where his order — the Society of Jesus — had established a mission. Of Fort Niagara at this time he says: "I found the place very agreeable; hunting and fishing were very productive; the woods in their greatest beauty, and full of walnut and chestnut trees, oaks, elms and some others, far superior to any we see in France." But not even the banks of the Niagara were to prove an earthly paradise. "The fever," he continues, "soon destroyed the pleasures we began to find, and much incommoded us, until the beginning of autumn, which season dispelled the unwholesome air. We passed the winter very quietly, and would have passed it very agreeably, if the vessel which was to have brought us refreshments had not encountered a storm on the lake, and been obliged to put back to Frontenac, which laid us under the necessity of drinking nothing but water. As the winter advanced, she dared not proceed, and we did not receive our stores till May."

Remember the utter isolation of this post and mission at the period we are considering. To be sure, it was a link in the chain of French posts, which included Quebec, Montreal, Kingston, Niagara, Detroit, Michillimackinac; but in winter the water route for transport was closed, and Niagara, like the upper posts, was thrown on its own resources for existence. There is no place in our domain to-day which fairly may be compared to it for isolation and remoteness. The upper reaches of Alaskan rivers are scarcely less known to the world than was the Niagara at the beginning of the last century. A little fringe of settlement — hostile settlement at that — stretched up the Hudson from New York. Even the Mohawk Valley was still unsettled. From the Hudson to the remotest West the wilderness stretched as a sea, and Fort Niagara was buried in its midst. Although a full century had gone by since Father Dallion first reached its shores, there was now no trace of white men on the banks of the Niagara save at the fort at its mouth, where Father Crespel ministered, and at the carrying-place, where Joncaire the interpreter lived with the Indians. Not even the first Indian villages on Buffalo Creek were to be established for half a century to come.

After Father Crespel's return from Detroit, he remained two years longer at Fort Niagara, caring for the spiritual life of the little garrison, and learning the Iroquois and Ottawah languages well enough to converse with the Indians. "This enabled me," he writes, "to enjoy their company when I took a walk in the environs of our post." The ability to converse with the Indians afterwards saved his life. When his three years of residence at Niagara expired he was relieved, according to the custom of his order, and he passed a season in the convent at Quebec. While he was undoubtedly immediately succeeded at Niagara by another chaplain, I have been unable to learn his name or aught of his ministrations. Indeed, there are but few glimpses of the post to be had from 1733 to 1759, when it fell into the hands of the English. One of the most interesting of these is of the visit of the Sulpitian missionary, the Abbé Piquet, who in 1751 came to Fort Niagara from his successful mission at La Présentation — now Ogdensburg. It is recorded of him that while here he exhorted the Senecas to beware of the white man's brandy; his name may perhaps stand as that of the first avowed temperance worker in the Niagara region.

But the end of the French *régime* was at hand. For more than a century our home region had been claimed by France; for the last thirty-three years the lily-strewn standard of Louis had flaunted defiance to the English from the banks of the Niagara. Now on a scorching July day the little fort found itself surrounded, with Sir Wm. Johnson's cannon roaring from the wilderness. There was a gallant defense, a baptism of fire and blood, an honorable capitulation. But in that fierce conflict at least one of the consecrated soldiers of the cross — Father Claude Virot — fell before British bullets; and when the triple cross of Britain floated over Fort Niagara, the last altar raised by the French on the east bank of the Niagara river had been overthrown.

On this eventful day in 1759, when seemingly the opportunities for the Catholic Church to continue its work on the Niagara were at an end, there was, in the poor parish of Maryborough, county Kildare, Ireland, a little lad of six whose mission it was to be to bring hither again the blessed offices of his faith. This was Edmund Burke, afterwards Bishop of Zion, and first Vicar-Apostolic of Nova Scotia, but whose name shines not less in the annals of his church because of his zeal as missionary in Upper Canada. Having come to Quebec in 1786, he was, in 1794, commissioned Vicar-General for the whole of Upper Canada — the province having then been established two years. In that year we find him at Niagara, where he was the first English-speaking priest to hold Catholic service. True, there was at the post that year a French missionary named Le Dru, who could speak English; but he had been ordered out of the province for cause. The field was ripe for a man of Father Burke's character and energy. His early mission was near Detroit; he was the first English-speaking priest in Ohio, and it is worthy of note that he was at Niagara on his way east, July 22, 1796 — only three weeks before the British finally evacuated Fort Niagara and the Americans took possession. Through his efforts in that year, the Church procured a large lot at Niagara, Ont., where he proposed a missionary establishment. There had probably never been a time, since the English conquest, when there had not been Catholics among the troops quartered on the Niagara; but under a British and Protestant commandant no suitable provision for their worship had been made. In 1798 — two years after the British had relinquished the fort on the east side of the river to the Americans — Father Burke, being at the British garrison on the Canadian side, wrote to Monseigneur Plessis:

> Here I am at Niagara, instead of having carried out my original design of going on to Detroit, thence returning to Kingston to pass the winter. The commander of the garrison, annoyed by the continual complaints of the civic officials against the Catholic soldiers, who used to frequent the taverns during the hours of service on Sunday, gave orders that officers and men should attend the Protestant service. They had attended for three consecutive Sundays when I represented to the commander the iniquity of this

order. He replied that he would send them to mass if the chaplain was there, and he thought it very extraordinary that whilst a chaplain was paid by the king for the battalion, instead of attending to his duty he should be in charge of a mission, his men were without religious services, and his sick were dying without the sacraments. You see, therefore, that I have reason for stopping short at Niagara; for we must not permit four companies, of whom three fourths both of officers and men are Catholics, to frequent the Protestant church.

The name of the priest against whom the charge of neglect appears to lie, was Duval; but it is not clear that he had ever attended the troops to the Niagara station. But after Father Burke came Father Désjardines and an unbroken succession, with the district fully organized in ecclesiastical jurisdiction.

And now, although our story of mission work in the Niagara region has been long — has reviewed the visitations of two centuries — the reader may have remarked the striking fact that every priest who came into our territory, up to the opening of the nineteenth century, came from Canada. This fact is the more remarkable when we recall the long-continued and vigorous missions of the Jesuits in what is now New York State, extending west nearly to the Genesee River. But the fact stands that no priest from those early establishments made his way westward to the present site of Buffalo. Fathers Lamberville and Milet had been stationed among the Onondagas and Oneidas before coming into our region at Fort Niagara; but they came thither from Canada, by way of Lake Ontario, and not through the wilderness of Western New York. The westernmost mission among the Iroquois was that of Fathers Carheil and Garnier at Cayuga, where they were at work ten years before La Salle built the Griffon on the Niagara. It is interesting to note that this mission, which was established nearest to our own region, was "dedicated to God under the invocation of St. Joseph," and that, two hundred years after, the first Bishop of Buffalo obtained from his Holiness, Pope Pius IX., permission that St. Joseph should be the principal patron saint of this diocese.

The earliest episcopal jurisdiction of the territory now embraced in the city of Buffalo, dating from the first visit of Dallion to the land of the Neuters, was directly vested in the diocese of Rouen — for it was the rule that regions new-visited belonged to the government of the bishop from a port in whose diocese the expedition bearing the missionary had sailed; and this stood until a local ecclesiastical government was formed; the first ecclesiastical association of our region, on the New York side, therefore, is with that grand old city, Rouen, the home of La Salle, scene of the martyrdom of the Maid of Orleans, and the center, through many centuries, of mighty impulses affecting the New World. From 1657 to 1670 our region was embraced in the jurisdiction of the Vicar Apostolic of New France; and from 1670 to the Conquest in the diocese of Quebec. There are involved here, of course, all the questions which grew out of the strife for possession of the Niagara region by the French,

The Cross Bearers.

English and Dutch. Into these questions we may not enter now further than to note that from 1684 the English claimed jurisdiction of all the region on the east bank of the Niagara and the present site of Buffalo. This claim was in part based on the Treaty of Albany at which the Senecas had signified their allegiance to King Charles; and by that acquiescence nominally put the east side of the Niagara under British rule. The next year, when the Duke of York came to the throne, he decreed that the Archbishop of Canterbury should hold ecclesiastical jurisdiction over the whole Colony of New York. It is very doubtful, however, if the Archbishop of Canterbury had ever heard of the Niagara — the first English translation of Hennepin did not appear for fourteen years after this date; and nothing is more unlikely than that the Senecas who visited the Niagara at this period, or even the Dutch and English traders who gave them rum for beaver-skins, had ever heard of the Archbishop of Canterbury, or cared a copper for his ecclesiastical jurisdiction, either on the Niagara or even in the settlements on the Hudson. In the New York Colony, and afterward State, the legal discrimination against Catholics continued down to 1784, when the law which condemned Catholic priests to imprisonment or even death was repealed. At the date of its repeal there was not a Catholic congregation in the State. Those Catholics who were among the pioneer settlers of Western New York had to go as far east as Albany to perform their religious duties or get their children baptized. Four years later — in

1788 — our region was included in the newly-formed diocese of Baltimore. In 1808 we came into the new diocese of New York. Not until 1821 do we find record of the visit of a priest to Buffalo. In 1829 the Church acquired its first property here — through its benefactor whose name and memory are preserved by one of our noblest institutions — Louis Le Couteulx — and the first Buffalo parish was established under the Rev. Nicholas Mertz.

We are coming very close to the present; and yet still later, in 1847, when the diocese of Buffalo was formed, there were but sixteen priests in the sixteen great counties which constituted it. It is superfluous to contrast that time with the present. There is nothing more striking, to the student of the history and development of our region during the last half century, than the increase of the Catholic Church — in parishes and schools, in means of propaganda, in material wealth with its vast resources and power for good, and especially in that personal zeal and unflagging devotion which know no limit and no exhaustion, and are drawn from the same source of strength that inspired and sustained Brébeuf and Chaumonot and their fellow-heroes of the cross on the banks of the Niagara.

The Paschal of the Great Pinch.

THE PASCHAL OF THE GREAT PINCH.

An Episode in the History of Fort Niagara; being an Extract from the hitherto unknown Memoirs of the Chevalier De Tregay, Lieutenant under the Sieur de Troyes, commanding at Fort Denonville (now called Niagara), in the Year of Starvation 1687; with Captain Désbergeres at that remote fortress from the joyfull Easter of 1688 till its abandonment; Soldier of His Excellency the Sr. de Brissay, Marquis de Denonville, Governor and Lieutenant General in New France; and humble Servitor of His Serene Majesty Louis XIV.

IT HAS BEEN my lot to suffer in many far parts of the earth; to bleed a little and go hungry for the King; to lie freezing for fame and France — and gain nothing thereby but a distemper; but so it is to be a soldier.

And I have seen trouble in my day. I have fought in Flanders on an empty stomach, and have burned my brain among the Spaniards so that I could neither fight nor run away; but of all the heavy employment I ever knew, naught can compare with what befel in the remote parts of New France, where I was with the troops that the Marquis de Denonville took through the wilderness into the cantons of the Iroquois, and afterwards employed to build a stockade and cabins at the mouth of the Strait of Niagara, on the east side, in the way where they go a beaver-hunting. "Fort

Denonville," the Sieur de Brissay decreed it should be called, for he held great hopes of the service which it should do him against both the Iroquois and the English; but now that he has fallen into the disfavor that has ever been the reward of faithful service in this accurséd land, his name is no more given even to that unhappy spot, but rather it is called Fort Niagara.

There were some hundreds of us all told that reached that fair plateau, after we left the river of the Senecas. It was mid-summer of the year of grace 1687, and we made at first a pleasant camp, somewhat overlooking the great lake, while to the west side of the point the great river made good haven for our batteaux and canoes. There was fine stir of air at night, so that we slept wholesomely, and the wounded began to mend at a great rate. And of a truth, tho' I have adventured in many lands, I have seen no spot which in all its demesne offered a fairer prospect to a man of taste. On the north of us, like the great sea itself, lay the Lake Ontario, which on a summer morning, when touched by a little wind, with the sun aslant, was like the lapis lazuli I have seen in the King's palace — very blue, yet all bright with white and gold. The river behind the camp ran mightily strong, yet for the most part glassy and green like the precious green-stone the lapidaries call verd-antique. Behind us to the south lay the forest, and four leagues away rose the triple mountains wherein is the great fall; but these are not such mountains as we have in Italy and Spain, being more of the nature of a great table-land, making an exceeding hard portage to reach the Strait of Erie above the great fall.

It was truly a most fit place for a fort, and the Marquis de Denonville let none in his command rest day or night until we had made a fortification, in part of earth, surmounted by palisades which the soldiers cut in the woods. There was much of hazard and fatigue in this work, for the whole plain about the fort had no trees; so that some of us went into the forest along the shore to the eastward and some cut their sticks on the west side of the river. It was hard work, getting them up the high bank; but so pressed were we, somewhat by fear of an attack, and even more by the zeal of our commander, that in three days we had built there a pretty good fort with four bastions, where we put two great guns and some pattareras; and we had begun to build some cabins on the four sides of the square in the middle of it. And as we worked, our number was constantly diminished; for the Sieurs Du Luth and Durantaye, with that one-handed Chevalier de Tonty of whom they tell so much, and our allies the savages who had come from the Illinois to join the Governor in his assault upon the Iroquois, as soon as their wounded were able to be moved, took themselves off up the Niagara and over the mountain portage I have spoken of; for they kept a post and place of trade at the Detroit, and at Michillimackinac. And then presently the Marquis himself and all whom he would let go sailed away around the great lake for Montreal. But he ordered that an hundred, officers and men, stay behind to hold this new Fort Denonville. He had placed in command over us the Sieur de Troyes, of whom it would not become me to speak in any wise ill.

There were sour looks and sad, as the main force marched to the batteaux. But the Marquis did not choose to heed anything of that. We were put on parade for the embarkation — though we made a sorry show of it, for there were even then more rags than lace or good leather — and His Excellency spoke a farewell word in the hearing of us all.

"You are to complete your quarters with all convenient expediency," he said to De Troyes, who stood attentive, before us. "There will be no lack of provision sent. You have here in these waters the finest fish in the world. There is naught to fear from these Iroquois wasps — have we not just torn to pieces their nests?"

He said this with a fine bravado, though methought he lacked somewhat of sincerity; for surely scattered wasps might prove troublesome enough to those of us who stayed behind. But De Troyes made no reply, and saluted gravely. And so, with a jaunty word about the pleasant spot where we were to abide, and a light promise to send fresh troops in the spring, the General took himself off, and we were left behind to look out for the wasps. As the boats passed the sandbar and turned to skirt the lake shore to the westward, we gave them a salvo of musketry; but De Troyes raised his hand — although the great Marquis was yet in sight

The Paschal of the Great Pinch. 47

and almost in hailing distance — and forbade another discharge.

"Save your powder," was all he said; and the very brevity of it seemed to mean more than many words, and put us into a low mood for that whole day.

Now for a time that followed there was work enough to keep each man busy, which is best for all who are in this trade of war, especially in the wilderness. It was on the third of August that M. de Brissay left us, he having sent off some of the militia ahead of him; and he bade M. de Vaudreuil stay behind for a space, to help the Sieur de Troyes complete the fort and cabins, and this he did right ably, for as all Canada and the King himself know, M. de Vaudreuil was a man of exceeding great energy and resources in these matters. There was a vast deal of fetching and carrying, of hewing and sawing and framing. And notwithstanding that the sun of that climate was desperately hot the men worked with good hearts, so that there was soon finished an excellent lodgment for the commandant; with a chimney of sticks and clay, and boards arranged into a sort of bedstead; and this M. de Troyes shared with M. de Vaudreuil, until such time as the latter gentleman quit us. There were three other cabins built, with chimneys, doors and little windows. We also constructed a baking-house with a large oven and chimney, partly covered with boards and the remainder with hurdles and clay. We also built an extensive framed building without chimney, and a large store-house with pillars eight feet high, and made from time to time yet other constructions for the men and goods — though, *Dieu défend!* we had spare room for both, soon enough. In the square in the midst of the buildings we digged a well; and although the water was sweet enough, yet from the first, for lack of proper curbing and protection, it was ever much roiled and impure when we drew it, a detriment alike to health and cookery.

M. de Vaudreuil seeing us at last well roofed, and having directed for a little the getting of a store of firewood, made his adieux. Even then, in those fine August days, a spirit of discontent was among us, and more than one spark of a soldier, who at the first camp had been hot upon staying on the Niagara, sought now to be taken in M. de Vaudreuil's escort. But that gentleman replied, that he wished to make a good report of us all to the Governor, and that, for his part, he hoped he might come to us early in the spring, with the promised detachment of troops. And so we parted.

Now the spring before, when we had all followed the Marquis de Denonville across Lake Ontario to harass the cantons of the Iroquois, this establishment of a post on the Niagara was assuredly a part of that gentleman's plan. It is not for me, who am but a mere lieutenant of marines, to show how a great commander should conduct his expeditions; yet I do declare that while there was no lack of provision made for killing such of the savages as would permit it, there was next to none for maintaining troops who were to be left penned up in the savages' country. We who were left at Fort Denonville had but few mattocks or even axes. Of ammunition there was none too much. In the Senecas' country we had destroyed thousands of minots[1] of corn, but had brought along scarce a week's rations of it to this corner. We had none of us gone a-soldiering with our pockets full of seed, and even if we had brought ample store of corn and pumpkin seed, of lentils and salad plants, the season was too late to have done much in gardening. We made some feeble attempts at it; but no rain fell, the earth baked under the sun so hard that great cracks came in it; and what few shoots of corn and pumpkin thrust upward through this parched soil, withered away before any strengthening juices came in them. To hunt far from the fort we durst not, save in considerable parties; so that if we made ourselves safe from the savages, we also made every other living thing safe against us. To fish was well nigh our only recourse; but although many of our men labored diligently at it, they met with but indifferent return.

Thus it was that our most ardent hopes, our very life itself, hung upon the coming of the promised supplies. There was joy at the fort when at length the sail of the little bark was seen; even De Troyes, who had grown exceeding grave and melancholy, took on again something of his wonted spirit. But we were not quite yet to be succored, for it was the season of the most light and trifling airs, so that the bark for two days hung idly on the shining lake, some leagues away from the

---

[1] A minot is an old French measure; about three bushels.

mouth of the river, while we idled and fretted like children, impatient for her coming. When once we had her within the bar, there was no time lost in unlading. It was a poor soldier indeed who could not work to secure the comfort of his own belly; and the store was so ample that we felt secure for the winter, come what might. The bark that fetched these things had been so delayed by the calms, that she weighed and sailed with the first favoring breeze; and it was not until her sail had fall'n below the horizon that we fairly had sight or smell of what she had brought.

From the first the stores proved bad; still, we made shift to use the best, eked out with what the near-by forest and river afforded. For many weeks we saw no foes. There was little work to do, and the men idled through the days, with no word on their lips but to complain of the food and wish for spring. When the frosts began to fall we had a more vigorous spell of it; but now for the first time appeared the Iroquois wasps. One of our parties, which had gone toward the great fall of the Niagara, lost two men; those who returned reported that their comrades were taken all unawares by the savages. Another party, seeking game to the eastward where a stream cuts through the high bank on its way to the lake,[1] never came back at all. Here we found their bodies and buried them; but their scalps, after the manner of these people, had been taken.

Christmas drew on, but never was a sorrier season kept by soldiers of France. De Troyes had fallen ill.

---

[1] Evidently at Four or Six Mile Creek.

Naught ailed him that we could see save low spirits and a thinning of the blood, which made him too weak to walk. The Father Jean de Lamberville, who had stayed with us, and who would have been our hope and consolation in those days, very early fell desperate ill of a distemper, so that the men had not the help of his ministrations and holy example. Others there were who either from feebleness or lack of discipline openly refused their daily duty and went unpunished. We had fair store of brandy; and on Christmas eve those of us who still held some soul for sport essayed to lighten the hour. We brewed a comfortable draught, built the blaze high, for the frosts were getting exceeding sharp, gathered as many as could be had of officers and worthy men into our cabin, and made brave to sing the songs of France. And now here was a strange thing: that while the hardiest and soundest amongst us had made good show of cheer, had eaten the vile food and tried to speak lightly of our ills, no sooner did we hear our own voices in the songs that carried us back to the pleasantries of our native land, than we fell a-sobbing and weeping like children; which weakness I attribute to the distemper that was already in our blood.

For the days that followed I have no heart to set down much. We never went without the palisades except well guarded to fetch firewood. This duty indeed made the burden of every day. A prodigious store of wood was needed, for the cold surpassed anything I had ever known. The snow fell heavily, and there were storms when for days the gale drave straight across our bleak plateau. There was no blood in us to withstand the icy blasts. Do what we would the chill of the tomb was in the cabins where the men lay. The wood-choppers one day, facing such a storm, fell in the deep drifts just outside the gate. None durst go out to them. The second day the wolves found them — and we saw it all!,

There was not a charge of powder left in the fort. There was not a mouthful of fit food. The biscuits had from the first been full of worms and weevils. The salted meat, either from the admixture of sea-water through leaky casks, or from other cause, was rotten beyond the power even of a starving man to hold.

Le scorbut broke out. I had seen it on shipboard, and knew the signs. De Troyes now seldom left his cabin; and when, in the way of duty, I made my devoirs, and he asked after the men, I made shift to hide the truth. But it could not be for long.

"My poor fellows," he sighed one day, as he turned feebly on his couch of planks, "it must be with all as it is with me — see, look here, De Tregay, do you know the sign?" and he bared his shrunken arm and side.

Indeed I knew the signs — the dry, pallid skin, with the purple blotches and indurations. He saw I was at a loss for words.

"*Sang de Dieu!*" he cried, "is this what soldiers of France must come to, for the glory of"——. He stopped short, as if lacking spirit to go on. "Now I be-

The Paschal of the Great Pinch. 53

think me," he added, in a melancholy voice, "it *is* what soldiers must come to." Then, after a while he asked:

"How many dead today, De Tregay?"

How many dead! From a garrison of gallant men-at-arms we had become a charnel-house. In six weeks we had lost sixty men. From a hundred at the beginning of autumn, we were now scarce forty, and February was not gone. A few of us, perhaps with stouter stomachs than the rest, did all the duty of the post. We brought the firewood and we buried the dead — picking the frozen clods with infinite toil, that we might lay the bones of our comrades beyond the reach of wolves. Sometimes it was the scurvy, sometimes it was the cold, sometimes, methinks, it was naught but a weak will — or as we say, the broken heart; but it mattered not, the end was the same. More than twenty died in March; and although we were now but a handful of skeletons and accustomed to death, I had no thought of sorrow or of grief, so dulled had my spirit become, until one morning I found the brave De Troyes drawing with frightful pains his dying breath. With the name of a maid he loved upon his lips, the light went out; and with heavy heart I buried him in that crowded ground, and fain would have lain down with him.

And now with our commander under the snow, what little spirit still burned in the best of us seemed to die down. I too bore the signs of the distemper, yet to no great extent, for of all the garrison I had labored by exercise to keep myself wholesome, and in the woods I had tasted of barks and buds and roots of little herbs, hoping to find something akin in its juices to the *herbe de scorbut*[1] which I have known to cure sick sailors. But now I gave over these last efforts for life; for, thought I, spring is tardy in these latitudes. Many weeks must yet pass before the noble Marquis at Montreal (where comforts are) will care to send the promised troop. And the Western savages, our allies the Illinois, the Ottawais, the Miamis, were they not coming to succor us here and to raid the Iroquois cantons? But of what account is the savage's word!

So I thought, and I turned myself on my pallet. I listened. There was no sound in all the place save the beating of a sleet. "It is appointed," I said within me. "Let the end come." And presently, being numb with the cold, I thought I was on a sunny hillside in Anjou. It was the time of the grape-harvest, and the smell of the vines, laughter and sunshine filled the air. Young lads and maids, playmates of my boyhood days, came and took me by the hand. . . .

A twinge of pain made the vision pass. I opened my eyes upon a huge savage, painted and bedaubed, after their fashion. It was the grip of his vast fist that had brought me back from Anjou.

"The Iroquois, then," I thought, "have learned of our extremity, and have broken in, to finish all. So much the better," and I was for sinking back upon the boards, when the savage took from a little pouch a handful of the parched corn which they carry on their expeditions. "Eat," he said, in the language of the

---

[1] Probably what the English call scurvy-grass.

Miamis. And then I knew that relief had come — and I knew no more for a space.

Now this was Michitonka himself, who had led his war party from beyond Lake Erie, where the Chevalier de Tonty and Du Luth were, to see how we fared at Fort Denonville, and to make an expedition against the Senecas — of whom we saw no more, from the time the Miamis arrived. There were of all our garrison but twelve not dead, and among those who threw off the distemper was the Father de Lamberville. His recovery gave us the greatest joy. He lay for many weeks at the very verge of the grave, and it was marvelous to all to see his skin, which had been so empurpled and full of malignant humors, come wholesome and fair again. I have often remarked, in this hard country, that of all Europeans the Fathers of the Holy Orders may be brought nearest to death, and yet regain their wonted health. They have the same prejudice for life that the wildest savage has. But as for the rest of us, who are neither savage nor holy, it is by a slim chance that we live at all.

Now the Father, and two or three of the others who had the strength to risk it, set out with a part of Michitonka's people to Cataracouy[1] and Montreal, to carry the news of our extremity. And on a soft April day as we looked over lake, we saw a sail; and we knew that we had kept the fort until the relief company was sent as had been commanded. But it had been a great pinch.

. . . .

---
[1] Otherwise Fort Frontenac, now Kingston, Ont.

Now I am come to that which after all I chiefly set out to write down; for I have ever held that great woes should be passed over with few words, but it is meet to dwell upon the hour of gladness. And this hour was now arrived, when we saw approach the new commandant, the Sieur Désbergeres, captain of one of the companies of the Detachment of the Marine, and with him the Father Milet, of the Society of Jesus. There was a goodly company, whose names are well writ on the history of this New France: the Sieurs De la Mothe, La Rabelle, Demuratre de Clerin and de Gemerais, and others, besides a host of fine fellows of the common rank; with fresh food that meant life to us.

Of all who came that April day, it was the Father Milet who did the most. The very morning that he landed, we knelt about him at mass; and scarce had he rested in his cabin than he marked a spot in the midst of the square, where a cross should stand, and bade as many as could, get about the hewing of it; and although I was yet feeble and might rest as I liked, I chose to share in the work, for so I found my pleasure. A fair straight oak was felled and well hewn, and with infinite toil the timber was taken within the palisades and further dressed; and while the carpenters toiled to mortise the cross-piece and fasten it with pins, Father Milet himself traced upon the arms the symbols for the legend:

Regnat, Vincit, Imperat Christus.

And these letters were well cut into the wood, in the

The Paschal of the Great Pinch.   57

midst of them being the sign of the Sacred Heart. We had it well made, and a place dug for it, on a Thursday; and on the next morning, which was Good Friday, the reverend Father placed his little portable altar in the midst of the square, where we all, officers and men, and even some of the Miamis who were yet with us, assembled for the mass. Then we raised the great cross and planted it firmly in the midst of the little square. The service of the blessing of it lay hold of my mind mightily, for my fancy was that this great sign of victory had sprung from the midst of the graves where De Troyes and four score of my comrades lay; and being in this tender mood (for I was still weak in body) the words which the Father read from his breviary seemed to rest the more clearly in my mind.

"*Adjutorium nostrum in nomine Domini.*" Father Milet had a good voice, with a sort of tenderness in it, so that we were every one disposed to such silence and attention, that I could even hear the little waves lapping the shore below the fort. And when he began with the "*Oramus*"—"*Rogamus te Domine sancte Pater omnipotens,*"—I was that moved, by the joy of it, and my own memories, that I wept—and I a soldier!

It may be believed that the Sunday which followed, which was the Paschal, was kept by us with such worship and rejoicing as had never yet been known in those remote parts. Holy men had been on that river before, it is true; but none had abode there for long, nor had any set up so great a cross, nor had there ever such new life come to men as we knew at Fort Denonville that Easter.

For a space, all things went well. What with the season (for spring ever inspires men to new undertakings) and the bitter lessons learned in the great pinch of the past winter, we were no more an idle set, but kept all at work, and well. Yet the Iroquois pestered us vastly, being set on thereto by the English, who claimed this spot. And in September there came that pilot Maheut, bringing his bark La General over the shoal at the river's mouth all unexpected; and she was scarce anchored in the little roadstead than Désbergeres knew he was to abandon all. It was cause of chagrin to the great Marquis, I make no doubt, thus to drop the prize he had so tried to hold; but some of us in the fort had no stomach for another winter on the Niagara, and we made haste to execute the orders which the Marquis de Denonville had sent. We put the guns on board La General. We set the gate open, and tore down the rows of pales on the south and east sides of the square. Indeed the wind had long ago begun this work, so that towards the lake the pales (being but little set in the earth) had fallen or leaned over, so they could readily have been scaled, or broken through. But as the order was, we left the cabins and quarters standing, with doors ajar, to welcome who might come, Iroquois or wolf, for there was naught within. But Father Milet took down from above the door of his cabin the little sun dial. "The shadow of the great cross falls divers ways," was his saying.

The Paschal of the Great Pinch. 59

Early the next morning, being the 15th of September, of the year 1688, being ready for the embarkation, Father Milet summoned us to the last mass he might say in the place. It was a sad morning, for the clouds hung heavy, the lake was of a somber and forbidding cast, and the very touch in the air forebode autumnal gales. As we knelt around the cross for the last time, the ensign brought the standards which Désbergeres had kept, and holding the staves, knelt also. Certain Miamis, too, who were about to make the Niagara portage, stayed to see what the priest might do. And at the end of the office Father Milet did an uncommon thing, for he was mightily moved. He turned from us toward the cross, and throwing wide his arms spoke the last word — "Amen."

There were both gladness and sorrow in our hearts as we embarked. Lake and sky took on the hue of lead, foreboding storm. We durst carry but little sail, and at the sunset hour were scarce a league off shore. As it chanced, Father Milet and I stood together on the deck and gazed through the gloom toward that dark coast. While we thus stood, there came a rift betwixt the banked clouds to the west, so that the sun, just as it slipped from sight, lighted those Niagara shores, and we saw but for an instant, above the blackness and the desolation, the great cross as in fire or blood gleam red.

With Bolton at Fort Niagara.

WITH BOLTON AT FORT NIAGARA.

ONE PLEASANT September day in 1897 it was my good fortune, under expert guidance, to follow for a little the one solitary trail made by the American patriots in Western New York during the Revolutionary War, the one expedition of our colonial forces approaching this region during that period. This was the famous "raid" led by Gen. John Sullivan in the summer of 1779. Our quest took us up the long hill slope west of Conesus Lake, in what is now the town of Groveland, Livingston Co., to a spot — among the most memorable in the annals of Western New York, yet unmarked and known to but a few — where a detachment of Sullivan's army, under Lieut. Boyd, were waylaid and massacred by the Indians. It was on the 13th of September that this tragedy occurred. Two days later Gen. Sullivan, having accomplished the main purpose of his raid — the destruction of Indian villages and crops — turned back towards Pennsylvania, returning to Easton, whence the expedition had started. He had come within about eighty miles of the Niagara. "Though I had it not in command," wrote Gen. Sullivan in his report to the Secretary of War, "I should have ventured to have paid [Fort] Niagara a visit, had I been supplied with fifteen days' provisions in addition to what I had, which I am persuaded from the bravery and ardor of our troops would have fallen into our hands."[1] This was the nearest approach to any attempt made by the Americans to enter this region during that war.

The events of Sullivan's expedition are well known. Few episodes of the Revolution are more fully recorded. But what is the reverse of the picture? What lay at the other side of this Western New York wilderness which Sullivan failed to penetrate? What was going on, up and down the Niagara, and on Buffalo Creek, during those momentous years? We know that the region was British, that old Fort Niagara was its garrison, the principal rendezvous of the Indians and the base from which scalping parties set out to harry the frontier settlements. The most dreadful frontier tragedies of the war — Wyoming, Cherry Valley, and others — were planned here and carried out with British coöperation. But who were the men and what were the incidents of the time, upon our Niagara frontier? So far as I am aware, that period is for the most part a blank in our histories. One may search the books in vain for any adequate narrative — indeed for any but the most meager data — of the history of the Niagara region during the Revolution. The materials are not lacking, they are in fact abundant. In this paper I undertake only to give an inkling of

---

[1] Sullivan to Jay, Teaogo (Tioga), Sept. 30, 1779.

the character of events in this region during that grave period in our nation's history.[1]

In 1778, Colonel Haldimand, afterward Sir Frederick, succeeded Gen. Guy Carleton in the command of the British forces in Canada. He was Commander in Chief, and Governor of Canada, until his recall in 1784. Lord North was England's Prime Minister, Lord George Germaine in charge of American affairs in the Cabinet. Haldimand took up his residence at Quebec, and therefrom, for a decade, administered the affairs of the Canadian frontier with zeal and adroitness. He was a thorough soldier, as his letters show. He was also an adept in the treatment of matters which, like the retention by the British of the frontier posts for thirteen years after they had been ceded to the Americans by treaty, called for dogged determination, veiled behind diplomatic courtesies. The troops which he commanded were scattered from the mouth of the St. Lawrence to Lake Michigan; but to no part of this

---

[1] I first struck the trail in London, among the Colonial Papers preserved in the Public Records Office. Subsequently, in the Archives Department at Ottawa, I found that trail broaden into a fair highway. Something has been gleaned at Albany; more, no doubt, is to be looked for at Washington; but it is an amazing fact that our Government is far less liberal in granting access for students to its official records than is either England or Canada. But the Niagara region was British during the Revolution, and its history is chiefly to be sought in British archives. Especially in the Haldimand Papers, preserved in the British Museum, but of which verified copies are readily accessible in the Archives at Ottawa, is the Revolutionary history of the Niagara to be found. Besides the 232 great volumes in which these papers are gathered, there are thousands of other MSS. of value to an inquirer seeking the history of this region; especially the correspondence, during all that term of years, between the commandants at Fort Niagara and other upper lake posts, and the Commander in Chief of the British forces in America; between that general and the Ministry in London, and between the commandants at the posts and the Indian agents, fur traders and many classes and conditions of men. For the incidents here recorded I have drawn, almost exclusively, on these unpublished sources.

long line of wilderness defense — a line which was substantially the enemy's frontier — did he pay more constant attention than to Fort Niagara. There were good reasons for this. Fort Niagara was not only the key to the upper lakes, the base of supplies for Detroit, Michillimackinac and minor posts, but it had long been an important trading post and the principal rendezvous of the Six Nations, upon whose peculiarly efficient services against the American frontiers Sir Frederick relied scarcely less than he did upon the British troops themselves. It was, therefore, with no ordinary solicitude that he made his appointments for Niagara.

I cannot state positively the names of all officers in command at Fort Niagara from the time war was begun, down to 1777. Lieut. Lernault, afterwards at Detroit, was here for a time; but about the spring of '77 we find Fort Niagara put under the command of Lieut. Col. Mason Bolton, of the 34th Royal Artillery. He had then seen some years of service in America; had campaigned in Florida and the West Indies; had been sent to Mackinac and as far west as the Illinois; and it was no slight tribute to his ability and fidelity, when Haldimand put the Niagara frontier into his hands. Here, for over three years, he was the chief in command. In military rank, even if in nothing else, he was the principal man in this region during the crucial period of the Revolution. He commanded the garrison at Fort Niagara, and its dependencies at Schlosser and Fort Erie. Buffalo was then unthought of — it was merely Te-hos-e-ro-ron, the place of the basswoods; but at the Indian villages farther up Buffalo Creek, which came into existence in 1780, the name of Col. Bolton stood for the highest military authority of the region. And yet, incredible as it may seem, after all these years in which — to adapt Carlyle's phrase — the Torch of History has been so assiduously brandished about, I do not know of any printed book which offers any information about Col. Mason Bolton or the life he led here. Indeed, with one or two exceptions, in which he is barely alluded to, I think all printed literature may be searched in vain for so much as a mention of his name.

Other chief men of this frontier, at the period we are considering, were Col. Guy Johnson, Superintendent of Indian Affairs; Sir John Johnson, son of the Sir William who captured Fort Niagara from the French in 1759; Col. John Butler, of the Queen's Rangers; his son Walter; Sayenqueraghta, the King of the Senecas; Rowland Montour, his half-breed son-in-law; and Brant, the Mohawk hero, who, equipped with a New England schooling and enlightened by a trip to England, here returned to lead out scalping parties in the British interests.

Col. Bolton had been for some time without authentic news of the enemy, when on the morning of December 14, 1777, the little garrison was thrown into unwonted activity by the arrival of Capt. La Mothe, who reported that Gen. Howe had taken Philadelphia, and that the rebels had "sustained an incredible loss." By a forced march of Howe, La Mothe averred, Gen. Washington had been defeated, "with 11,000 rebels killed, wounded and prisoners." Two days later the excitement was increased by the arrival at the fort of some Delaware Indians, who brought the great news that Washington was killed and his army totally routed. "I had a meeting of the chiefs of the Six Nations," wrote Bolton to Gen. Carleton, "about an hour after the express arrived and told them the news. They seemed extremely pleased and have been in good temper ever since their arrival." Oddly enough, this news was confirmed by a soldier of the 7th Regiment, who had been taken prisoner by the Americans, but had escaped and made his way to Niagara. He further embellished the report by declaring that 9,000 men under Lord Percy defeated 13,000 rebels at Bear's Hill on December 20th, under Washington, that Gates was sent for to take the command when Washington was killed, and that 7,000 volunteers from Ireland had joined Howe's army. Washington at this time, the reader will remember, had gone into winter quarters with his army at Valley Forge.

There were 2,300 Indians at Fort Niagara at this period, all making perpetual demands for beef, flour and rum. The license of the jubilee over Washington's death probably was limited only by the scantiness of provisions and the impossibility of adding to the store. Cold weather shut down on the establishment, the vessels were laid up, and all winter long Col. Bolton and his men had no word contradicting the report of Washington's death. As late as April 8th, the following spring, he wrote to Gen. Carleton that "all accounts confirm Washington being killed and his army defeated in December last, and that Gates was sent for to take the command."

The British early were apprised of Sullivan's intended raid, and although powerless to prevent it, kept well posted as to its progress. The various parties which Sullivan encountered, were directed from Fort Niagara. "Since the rebels visit the Indian country," wrote Gen. Haldimand to Sir John Johnson, September 14, 1779, "I am happy they are advancing so far. They can never reach Niagara and their difficulties and danger of retreat will, in proportion as they advance, increase." Again he wrote twelve days later: "You will be able to make your way to Niagara, and if the rebels should be encouraged to advance as far as that place, I am convinced that few of them will escape from famine or the sword. All in my power to do for you is to push up provisions, which shall be done with the utmost vigor, while the river and lake remain navigable, although it may throw me into great distress in this part of the province, should anything happen to prevent the arrival of the fall victuallers." There was however genuine alarm at Fort Niagara, and even Sir Frederick himself, though he wrote so confidently to Bolton, in his letters to the Ministry expressed grave apprehensions of what might happen.

What did happen was bad enough for British interests, for though the Americans turned back, the raid had driven in upon Bolton a horde of frightened, hungry and irresponsible Indians, who had to be fed at the King's expense and were a source of unmeasured concern to the overworked commandant, notwithstanding the independent organization of the Indian Department which was effected.

To arrive at a just idea of conditions hereabouts at this period, we must keep in mind the relation of the fluctuating population, Indians and whites, to the uncertain and often inadequate food supply.

Fort Niagara at this time — the fall of '78 — was a fortification 1,100 yards in circumference, with five bastions and two blockhouses. Capt. John Johnson thought 1,000 men were needed to defend it; "the present strength," he wrote, "amounting to no more than 200 rank and file, including fifteen men of the Royal Artillery and the sick, a number barely sufficient to defend the outworks (if they were in a state of defense) and return the necessary sentries, should the place be infested by a considerable force. . . . . With a garrison of 500 or a less number, it is impregnable against all the savages in America, but if a strong body of troops with artillery should move this way, I believe no engineer who has ever seen these works will say it can hold out any considerable time."

On May 1st, 1778, there had been in the garrison at Fort Niagara 311 men. Half a dozen more were stationed at Fort Schlosser, and thirty-two at Fort Erie, a total of 349, of whom 255 were reported as fit for duty. At this time Maj. Butler's Rangers, numbering 106,

With Bolton at Fort Niagara. 71

had gone on "an expedition with the Indians towards the settlements of Pennsylvania or New York, whichever he finds most practicable and advantageous to the King's service." These raids from Fort Niagara were far more frequent than one would infer from the histories — even from the American histories whose authors are not to be suspected of purposely minimizing either their number or effect. But it appears from the records that not infrequently the expeditions accomplished nothing of more consequence than to steal stock. Horses, cattle and sheep were in more than one instance driven away from settlements far down on the Mohawk or Susquehanna, and brought back alive or dead along the old trails, to Fort Niagara.

To illustrate the methods of the time: In a report to Brig. Gen. Powell, Maj. Butler wrote: "In the spring of 1778 I found it absolutely requisite for the good of His Majesty's service, with the consent and approbation of Lt. Col. Bolton, and on the application of the chiefs and warriors of the five united nations . . . ., to proceed to the frontiers of the colonies in rebellion, with as many officers and men of my corps as were then raised, in order to protect the Indian settlements and to annoy the enemy." At this time many of his men were new recruits from the colonies, sons or heads of Loyalist — or as we used to say, on this side the border, of Tory — families. As they approached American frontier settlements, the loyalty to King George of some of his men became suspicious, so that Butler issued a proclamation that all deserters, if apprehended, were to be shot. In the letter just quoted from he reports that this order had a good effect. Many curious circumstances arose at the time, due to the British or American allegiance of men who before the war had been friendly neighbors, but who now met as hostiles, as captor and captive, sometimes as victor and victim. There was a constant flight, by one route and another, of Loyalist refugees to Fort Niagara. Thus, by a return of Feb. 12, 1779, 1,346 people were drawing rations from the stores of that place, of whom sixty-four were "distressed families," that is, Tories who had fled from the colonies (mostly from the Mohawk Valley); and 445 Indians. The war parties left early in the spring, and during the summer the supply boats could get up from the lower stations. Then came that march of destruction up the Genesee Valley; winter shut down on lake and river communication, and the most distressed period the frontier had known under British rule set in. In October, immediately after the invasion, Col. Bolton wrote (I quote briefly from a very full report): "Joseph Brant . . . . assures me that if 500 men had joined the Rangers in time, there is no doubt that instead of 300, at least 1,000 warriors would have turned out, and with that force he is convinced that Mr. Sullivan would have had some reason to repent of his expedition; but the Indians not being supported as they expected, thought of nothing more than carrying off their families, and we had at this Post the 21st of last month 5,036 to supply with provisions, and notwithstanding a number of parties have been sent out since, we have still on the ground 3,678 to maintain. I am convinced your Excellency will not be surprised, if I am extremely alarmed, for to support such a multitude I think will be absolutely impossible. I have requested of Major Butler to try his utmost to prevail on the Indians whose villages have been destroyed to go down to Montreal for the winter, where, I have assured him, they would be well taken care of; and to inform all the rest who have not suffered by the enemy that they must return home and take care of their corn."

Neither plan worked as hoped for. It was difficult to get the Indians to consent to go down the river, or even to Carleton Island; and as Sullivan had destroyed every village save two, few of the Senecas could be induced to return into the Genesee country. Bolton's urgent appeals for extra provisions were also doomed to disappointment, owing to the lateness of the season or the lack of transports.

The winter after Sullivan's raid, Guy Johnson distributed clothing to more than 3,000 Indians at Fort Niagara. But the cost of clothing them was trifling compared with the cost of feeding them. Expeditions against the distant American settlements were planned, not more through the desire for retaliation, than from the necessity of reducing the number of dependents on Fort Niagara. When the inroads on provisions grew serious, the Indians were encouraged to go on the war-path. But so exceedingly severe was the winter, so deep was the snow on the trails, that not until the middle of February could any parties be induced to set out. The number camped around the fort, consuming the King's pork, beef, flour and rum, rose as we have seen, to more than 5,000. Many starved and many froze.

Much could be said regarding the British policy of dealing with the Indians at Fort Niagara, but I may only touch upon the subject at this time. Haldimand, and behind him the British Ministry, placed great reliance upon them. The uniform instruction was that the Indians should be maintained as allies. On April 10, 1778, Lord George Germaine wrote to Gen. Haldimand that the designs of the rebels against Niagara and Detroit were not likely to be successful as long as the Six Nations continued faithful. Presents, honors, and the full license of the tomahawk and scalping-knife were allowed them. With a view to promoting their fidelity, Joseph Brant was made a colonel. Significant, too, was the settling of a generous allowance for life upon Brant's sister, Sir William Johnson's consort; which act was approved, about this time, by the august council at Whitehall.

The British watched the state of the Indian mind as the sailor watches his barometer at the coming of a storm. And the Indian mind, though always cunning, was sometimes childlike in the directness and simplicity of its conclusions. The constant flight to Fort Niagara of refugee Tories was remarked by the savages, and in turn noted and reported to Gen. Haldimand. "The frequent passing of white people to Niagara," wrote Capt. John Johnson to Gen. Carleton, October

With Bolton at Fort Niagara. 75

6, 1778, "is much taken note of by the Indians, who say they are running away and that they (the Tories) have begun the quarrel and leave them (the Indians) to defend it." However, Johnson counted on being able to change their minds, for he added: "I hope in my next to inform you of giving the rebels an eternal thrashing."

The usual British good sense — the national tradesman's instinct — seems to have been temporarily suspended, held in abeyance, at the demands of these Indians. In his report of May 12, '78, Col. Bolton writes that he has approved bills for nearly £18,000 "for sundries furnished savages which Maj. Butler thought absolutely necessary, notwithstanding all the presents sent to their posts last year; 2,700 being assembled at a time when I little expected such a number, obliged me to send to Detroit for a supply of provisions, and to buy up all the cattle, etc., that could possibly be procured, otherwise this garrison must have been distressed or the savages offended, and of course, I suppose, would have joined the rebels. Even after all that was done for them they scarce seemed satisfied." In June he writes that only eight out of twenty puncheons of rum ordered for Fort Niagara had been received, and that "much wine has been given to the savages that was intended for this post."

One reads in this old correspondence, with mingled amusement and amazement, of the marvelous attentions paid these wily savages. Childlike, whatever they saw in the cargoes of the merchants, they wanted, and

England humored and pampered them, lest they transfer their affections. We have Guy Johnson's word for it, under date of Niagara, July 3, 1780, that "many of the Indians will no longer wear tinsel lace, and are become good judges of gold and silver. They frequently demand and have received wine, tea, coffee, candles and many such articles, and they are frequently nice in the choice of the finest black and other cloth for blankets, and the best linnen and cambrick with other things needless to enumerate. . . . The Six Nations are not so fond of gaudy colors as of good and substantial things, but they are passionately fond of silver ornaments and neat arrows." Elsewhere in these letters a requisition for port wine is explained on the ground that it was demanded by the chiefs when they were sick — dainty treatment, truly, for stalwart savages whose more accustomed diet was cornmeal and water, and who could feast, when fortune favored, on the recking entrails of a dead horse.

Now and then, it is true, advantages were taken of the Indians in ways which, presumably, it was thought they would not detect; all, we must grant, in the interest of economy. One was in the matter of powder. The Indians were furnished with a grade inferior to the garrison powder. This was shown by a series of tests made at Fort Niagara by order of Brig. Gen. Powell — Col Bolton's successor — on July 10, 1782. We may suppose it to have been an agreeable summer day, that there was leisure at the fort to indulge in experiments, and that there were no astute Indians on

With Bolton at Fort Niagara. 77

hand to be unduly edified by the result. At Gen. Powell's order an eight-inch mortar was elevated to forty-five degrees, and six rounds fired, to find out how far one half a pound of powder would throw a forty-six pound shell. The first trial, with the garrison powder, sent the shell 239 yards. For rounds two and three Indian Department powder was used; the fine-glazed kind sent the shell eighty-two yards, the coarser grain carried it but seventy-nine yards. Once more the garrison powder was used; the shell flew 243 yards, while a second trial of the two sorts of Indian Department powder sent it but eighty-four and seventy-six yards, or about three to one in favor of the white man. With the garrison powder, a musket and carbine ball went through a two and one-quarter-inch oak plank, at the distance of fifty yards, and lodged in one six inches behind it; but with the Indian powder these balls would not go through the first plank.

This seems like taking a base advantage of the trustful Indian ally, especially since he was to use his powder against the common foe, the American rebel; in reality, however, the Indians were wasteful and irresponsible, and squandered their ammunition on the little birds of the forest and even in harmless but expensive salvos into the empty air.

Another economy was practiced in the Indian Department: when the stock ran low the rum was watered. Sometimes the precious contents of the casks were augmented one third, sometimes even two thirds, with the more abundant beverage from Niagara River, so that the garrison rum, like the garrison powder, "carried" two or three times as well as did that of the Indian Department; but whether this had a salutary effect upon the thirsty recipients is a problem the solution of which lies outside the range of the exact historian.

Difficult as it was to hold the allegiance of the savage, it was harder yet — nay, it was impossible — to make him fight according to the rules of civilized warfare. The British Government from the Ministry down stand in history in an equivocal position in this matter. Over and over again in the correspondence which I have examined, one finds vigorous condemnation of the Indian method of slaughter of women and children, and the torture of captives. Over and over again the officers are urged not to allow it; and over and over again they report, after a raid, that they deplore the acts of wantonness which were committed, and which they were unable to prevent. But nowhere do I find any suggestion that the services of the Indians be dispensed with. Throughout the Revolution, the Senecas, Cayugas, Onondagas and Delawares — for the last, also, were often at Fort Niagara — were sent against the Americans, by the British. The Oneidas, as is well known, were divided and vacillating in their allegiance. In August, 1780, 132 of them who hitherto had been ostensibly friendly to the Americans, were induced to go to Niagara and give their pledges to the British. When they arrived Guy Johnson put on a severe front and censured them for their lack of

With Bolton at Fort Niagara.   79

steadfastness to the King. According to him, some 500 Oneidas in all came to the fort that year and declared themselves ready to fight the Americans. The last party that arrived delivered up to the Superintendent a commission which, he says, "the Rebels had issued with a view to form the Oneidas into a corps, . . . they also delivered up to me the Rebel flag."

So far as I am aware this is the first mention of the Stars and Stripes on the banks of the Niagara. By resolution of June 14, 1777, the American Congress had decreed "That the flag of the thirteen United States be thirteen stripes alternate red and white; that the union be thirteen stars, white in a blue field, representing a new constellation." A little over three years had passed since John Paul Jones had first flung to the breeze, at the mast of his ship Ranger, this bright banner of the new nation. It was not to appear in a British port for two and a half years to come; sixteen years were to pass before it could fly triumphant over the old walls of Fort Niagara; but France had saluted it, Americans were fighting for it, and although it is first found here in hostile hands, yet I like to reckon from that August day in 1780, the beginning, if in prophecy only, of the reign of that new constellation over the Niagara region.

Col. Bolton's life at Fort Niagara was one of infinite care. Besides the routine of the garrison, he was constantly harrassed by the demands of the Indians, whom the British did not wish to feed, but whom they dared not offend. The old fort, which now sleeps so quietly at the mouth of the river, was a busy place in those days. There was constant coming and going. Schooners, snows[1] and batteaux with provisions from Quebec, or with munitions of war or detachments of troops for Detroit or Michillimackinac, were constantly arriving. I question if the lower Niagara were not busier in that period than it is now. The transfer of supplies around the falls — the "great portage" — was hard and tedious work. Not Quebec, but Great Britain, was the real base of supplies. There were many detentions, and constant interruption in shipment, at every stage of the way. Sometimes a cargo of salt pork from Ireland or flour from London would reach Quebec too late in the summer to admit of transfer to the posts until spring. Sometimes, in crossing Lake Ontario, the provisions would be damaged so as to be unfit for use; sometimes they would be lost. Then not only the garrison at Niagara had to face starvation, but Col. Bolton soon had his ears ringing with messages and maledictions from Detroit and Mackinac, buried still farther in the wilderness, and all looking to Niagara for food and clothing. At such times of distress the upper posts questioned whether goods intended for them were not irregularly held at Niagara; the meanwhile, Col. Bolton would be straining every effort to get provisions enough to keep his own command from star-

---

[1] A snow is a three-masted craft, the smallest mast abaft the mainmast being rigged with a try-sail. Possibly, on the lakes where shipyards were primitive, this type was not always adhered to; but the correspondence and orders of the period under notice carefully discriminate between snows and schooners.

vation. Indian supplies and traders' goods, too, were liable to loss and detention; and on very slight provocation, the demands of the Indians grew insolent.

There were constant desertions, too, among the troops. Indeed, there seems never to have been a time at Fort Niagara when desertions were not frequent, and, more than once, so numerous as to threaten the very existence of the garrison. This, however, not in Bolton's time. As the correspondence shows, he enjoyed the utmost confidence of his superiors, and there is nothing to indicate that his men were not as devoted to him as any officer could expect at a frontier post where service meant hard work and possible starvation.

Frequent as had been the raids against the settlements before the expedition of Sullivan, they became thereafter even more frequent; and, if less disastrous, they were so merely because the American frontier settlements had already paid their utmost tribute to Butler and Brant. The expeditions, along certain much-worn trails, had to go farther and farther in order to find foes to attack or cattle to steal. This was especially so in the valleys of the Mohawk and Susquehanna; yet in one quarter and another this border warfare went on, and there is no lack of evidence, in the official correspondence, of its effectiveness. Thus, writing from Fort Niagara, August 24, 1780, Guy Johnson reports: "I have the pleasure to inform your excellency that the partys who subdivided after Capt. Brant's success at the Cleysburg"—an expedition which he had previously reported—"have all been successful; that Capt. Brant has destroyed twenty houses in Schoharie and taken and killed twelve persons, besides releasing several women and children. Among the prisoners is Lieut. Vrooman, the settlement of that name being that which was destroyed. The other divisions of that party have been also successful, particularly Capt. David's party, and the number of killed and taken by them within that time, so far as it has come to my hands, is, killed, thirty-five, taken, forty-six, released, forty. . . . The remaining inhabitants on the frontiers are drawing in so as to deprive the rebels of any useful resources from them. I have at present on service, several partys that set out within one and the same week, and I apprehend that falling on the frontiers in different places at the same time will have a good effect." September 18th he writes, telling of the destruction of "Kleysberg," "containing a church, 100 houses and as many barnes, besides mills and 500 cattle and horses." In the same letter he wrote: "I have now 405 warriors out in different parties and quarters, exclusive of some marched from Kadaragawas. . . . The greater part of the rest are at their planting grounds, and many sick here, as fevers and fluxes have for some time prevailed at this Post." October 1st he reports the number of men in the war parties sent out from Fort Niagara as 892. A return, dated June 30, 1781, shows that the war parties "have killed and taken during the season already 150 persons." September 30th he reports an expedition under Walter Johnson and Montour, in which about

With Bolton at Fort Niagara. 83

"twenty rebels" were killed; and on that day Capt. Nelles arrived with eleven prisoners taken in Pennsylvania. A postscript to this letter says: "Since writing, I have received the disagreeable news of the death of the gallant Montour, who died of the wounds he received in the action before related. He was a chief of the greatest spirit and readiness, and his death is a loss." We can well believe that; for Montour, who, from the American view-point, had the reputation of being a fiend incarnate, had indeed shown "spirit and readiness" in stealing cattle, burning log cabins, killing and scalping their occupants or bringing them captive to Fort Niagara.

In another paper [1] I have stated that I have traced out the individual experiences in captivity of thirty-two of these Americans, who were taken by the Indians and British and brought as prisoners to Fort Niagara. How much might be done on this line may be judged from a review of Col. Johnson's transactions, furnished by that officer at Montreal, March 24, 1782, in which it is stated that the number of Americans killed and taken captive by parties from Fort Niagara, amounted at that time to near 900. The time was rife with like experiences. For instance, there was the famous raid on Cherry Valley, from which Mrs. Jane Campbell and her four children, after a long detention among the Indians, were brought to Fort Niagara. There was Jane Moore, who was also taken at Cherry Valley, and who subsequently was married to Capt. Powell of the

---

[1] See "What Befel David Ogden," in this volume.

Niagara garrison in the winter of 1779 — the ceremony, by the Church of England service, so impressing Joseph Brant that he immediately led up to the minister the squaw with whom he had been living for a long time, and insisted on being married over again, white man's fashion. There was Lieut. Col. Stacia, another prisoner from Cherry Valley, whose head Molly Brant wanted for a football. Some of the stories of these captives, like that of Alexander Harper, who ran the gauntlet at Fort Niagara (the ordeal apparently being made light in his case), are familiar to readers of our history; others, I venture to say, are unknown. For instance, there were John and Robert Brice, two little boys, who were taken in 1779 near Rensselaerville by a scouting party, and brought, with other prisoners and eight scalps, to Fort Niagara. But they did not come together. Robert, who was but eleven years old, was taken to Fort Erie and sold to a lake sailor for the sum of £3. This little Son of the Revolution was kept on the upper lakes until 1783, when he was summoned to Fort Niagara where he met his brother John, from whom he had parted near the mouth of the Unadilla River some four years before. They were sent to Montreal with nearly 200 liberated captives, and ultimately the boys reached Albany and their friends. Then there is the story of Nancy Bundy, who, her husband and children being killed, was brought to Fort Niagara and sold into servitude for $8. There was the famous Indian fighter, Moses Van Campen, whose adventures and captivity in our region are the subject

With Bolton at Fort Niagara. 85

of a whole book. There were Horatio Jones and Jasper Parrish, who passed from Indian captives into the useful rôle of interpreters for the whites.

Thus I might go on, naming by the score the heroes and heroines of Indian captivities whose sufferings and whose adventures make up the most romantic chapter in our home annals, as yet for the most part unwritten. But I take time now to dwell, briefly as possible, upon but one of these captivities — one of the notable incidents during Col. Bolton's time at Fort Niagara. This was the capture of the Gilbert family. It made so great a stir, even in those days accustomed to war and Indian raids, that in 1784 a little book was published in Philadelphia giving the history of it. The original edition[1] has long since been one of the scarcest of Americana. But in the unpublished correspondence between Gen. Haldimand and the officers at Fort Niagara, I find sundry allusions to "the Quaker's family," and statements which go to show that the British at least were disposed to treat them well, and

[1] "A Narrative of the Captivity and Sufferings of Benjamin Gilbert and his Family; Who were surprised by the Indians, and taken from their Farms, on the Frontiers of Pennsylvania, in the Spring, 1780. Philadelphia: Printed and sold by Joseph Crukshank, in Market-street, between Second and Third-streets. M DCC LXXXIV." 12mo, pp. iv-96. It was reprinted in London (12mo, pp. 123) in 1785, and again (12mo, pp. 124, "Reprinted and sold by James Phillips, George-Yard, Lombard street") in 1790. A "third edition, revised and enlarged," 16mo, pp. 240, bears date Philadelphia, 1848. Of a later edition (8vo, pp. 38. Lancaster, Pa., 1890) privately printed, only 150 copies were issued. The work was written by William Walton, to whom the facts were told by the Gilberts after their return. (Field.) Ketchum made some use of the "Narrative" in his "Buffalo and the Senecas," as has Wm. Clement Bryant and perhaps other local writers. See also "Account of Benjamin Gilbert," Vol. III., Register of Pennsylvania. A reissue of the original work, carefully edited, would not only be a useful book for students of the history of Buffalo and the Niagara region, but would offer much in the way of extraordinary adventure for the edification of "the general reader."

to effect their exchange as soon as possible. Notwithstanding, it was a long and cruel captivity, and presents some features of peculiar significance in our local history.

About sunrise on the morning of April 25, 1780, a party of eleven painted Indians suddenly issued from the woods bordering Mahoning Creek, in Northampton County, Penn. They had come from Fort Niagara, and were one of those scalping parties for the success of which so many encouraging messages had passed from Whitehall to Quebec, and from Quebec to the frontier, and to stimulate which Guy Johnson had been so lavish with the fine linen, silver ornaments and port wine. The party was commanded by Rowland Montour, John Montour being second in command. Undiscovered, they surrounded the log house of the old Quaker miller, Benjamin Gilbert. With tomahawk raised and flint-locks cocked they suddenly appeared at door and windows. The old Quaker offered his hand as a brother. It was refused. Partly from the Quaker habit of non-resistance, partly from the obvious certainty that to attempt to escape meant death, the whole household submitted to be bound, while their home was plundered and burned. Loading three of Gilbert's horses with booty, and placing heavy packs on the back of each prisoner old enough to bear them, the expedition took the trail for Fort Niagara, more than 200 miles away. This was "war" in "the good old days."

There were twelve prisoners in the party, of whom

but five were men. The patriarch of the household, Benjamin, was sixty-nine years old; Elizabeth, his wife, was fifty-five; Joseph, Benjamin's son by a former wife, aged forty-one; another son, Jesse, aged nineteen, and his wife Sarah, the same age. There were three younger children, Rebecca, Abner and Elizabeth, respectively sixteen, fourteen and twelve; Thomas Peart, son to Benjamin Gilbert's wife by a former husband, aged twenty-three; a nephew, Benjamin Gilbert, aged eleven; a hired man, Andrew Harrigar, twenty-six; and Abigail Dodson, the fourteen-year-old daughter of a neighbor; she had had the ill-luck to come to Gilbert's mill that morning for grist, and was taken with the rest. Half a mile distant lived Mrs. Gilbert's oldest son, Benjamin Peart, aged twenty-seven, his wife Elizabeth, who was but twenty, and their nine-months-old child. Montour added these to his party, making fifteen prisoners in all, burned their house and urged all along the trail, their first stop being near "Mochunk." (Mauch Chunk.)

I must omit most of the details of their march northward. On the evening of the first day Benjamin Peart fainted from fatigue and Rowland Montour was with difficulty restrained from tomahawking him. At night the men prisoners were secured in a way which was usual on these raids, throughout Western New York and Pennsylvania, during those dismal years. The Indians cut down a sapling five or six inches in diameter, and cut notches in it large enough to receive the ankles of the prisoners. After fixing their legs in these notches, they placed another pole over the first, and thus secured them as in stocks. This upper pole was then crossed at each end by stakes driven into the ground. The prisoners thus lay on the ground, on their backs. Straps or ropes around their necks were made fast to near-by trees. Sometimes a blanket was granted them for covering, sometimes not. What rest might be had, preparatory to another day's forced march, I leave to the imagination.

During the early stages of this march the old couple were constantly threatened with death, because unable to keep up. On the fourth day four negroes who claimed that they were loyal to the King, that they had escaped from the Americans and had set out for Fort Niagara, were taken up by Montour from a camp where he had left them on his way down the valley. These negroes frequently whipped and tortured the prisoners for sport, Montour making no objection. On the 4th of May, the Indians separated into two companies; one taking the westward path, and with this party went Thomas Peart, Joseph Gilbert, Benjamin Gilbert — the little boy of eleven — and Sarah, wife of Jesse. The others kept on the northerly course. Andrew Harrigar, terrified by the Indian boast that those who had gone with the other party "were killed and scalped, and you may expect the same fate tonight," took a kettle, under pretence of bringing water, but ran away under cover of darkness. After incredible hardships he regained the settlements. His escape so angered Rowland Montour that he threw

Jesse Gilbert down, and lifted his tomahawk for the fatal blow; Elizabeth, Jesse's mother, knelt over him, pressed her head to her son's brow and begged the captain to spare his life. Montour kicked her over and tied them both by their necks to a tree; after a time, his passion cooling, he loosed them, bade them pack up and take the trail. This is but a sample incident. I pass over many.

None suffered more on the march than Elizabeth Peart, the girl mother. The Indians would not let her husband relieve her by carrying her child, and she was ever the victim of the whimsical moods of her captors. At one time they would let her ride one of the horses; at another, would compel her to walk, carrying the child, and would beat her if she lagged behind. By the 14th of May Elizabeth Gilbert had become so weak that she could only keep the trail when led and supported by her children. On this day the main party was rejoined by a portion of the party that had branched off to westward; with them were two of the four captives, Benjamin Gilbert, Jr., and Sarah, wife of Jesse. On this day old Benjamin was painted black, the custom of the Indians with prisoners whom they intended to kill. Later on they were joined by British soldiers, who took away the four negroes and did something to alleviate the sufferings of the white prisoners. The expedition had exhausted its provisions and all that had been taken from the Gilberts. A chance hedgehog, and roots dug in the woods, sustained them for some days. May the 17th they ferried across the Genesee River on a log raft. Provisions were brought from Fort Niagara, an Indian having been sent ahead, on the best horse; and on the morning of the 21st of May they heard, faintly booming beyond the intervening forest, the morning gun at Fort Niagara. An incident of that day's march was a meeting with Montour's wife. She was the daughter of the great Seneca Sayenqueraghta, the man who led the Indians at Wyoming,[1] and whose influence was greater in this region, at the time we are studying, than even that of Brant himself. He was the Old King of the Senecas, called Old Smoke by the whites. Smoke's Creek, the well-known stream which empties into Lake Erie just beyond the southwest limit of Buffalo, between South Park and Woodlawn Beach, preserves his name to our day. It was there that he lived in his last years; and somewhere on its margin, in a now unknown grave, he was buried. His daughter the "Princess," was, next to Molly Brant, the grandest Indian woman of the time on the Niagara. As she met the wretched Gilberts, "she was dressed altogether in the Indian costume, and was shining with gold lace and silver baubles." To her Rowland Montour presented the girl Rebecca, as a daughter. The princess took a silver ring from her finger and put it on Rebecca's, which act completed the adoption of this little

---

[1] Ketchum says he could not have done so. ("History of Buffalo," Vol. I., p. 328.) But Ketchum was misled, as many writers have been ascribing the leadership to Brant. My assertion rests on the evidence of contemporary documents in the Archives at Ottawa, especially the MS. "Anecdotes of Capt. Joseph Brant, Niagara, 1778," in the handwriting of Col. Daniel Claus. Wm. Clement Bryant published a part of it in his "Captain Brant and the Old King," *q. v.*

With Bolton at Fort Niagara. 91

Quaker maid of sixteen into one of the most famous — possibly the most infamous — family of the Niagara region during the Revolutionary period.

At a village not far from Fort Niagara, apparently near the present Tuscarora village on the heights east of Lewiston, Montour painted Jesse, Abner, Rebecca and Elizabeth Gilbert, Jr., as Indians are painted, and gave each a belt of wampum; but while these marks of favor were shown to the young people, the mother, because of her feebleness, was continually the victim of the displeasure and the blows of the Indians. On May 23d, being at the Landing — what is now Lewiston — they were visited by Captains Powell and Dace from the fort, and the next day, just one month from the time of their capture, they trudged down the trail which is now the pleasant river road, towards the old fort, protected with difficulty from the blows of the Indians along the way.

Now followed the dispersion of this unhappy family. After the Indian custom, the young and active prisoners were sought by the Indians for adoption. Many brave American boys went out to live, in the most menial servitude, among the Senecas and other tribes who during the later years of the Revolution lived on the Genesee, the Tonawanda, Buffalo, Cazenove, Smoke's, and Cattaraugus creeks. The old man and his wife and their son Jesse were surrendered to Col. Johnson. Benjamin Peart, Mrs. Gilbert's son, was carried off to the Genesee. The other members of the party were held in captivity in various places; but I may only stay now to note what befel the little Rebecca and her sister-in-law, Elizabeth Peart.

As already stated, Rebecca had been adopted by Rowland Montour's wife. In the general allotment of prisoners, her cousin, Benjamin Gilbert, the lad of eleven, also fell to this daughter of Sayenqueraghta. She took the children to a cabin where her father's family, eleven in number, were assembled. After the usual grand lamentation for the dead, whose places were supposed now to be filled by the white prisoners, this royal household departed by easy stages for their summer's corn-planting. They tarried at the Landing, while clothing was had from the fort. The little Quaker girl was dressed after the Indian fashion, "with short-clothes, leggins and a gold-laced hat"; while Benjamin, "as a badge of his dignity, wore a silver medal hanging from his neck." They moved up to Fort Schlosser (just above the falls, near where the present power-house stands), thence by canoe to Fort Erie; then "four miles further, up Buffalo Creek, where they pitched their tent for a settlement." Here the women planted corn; but the little Rebecca, not being strong, was allowed to look after the cooking. The whole household, queen, princess and slave, had to work. The men of course were exempt; but the chief advantage of Sayenqueraghta's high rank was that he could procure more provisions from the King's stores at Fort Niagara than could the humbler members of the tribe. The boy Ben had an easy time of it. He roamed at will with the Indian boys over the territory that is now Buffalo; fished in the lake, hunted or idled without constraint, and it is recorded that he was so pleased with the Indian mode of life, that but for his sister's constant admonition he would have dropped all thought of return to civilization, and cheerfully have become as good an Indian as the best of them. At eleven years of age savagery takes easy hold.

These children lived with Montour's Indian relatives for over two years; sharing in the feasts when there was plenty, going pinched with hunger on the frequent occasions when improvidence had exhausted the supply. There were numerous expeditions, afoot and by canoe, to Fort Niagara. On one occasion Rebecca, with her Indian family, were entertained by British officers at Fort Erie, when Old Smoke drank so much wine that when he came to paddle his canoe homeward, across the river, he narrowly escaped an upset on the rocky reef, just outside the entrance to Buffalo Creek. On every visit to Fort Niagara Rebecca would look for release; but although the officers were kind to her, they did not choose to interfere with so powerful a family as Montour's. It was shortly after one of these disappointments that she heard of her father's death. For some months she was sick; then came news of the death of her Indian father, Rowland Montour, who succumbed to wounds received in the attack already noted. There was great mourning in the lodge on Buffalo Creek, and Rebecca had to make a feint of sorrow, weeping aloud with the rest.

In the winter of '81–'82 a scheme was devised by

friends at the fort for abducting her from the Indians, but it was not undertaken. In the spring of '82 peremptory orders came from Gen. Haldimand that all the remaining members of the Gilbert family who were still in captivity should be taken from the Indians; but after a council fire had been lighted, Old Smoke, Montour's widow, and the rest of the family, Rebecca and Ben included, moved six miles up the lake shore — apparently to Smoke's Creek — where they stayed several weeks making maple sugar. Then, a great pigeon roost being reported, men and boys went off to it, some fifty miles, and the delighted young Ben went too. Of all the Gilbert captives he alone seems to have had experiences too full of wholesome adventure and easy living to warrant the expenditure of the least bit of sympathy upon him. But sooner or later the wily Indians had to heed Sir Frederick's command, and on the 1st of June, 1782, after upwards of two years of captivity, Rebecca and her cousin were released at Fort Niagara, and two days later, with others, embarked for Montreal.

Far more cheerless were the experiences of Elizabeth Peart. She was parted from her husband, adopted by a Seneca family, and was also brought to raise corn on Buffalo Creek. Early in her servitude among the Indians her babe was taken from her and carried across to Canada. She was but twenty years old herself; the family that had taken her came by canoe to Buffalo Creek, where they settled for the corn-planting. This was in the spring of 1780. All manner of drudgery

With Bolton at Fort Niagara.   95

and burdens were put upon her. Her work was to cultivate the corn. Falling sick, the Indians built a hut for her by the side of the cornfield, and then utterly neglected her. Here she remained through the summer, regaining strength enough to care for and gather the corn; when this was done, her Indian father permitted her to come and live again in the family lodge. At one time a drunken Indian attacked her, knocked her down, and dragged her about, beating her. At another, all provision failing, she tramped with others four days through the snow to Fort Niagara. Here Capt. Powell's wife — who had been a prisoner herself — interceded in Elizabeth's behalf, but to no avail. She was however given an opportunity to see her babe, which was being cared for by an Indian family on the Canadian side of the river, opposite Fort Niagara. This privilege was gained for the poor mother by bribing her Indian father with a bottle of rum. So far as I am aware, this was the best use to which a bottle of rum was put during the Revolutionary War. But back to Buffalo Creek the unhappy mother had to come. Her release was finally obtained by artifice. Being allowed to visit Fort Niagara, where she had some needlework to do for the white people, she feigned sickness, and by one excuse and another the Indians were put off until she could be shipped away to Montreal.

Of the Gilbert family and those taken with them by Montour, only the old man died in captivity. The adventures of each one would make a long story, but may not be entered upon here. By the close of '82 they were all released from the Indians, and after a detention at Montreal, reached their friends in Pennsylvania and set about the reëstablishment of homes.

Beyond question, Elizabeth Peart and Rebecca Gilbert were the first white women ever on the site of the present city of Buffalo. They were brave, patient, patriotic girls; no truer Daughters of the American Revolution are known to history. It would seem fitting that their memory should be preserved and their story known — much fuller than I have here sketched it — by the patriotic Daughters of the Revolution of our own day, who give heed to American beginnings in this region.

I have dwelt at length on the Gilbert captivity, not more because of its own importance than to illustrate the responsibilities which constantly rested on the commandant at Niagara, at this period. We now turn to other phases of the service which engaged the attention and taxed the endurance of Col. Bolton.

From the time of the conquest of Canada in 1760 down to the opening of the Revolution, there had been a slow but steady growth of shipping on the lakes, especially on Lake Ontario. On this lake, as early as 1767, there were four brigs of from forty to seventy tons, and sixteen armed deck-cutters. Besides the "King's ships" there were still much travel and traffic by means of canoes and batteaux. One of the first effects of the war with the American colonies was to beget active ship-building operations by the British;

With Bolton at Fort Niagara. 97

for Lake Ontario, at Oswegatchie, Oswego and Niagara; and for Lake Erie, at Navy Island, Detroit and Pine River. An official return made in July, 1778, the summer after Col. Bolton assumed command at Niagara, enumerates twelve sailing craft built for Lake Ontario since the British gained control of that lake in 1759, and sixteen for Lake Erie; seven of the Lake Ontario boats had been cast away, two were laid up and decayed; so that at this time — midsummer of '78 — there were still in service only the snow Haldimand, eighteen guns, built at Oswegatchie in 1771; the snow Seneca, eighteen guns, built in 1777; and the sloop Caldwell, two guns, built in 1774. A memorandum records that Capt. Andrews, in the spring of 1778, sought permission to build another vessel at Niagara, to take the place of the Haldimand, which, he was informed, could not last more than another year. The vessel built, in accordance with this recommendation, was a schooner; her construction was entrusted to Capt. Shank, at Niagara, across the river from the fort. We may be sure that Col. Bolton visited the yard from time to time to note the progress of the work. There was discussion over her lines. "Capt. Shank was told that he was making her too flat-bottomed, and that she would upset." The builder laughed at his critics and stuck to his model. She was launched, named the Ontario, and was hastened forward to completion, for the King's service had urgent need of her.

Col. Bolton had long been in bad health, wearied with the cares and perplexities of his position and eager to get away from Fort Niagara. One source of constant annoyance to his military mind was the traders' supplies, which turned the fort into a warehouse and laid distasteful duties upon its commandant. His letters contain many allusions to the "incredible plague and trouble caused by merchants' goods frequently sent without a single person to care for them." "Last year," so he wrote in May, '78, "every place in this fort was lumbered with them, and vessels were obliged to navigate the lakes until Nov. 30th." The vessels were primarily for the King's service, but when unemployed were allowed to be used in transporting merchants' goods, under certain regulations. The next statement in the same letter gives some idea of the magnitude of the transactions involved in the various departments in this region at the period: "I have drawn a bill of £14,760-9-5"—nearly $74,000—"on acct. of sundries furnished Indians by Maj. Butler, also another on acct. of Naval Dept. at Detroit for £4,070-18-9. Between us I am heartily sick of bills and accounts and if the other posts are as expensive to Government as this has been I think Old England had done much better in letting the savages take possession of them than to have put herself to half the enormous sum she has been at in keeping them. Neither does the climate agree with my constitution, which has already suffered by being employed many years in the West Indies and Florida, for I have been extremely ill the two winters I have spent here with rheumatism and a disorder in my breast."

One source of annoyance to Bolton was a detachment of Hessians which was sent to augment the garrison at Fort Niagara. Col. Bolton did not find them to his liking, nor was life at a backwoods post at all congenial to these mercenaries, fighting England's battles to pay their monarch's debts. They refused to work on the fortifications at Niagara; whereupon, in November, 1779, Col. Bolton packed them off down to Carleton Island. Alexander Fraser, in charge of that post, wrote to Gen. Haldimand that he had ordered the "jagers" to be replaced by a company of the 34th. " Capt. Count Wittgenstein," he added, "fears bad consequences should the Jagers be ordered to return." Nowhere in America does the British employment of Hessian troops appear to have been less satisfactory than on this frontier. At Carleton Island, as at Niagara, they refused to work, many of them were accused of selling their necessaries for rum, and the Count de Wittgenstein himself was reprimanded.

There were difficulties, too, with the lake service. Desertion and discontent followed an attempt to shorten the seamen's rations. In the summer of '78, the sailors on board the snow Seneca, at Niagara, asked to be discharged, alleging that their time had expired the preceding November, and the yet more remarkable reason that they objected to the service because they had been brought up on shore and life on the rolling deep of Lake Ontario afforded "no opportunity of exercising our Religion, neither does confinement agree with our healths." Like many lake sailors at this period they were probably French Canadian Catholics, with loyalty none too strong to the British cause.

Bolton stuck to his post throughout that season, the year of alarm that followed, and the succeeding period of distress. The most frequent entries in his letters record the arrival of war parties, and his anxiety over the enormous expense incurred for the Indians by Maj. Butler. "Scalps and prisoners are coming in every day, which is all the news this place affords," he writes in June, '78; and again, the same month: "Ninety savages are just arrived with thirteen scalps and two prisoners, and forty more with two scalps are expected. All of these gentry, I am informed, must be clothed."[1] While there does not seem ever to have been an open break between Bolton and Butler, yet the former looked with dismay, if not disapproval, upon the endless expenditure incurred for the Indians. In August, 1778, he wrote: "Maj. Butler, chief of the Indian Department, gives orders to the merchants to supply the savages with everything to answer their demands, of which undoubtedly he is the best judge and only person who can satisfy them or keep them in temper. He also signs a certificate that the goods and cash issued and paid by his order were indispensably necessary for the government of His Majesty's service. The

---

[1] What became of all the scalps brought in to Fort Niagara during these years, and delivered up to the British officers, if not for pay, certainly for presents? The human scalp, properly dried, is not readily perishable, if cared for. Very many of them — from youthful heads or those white with age, the long tresses of women and the soft ringlets of children — became the property of officers at this post. Little is said on this subject in the correspondence; we do not see them with flags and other trophies in the cathedrals and museums of England. What became of them?

commanding officer of this post is thus obliged to draw bills for the amount of all these accounts, of which it is impossible he can be a judge or know anything about. . . . I only mention these things to show Yr Excellency the disagreeable part that falls to my lot as commanding officer; besides this is such a complicated command that even an officer of much superior abilities than I am master of, would find himself sometimes not a little embarrassed at this Post.''

Bolton was seriously ill during the winter of '79-'80, as indeed were many of his garrison. In April, 1780, he reports his wretched health to Gen. Haldimand. All through the succeeding summer he stuck to his post; but on September 13th, worn out and discouraged, he asked to be allowed to retire from the command of the upper posts and lakes. September 30th he again wrote, begging for leave of absence. Some weeks later the desired permission was sent, and Bolton determined to stay no longer. Late in October the new Ontario, which Capt. Shank had built across the river from the fort, was finished and rigged; she carried sixteen guns, and was declared ready for service. She was ordered to convey a company of the 34th down to Carleton Island. It was a notable departure. The season was so late, no other opportunity for crossing Lake Ontario might be afforded until spring. Lieut. Royce, with thirty men of the 34th, embarked, under orders; so did Lieut. Colleton of the Royal Artillery. Capt. Andrews, superintendent of naval construction, at whose solicitations the Ontario had been built, being at Fort

Niagara at the time, also took passage. There was the full complement of officers and crew. Several passengers — licensed Indian traders and fur merchants, probably — crowded aboard; and among those who sailed away from Fort Niagara that last October day, was Col. Bolton. It was the Ontario's first voyage; and we may be sure that there was no lack of speculation and wise opinion in the throng of spectators who watched her round the bar at the mouth of the river and take her course down the lake. The old criticism about her flat bottom and lack of draught was sure to be recalled. But the Ontario, with her notable passenger list, had sailed, and the only port she ever reached was the bottom of the lake. It is supposed she foundered, some forty miles east of Niagara, near a place called Golden Hill. On the beach there, some days after, a few articles were found, supposed to have come ashore; but no other sign, no word of the Ontario or of any of the throng that sailed in her has been had from that day to this. In due time news of the loss reached Quebec. Sincere but short were the expressions of sorrow in the correspondence that followed. "The loss of so many good officers and men," wrote Haldimand, "particularly at this period, and the disappointment of forwarding provisions for the great consumption at the upper posts, will be severely felt."[1] It

---

[1] In another letter to Lord George Germaine, dated Nov. 20, 1780, we have a few additional particulars. It is probably the fullest account of this calamity in existence. "It is with great concern," wrote Haldimand, "I acquaint your Lordship of a most unfortunate event which is just reported to me to have happened upon Lake Ontario about the 1st. [Nov., 1780.] A very fine snow [schooner] carrying 16 guns, which was built last winter, sailed the 31st ultimo from Niagara and was seen several

was the fortune of war, and already the thought turned to those who had depended upon a return cargo of provisions by the Ontario. And so passes Mason Bolton out of the history of Fort Niagara.

---

times the same day near the north shore. The next day it blew very hard, and the vessel's boats, binnacle, gratings, some hats, etc., were found upon the opposite shore, the wind having changed suddenly, by Lt. Col. Butler about forty miles from Niagara, on his way from Oswego, so there cannot be a doubt that she is totally lost and her crew, consisting of forty seamen, perished, together with Lt. Col. Bolton of the King's Regiment, whom I had permitted to leave Niagara on account of his bad state of health, Lt. Colleton of the Royal Artillery, Lt. Royce and thirty men of the 34th Regiment, who were crossing the lake to reinforce Carleton Island. Capt. Andrews who commanded the vessel and the naval armament upon that lake was a most zealous, active, intelligent officer. The loss of so many good officers and men is much aggravated by the consequences that will follow this misfortune in the disappointment of conveying provisions across the lake for the garrison of Niagara and Detroit, which are not near completed for the winter consumption, and there is not a possibility of affording them much assistance with the vessels that remain, it being dangerous to navigate the lake later than the 20th inst., particularly as the large vessels are almost worn out. The master builder and carpenters are sent off to repair this evil."

What Befel David Ogden.

WHAT BEFEL DAVID OGDEN.

IT WAS my privilege, in the summer of 1896, to share in the exercises which marked the Centennial of the delivery of Fort Niagara by Great Britain to the United States. As I stood in that old stronghold on the bank above the blue lake, strolled across the ancient parade ground, or passed from one historic building to another, I found myself constantly forgetting the actual day and hour, and slipping back a century or two. There was a great crowd at Fort Niagara on this August day; thousands of people — citizens, officials, soldiers and pleasure-seekers; but with them came and went, to my retrospective vision, many more thousands yet: missionary priests, French adventurers, traders, soldiers of the scarlet, and of the buff and blue. I saw Butler's Rangers in their green suits; and I saw a horde of savages, now begging for rations from the King's stores, now coming in from their forays, famished but exultant, displaying the scalps they had taken, or leading their ragged and woebegone captives. It was upon these captives, whose romantic misfortunes make a long and dramatic chapter in the history of Fort Niagara, that my regard was prone to center. Their stories have nowhere been told, so far as I am aware, as a part of the history of the place; many of them never can be told; but of others some details may be recorded.

Throughout the whole period of the Revolutionary War, Fort Niagara was a garrisoned British post, of varying strength. It was the supply depot for all arms and provisions which were destined for the upper posts of Detroit and Michillimackinac; it was the rendezvous of the Senecas, who worked the Government for all the blankets and guns, trinkets and provisions which they could get; it was the headquarters of Col. Guy Johnson, Indian Superintendent; and it was the resting-place and base of operations of They-en-dan-e-gey-ah — in English, Joseph Brant; of Butler and his rangers, and of numerous other less famous but more cruel Indians, British and Tory leaders. No American troops reached Fort Niagara to attack it. Only once was it even threatened. Yet throughout the whole period of the war parties sallied forth from Fort Niagara to plunder, capture or kill the rebel settlers wherever they could be reached.

Sixty years ago Judge Samuel De Veaux wrote of this phase of the history of Fort Niagara:

> This old fort is as much noted for enormity and crime, as for any good ever derived from it by the nation in occupation. . . . During the American Revolution it was the headquarters of all that was barbarous, unrelenting and cruel. There, were congregated the leaders and chiefs of those bands of murderers and miscreants, that carried death and destruction into the remote American settlements. There, civilized Europe revelled with savage America; and ladies of education and refinement mingled in the

society of those whose only distinction was to wield the bloody tomahawk and scalping-knife. There, the squaws of the forest were raised to eminence, and the most unholy unions between them and officers of the highest rank, smiled upon and countenanced. There, in their strong hold, like a nest of vultures, securely, for seven years, they sallied forth and preyed upon the distant settlements of the Mohawks and Susquehannahs. It was the depot of their plunder; there they planned their forays, and there they returned to feast, until the hour of action came again.[1]

This striking passage, which the worthy author did not substantiate by a single fact, may stand as the present text. I have undertaken to trace some of the flights of the birds of prey from this nest, and to bring together the details relating to the captives who were brought hither. From many sources I have traced out the narratives of thirty-two persons who were brought to Fort Niagara captive by the Indians, during the years 1778 to 1783. Among them is my boy hero Davy Ogden, whose adventures I undertake to tell with some minuteness. Just how many American prisoners were brought into Fort Niagara during this period I am unable to say, though it is possible that from the official correspondence of the time figures could be had on which a very close estimate could be based. My examination of the subject warrants the assertion that several hundred were brought in by the war parties under Indian, British and Tory leaders. In this correspondence, very little of which has ever been published, one may find such entries as the following:

---
[1] "The Falls of Niagara, or Tourist's Guide," etc., by S. De Veaux. Buffalo, 1839.

Guy Johnson wrote from Fort Niagara, June 30, 1781:

In my last letter of the 24th inst. I had just time to enclose a copy of Lieut. Nelles's letter with an account of his success, since which he arrived at this place with more particular information by which I find that he killed thirteen and took seven (the Indians not having reckoned two of the persons whom they left unscalped). . . .

Again:

I have the honor to transmit to Your Excellency a general letter containing the state of the garrison and of my Department to the 1st inst., and a return, at the foot, of the war parties that have been on service this year, . . . by which it will appear that they have killed and taken during the season already 150 persons, including those last brought in. . . .

Again he reports, August 30, 1781:

The party with Capt. Caldwell and some of the Indians with Capt. Lottridge are returning, having destroyed several settlements in Ulster County, and about 100 of the Indians are gone against other parts of the frontiers, and I have some large parties under good leaders still on service as well as scouts towards Fort Pitt. . . .

Not only are there many returns of this sort, but also tabulated statements, giving the number of prisoners sent down from Fort Niagara to Montreal on given dates, with their names, ages, names of their captors, and the places where they were taken. There were many shipments during the summer of '83, and the latest return of this sort which I have found in the archives is dated August 1st of that year, when eleven prisoners were sent from the fort to Montreal. It was probably not far from this time that the last American prisoner of the Revolution was released from Fort Niagara. But let the reader beware of forming hasty conclusions as to the cruelty or brutality of the British at Fort Niagara. In the first place, remember that harshness or kindness in the treatment of the helpless depends in good degree — and always has depended — upon the temperament and mood of the individual custodian. There were those in command at Fort Niagara who appear to have been capable of almost any iniquity. Others gave frequent and conspicuous proofs of their humanity. Remember, secondly, that the prisoners primarily belonged to the Indians who captured them. The Indian custom of adoption — the taking into the family circle of a prisoner in place of a son or husband who had been killed by the enemy — was an Iroquois custom, dating back much further than their acquaintance with the English. Many of the Americans who were detained in this fashion by their Indian captors, probably never were given over to the British. Some, as we know, like Mary Jemison, the White Woman of the Genesee, adopted the Indian mode of life and refused to leave it. Others died in captivity, some escaped. Horatio Jones and Jasper Parrish were first prisoners, then utilized as interpreters, but remained among the Indians.[1] And

---

[1] Capt. Parrish became Indian agent, but Capt. Jones held the office of interpreter for many years. "Their councils [with the Indians] were held at a council house belonging to the Senecas situated a few rods east of the bend in the road just this side of the red bridge across Buffalo Creek on the Aurora Plank Road, then little more than an Indian trail ; but much of their business was transacted at the store of Hart & Lay, situated on the west side of Main Street, midway between Swan and Erie streets, and on the common opposite, then known as Ellicott Square."—MS. narrative of Capt. Jones's captivity, by Orlando Allen, in possession of William L.

in many cases, especially of women and children, we know that they were got away from the Indians by the British officers at Fort Niagara, only after considerable trouble and expense. In these cases the British were the real benefactors of the Americans, and the kindness in the act cannot always be put aside on the mere ground of military exchange, prisoner for prisoner. Gen. Haldimand is quoted to the effect that he "does not intend to enter into an exchange of prisoners, but he will not add to the distresses attending the present war, by detaining helpless women and children from their families."[1]

I have spoken of Mrs. Campbell, who was held some months at Kanadasaga. The letter just cited further illustrates the point I would make:

> A former application had been made in behalf of Col. Campbell to procure the exchange of his family for that of Col. Butler, and the officer commanding the upper posts collected Mr. Campbell's and the family of a Mr. Moore, and procured their release from the Indians upon the above mentioned condition with infinite trouble and a very heavy expense. They are now at Fort Niagara where the best care that circumstances will admit of, is taken of them, and I am to acquaint you that Mrs. Campbell & any other women or children that shall be specified shall be safely conducted to Fort Schuyler, or to any other place that shall be thought most convenient, provided Mrs. Butler & her family consisting of a like number shall in the same manner have safe

Bryant of Buffalo. Horatio Jones was captured about 1777 near Bedford, Pa., being aged 14; was taken to a town on the Genesee River, where he ran the gauntlet, was adopted, and lived with the Indians until liberated by the Treaty of Fort Stanwix in 1784. The MS. narrative above quoted is Orlando Allen's chronicle of facts given to him by Capts. Jones and Parrish, and is of exceptional value.

[1] Brig. Powell to Col. van Schaick, Feb. 13, 1780; Haldimand Papers, "Correspondence relating to exchange of prisoners," etc., B. 175.

What Befel David Ogden. 113

conduct to my advance post upon Lake Champlain in order that she may cross the lake before the ice breaks up.

The official correspondence carried on during the years 1779 to '83, between Gen. Haldimand and the commanding officers at Fort Niagara shows in more than one instance that American prisoners were a burden and a trouble at that post. Sometimes, as in the case of Mrs. Campbell, who was finally exchanged for Mrs. Butler and her children, they were detained as hostages. More often, they were received from the Indians in exchange for presents, the British being obliged to humor the Indians and thus retain their invaluable services. Thus, under date of Oct. 2, 1779, we find Col. Bolton writing from Fort Niagara to Gen. Haldimand: "I should be glad to know what to do with the prisoners sent here by Capt. Lernault. Some of them I forwarded to Carleton Island, and Maj. Nairne has applied for leave to send them to Montreal. I have also many here belonging to the Indians, who have not as yet agreed to deliver them up."[1]

---

[1] I cannot better show the real state of affairs at Fort Niagara, towards the close of the Revolutionary War, than by submitting the following "Review of Col. Johnson's Transactions," which I copy from the Canadian Archives. [Series B, Vol. 106, p. 123, *et seq.*] I do not know that it has ever been printed. Obviously written at the instigation of Col. Johnson, it is perhaps colored to justify his administrative conduct; but in any event it is a most useful picture of conditions at the time. Except for some slight changes in punctuation in order to make the meaning more readily apparent, the statement is given verbatim:

MONTREAL, 24th March, 1782.

Before Colonel Johnson arrived at Niagara in 1779 the Six Nations lived in their original possession the nearest of which was about 100 and the farthest about 300 miles from that post. Their warriors were called upon as the service required parties, which in 1776 amounted to about 70 men, and the expenses attending them and a few occasional meetings ought to have been and he presumes were a mere Trifle when compared with what must attend their situation when all [were] driven to Niagara, exposed to

I could multiply at great length these citations from the official correspondence, but enough has been given to show that the wholesale condemnation of the British, into whose hands American prisoners fell, is not warranted by the facts. But there is no plainer fact in it all than that the British organized and aided the Indian raids, and were, therefore, joint culprits in general.

And this brings us to the subject of scalps. For many years Fort Niagara was called a scalp-market.

---

every want, to every temptation and with every claim which their distinguished sacrifices and the tenor of Soloman [solemn] Treaties had entitled them to from Government. The years 1777 & 1778 exhibited only a larger number occasionally employed and for their fidelity and attachment to Government they were invaded in 1779 by a rebel army reported to be from 5 to 600 men with a train of Artillery who forced them to retire to Niagara leaving behind them very fine plantations of corn and vegetables, with their cloathing, arms, silver works, Wampum Kettles and Implements of Husbandry, the collection of ages of which were distroyed in a deliberate manner and march of the rebels. Two villages only escaped that were out of their route.

The Indians having always apprehended that their distinguished Loyalty might draw some such calamity towards them had stipulated that under such circumstances they effected [expected] to have their losses made up as well as a liberal continuation of favors and to be supported at the expence of Government till they could be reinstated in their former possessions. They were accordingly advised to form camps around Niagara which they were beginning to do at the time of Colonel Johnson's arrival who found them much chagrined and prepared to reconcile them to their disaster which he foresaw would be a work of time requiring great judgement and address in effecting which he was afterwards successful beyond his most sanguine expectations, and this was the state of the Indians at Colonel Johnson's arrival. As to the state and regulation of Colonel Johnson's offices and department at that period he found the duties performed by 2 or three persons the rest little acquainted with them and considered as less capable of learning them, and the whole number inadequate to that of the Indians, and the then requisite calls of the service, and that it was necessary after refusing the present wants of the Indians to keep their minds occupied by constant military employment, all which he laid before the Commander in Chief who frequently honoured his conduct with particular approbation.

By His Instructions he was to apply to Lieut. Colonel Bolton, more especially regarding the modes of this place and the public accounts &c from whom he received no further information, than that they were kept, and made up by the established house at that post, and consider of goods, orders and all contingencies and disbursements for Indians, ranging parties, Prisoners, &c. That they were generally arranged half yearly as well as the nature of them and of the changeable people they had to deal with would permit; that he believed many demands were therefore outstanding and that he was glad to have done with passing [i. e., granting of passes] as it was impossible for him or any person that had other duties to

What Befel David Ogden.

The statement is frequent in early writers that the British officers offered about eight dollars for every American's scalp, and that it was this offer, more than anything else, which fired the Indians to their most horrible deeds. Many scalps were brought into Fort Niagara, but I have failed, as yet, to find any report, or figure, or allusion, in the British archives pointing to the payment of anything whatever. Further search may discover something to settle this not unimportant matter;

---

discharge to give them much attention. At which Colonel Johnson expressed his concern but was told that the house was established in the business and thro' the impossibility of having proper circulating cash in another channell they advanced all monies and settled all accounts and that that mode had been found most eligable. Colonel Johnson thereupon issued the best orders he could devise for the preventing abuses and the better regulation of matters relating to goods payment of expenses, and proceeding to the discharge of the principal objects of his duty, he, accordingly to a plan long since proposed, formed the Indians into Companies and by degrees taught them to feel the convenience of having officers set apart to each, which they were soon not only reconciled to but highly pleased with, by which means he gave some degree of method and form to the most Independent race of the Indians, greatly facilitated all business with them and by a prudent arrangement of his officers those who were before uninformed became in a little time some of the most approved and usefull persons in his department, being constantly quartered at such places or sent on some services as tended most to their improvement and the public advantage, whilst by spiriting up and employing the Indians with constant party's along the frontiers from Fort Stanwix to Fort Pitt he so harrassed the back settlements, as finally to drive numbers of them from their plantation destroying their houses, mills, graneries, &c, frequently defeating their scouting parties killing and captivating many of their people amounting in the whole to near 900 and all this with few or no instances of savage cruelty exclusive of what they performed when assisted by His Majesty's Troops as will appear from his returns. By these means he presented [? preserved] the spirit of the Indians and kept their minds so occupied as to prevent their being disgusted at the want of Military aid, which had been long their Topic and which could then be afforded according to their requisitions ; neither did he admit any point of negociation during this period of peculiar hurry, for knowing the importance the Oneidas &c., were off [of] to the rebels and the obstruction they gave to all means of intelligence from that quarter, he sent a private Belt and message on pretence of former Friendship for them, in consequence of which he was shortly joined by 430 of them of [whom] 130 were men who have since on all occasions peculiarly distinguished themselves, and after defeating the rebel Invitation to the Indians he by the renewal of the great covenant chain and war Belt which he sent thro' all the nations animation to the most western Indians.

Soon after with intention to reduce the vast consumption of provisions, he with much difficulty prevailed on part of the Indians to begin some new plantation, that they might supply themselves with grain, &c;

for we may readily believe that if such payments were made the matter would be passed over as unobtrusively as possible, especially in the reports to the Ministry. The facts appear to be that warriors who brought scalps into Fort Niagara gave them to the Superintendent of Indian Affairs, or his deputy, and then received presents from him. Probably these presents were proportioned to the success on the warpath.

but this being an object of the most serious and National concern, and urged in the strongest terms by the commander-in-chief, Col. Johnson, during the winter 1780, took indefatigable pains to persuade the whole to remove and settle the ensuing season on advantageous terms. He had himself visited for that purpose but finding that their treaties with and expectations from Government, combined with their natural Indulgence to render it a matter of infinite difficulty which would encrease by delay and probably become unsurmountable he procured some grain from Detroit and liberally rewarded the families of Influence at additional expence to sett the example to the rest and assisted their beginning to prevent a disappointment by which means he has enabled before the end of May last to settle the whole about 3500 souls exclusive of those who had joined the 2 farms that had not been distroyed by the rebels and thereby with a little future assistance, and good management to create a saving of £100,000 pr annum N. York currency at the rate of provision is worth there to Government, together with a reduction of rum and of all Indian Expenses, as will appear from the reduced accounts since these settlements were made. The peculiar circumstances above mentioned and the constant disappointment of goods from the Crown at the times they were most wanted will easily account for the occasional expence. The house which conducted the Business at Niagara was perpetually thronged by Indians and others. Lieut. Colonel Bolton often sent verbal orders for articles as did some other secretaries and sometimes necessity required it and often they were charged and others substituted of equal value with other irregularities, the consequence of a crew of Indians before unknown, of an encrease of duties, and the necessity for sending them to plant well satisfied.

The number of prisoners thrown upon Colonel Johnson from time to time and of Indian Chiefs and their families about his quarters was attended with vast trouble and an Expense which it was impossible to ascertain with exactness and when he directed the moiety of certain articles of consumption to be placed to the account of the Crown, he soon found himself lower. The merchants have since been accused of fraud by a clerk who lived some time with them, the investigation of which he was called suddenly to attend and he now finds that many articles undoubtedly issued have been placed to his account instead of their [the] Crown, and many false and malicious insinuations circulated to the prejudice of his character and his influence with the Indians which is rendered the more injurious by his abrupt departure from the shortness of the time, which did not permit his calling and explaining to the chiefs the reasons for his leaving them as [he] undoubtedly should have done, and therefore, and on every public account, his presence is not only effected [expected], but is become more necessary among them than ever. This brief summary is candidly prepared and is capable of sufficient proof and Illustration.

What Befel David Ogden.

These facts and reflections are offered to assist the reader's ready understanding and imagination in following in detail the adventures of one out of the many prisoners whose paths we have glanced at; for of all these unfortunate patriots who were thus brought to the "vultures' nest" none has laid hold of my interest and my imagination more strongly than has David Ogden. He was born in a troublous time, and the hazards of border life were his sole heritage, save alone a sturdy intrepidity of character which chiefly commends him to me as the typical hero of all the heroic souls, men, women, and children, who came through great bereavements and hardships, into old Fort Niagara as prisoners of war. Davy was born at Fishkill, Dutchess Co., New York, in 1764. His parents made one remove after another, in the restless American fashion, for some years taking such chances of betterment as new settlements afforded; first at Waterford, Saratoga Co.; then in the wilderness on the head-waters of the Susquehanna near the present village of Huntsville; then up the river to the settlement known in those days as Newtown Martin, now Middlefield; and later, for safety, to Cherry Valley. Here David's mother and her four boys were at the time of the famous massacre of November, 1778. When the alarm was given Mrs. Ogden snatched a blanket, and with her little ones began a flight through the woods towards the Mohawk. With them also fled Col. Campbell, of the patriot militia. Coming to a deserted cabin whose owner had fled, they did not scruple to help themselves to a loaf of bread, which Col. Campbell cut up with his sword. After another flight of some hours through a storm of mingled snow and rain, they came to the house of one Lyons, a Tory, who was absent, presumably because busied in the black work at Cherry Valley. Mrs. Lyons, who seems to have shared her husband's sentiments, refused the refugees anything to eat, but finally let the mother and children spend the night on the floor. Col. Campbell left the Ogdens here and pushed on alone towards Canajoharie; while Mrs. Odgen and her hungry little ones went on by themselves through the snow. That day they came to a more hospitable house, where the keen suffering of that adventure ended; and some days later, on the Mohawk, the father rejoined the family, he also having escaped the massacre at Cherry Valley.

This incident may be reckoned the mere prelude of our Davy's adventures; for the next spring, having reached the mature age of fourteen, he volunteered in the service of his country, entered upon the regular life of a soldier, and began to have adventures on his own account. The year that followed was spent in arduous but not particularly romantic service. He was marched from one point to another on the Mohawk and the Hudson; saw André hanged at Tappan, and finally was sent to the frontier again, where at Fort Stanwix,[1] in the spring of 1781, what we may regard as the real adventures of Davy Ogden began.

A party of eleven wood-choppers were at work in

---

[1] Site of Rome, N. Y.

the heavy timber about two miles from the fort, and every day an armed guard was sent out from the garrison to protect them. On March 2d, Corporal Samuel Betts and six soldiers, Davy among them, were detailed on this service. I conceive of my hero at this time as a sturdy, well-seasoned lad, to whom woodcraft and pioneer soldiering had become second nature. I would like to see him among city boys of his own age to-day. Most things that they know, and think of, would be quite out of his range. But there is a common ground on which all healthy, high-minded boys, of whatever time or station in life, stand on a level. I do not know that he had ever been to school, or that he could read, though I think his mother must have looked to that. But I do know that he was well educated. He was innocent of the bicycle, but I'll warrant he could skate. I know he could swim like an otter—as I shall presently record—and when it came to running, he would have been a champion of the cinder-path, to-day. He knew the ways of poverty and of self-denial; knew the signs of the forest, of wild animal and Indian; and best of all, I am sure he knew just why he was carrying a heavy flint-lock in the ragged, hungry ranks of the American "rebels." It must be admitted, I linger somewhat over my hero; but I like the lad, and would have the reader come into sympathy with him. I can see him now as he followed the corporal out of the fort that March morning. He wore the three-cornered cocked-up hat of the prescribed uniform, and his powder-horn was slung at his side. The whole guard very likely wore snow-shoes, for the snow lay three feet deep in the woods, and a thaw had weakened the crust.

Late in the afternoon, soldiers and wood-choppers were startled by the yells of Indians and Tories, who had gained a hill between them and the fort. Brant had achieved another of his surprises, and there was no escape from his party, which seemed to fill the woods. His evident intent was to make captives and not to kill, though his men had orders to shoot or tomahawk any who fired in self-defense. Two of Davy's companions were wounded by the enemy. One of them, Timothy Runnels, was shot in the mouth, "the ball coming through his cheek; and yet not a tooth was disturbed, a pretty good evidence, in the opinion of his comrades, that his mouth was wide open when the ball went in." It fared more seriously with the other wounded soldier. This man, whose name was Morfat, had his thigh broken by a bullet. The Indians rushed upon him as he fell at Davy's side, tomahawked him, scalped him, stripped him and left him naked upon the snow, thus visiting a special vengeance upon one who was said to be a deserter from the British. It is further chronicled that Morfat did not immediately die, but lived until he was found, hours after, by a party from the fort, finally expiring as his comrades bore him through the gate of Fort Stanwix.

Davy Ogden had seen this dreadful thing, but with no sign of fear or sickness. He had already mastered that scorn of suffering and death which always commended the brave to their Indian captors. He was ranged up with the other prisoners, and Brant asked of each his name. When Davy gave his, the great chief exclaimed:

"What, a son of Ogden the beaver-hunter, that old scouter? Ugh! I wish it were he instead of you! But we will take care of his boy or he may become a scouter too!"

Thus began David's captivity, as the prisoner, and perhaps receiving some of the special regard, of Brant himself. There could have been little doubt in Davy's mind, from the moment of his capture, that he was to be carried to Fort Niagara; yet the first move of the party was characteristic of Indian strategy; for instead of taking the trail westward, they all marched off to the eastward, coming upon the Mohawk some miles below Fort Stanwix. They forded the river twice, the icy water coming above their waists. On emerging upon the road between Fort Stanwix and Fort Herkimer, Brant halted his sixteen prisoners and caused the buckles to be cut from their shoes. These he placed in a row in the road, where the first passing American would be sure to see them. There was something of a taunt in the act, and a good deal of humor; and we may be sure that Joseph Brant, who was educated enough, and of great nature enough, to enjoy a joke, had many a laugh on his way back to Niagara as he thought of those thirty-two buckles in a row.

The prisoners tied up their shoes with deerskin strings, and trudged along through the night until the gleam of fires ahead and a chorus of yells turned their thoughts towards the stake and an ignominious martyrdom. But their fate was easier to meet. In a volley of sixteen distinct yells for the prisoners and one for the scalp, the party — said to number 100 Indians and fifty Tories — entered the first camp, where squaws were boiling huge kettles of samp — pounded corn — eaten without salt. All fared equally well, and all slept on the ground in the snow, Davy and his fellows being guarded by British soldiers.

The next day's march brought them to Oneida Castle, often the headquarters of Brant in his expeditions. Here the Indians dug up from the snow a store of unhusked corn, and shelled and pounded a quantity for their long march. Here, too, Davy's three-cornered Revolutionary hat was taken from him, and in its place was given him a raccoon skin. All of the captives except the corporal were similarly treated and the Indians showed them how to tie the head and tail together. On some the legs stuck up and on others the legs hung down. I do not know how Davy wore his — with a touch of taste and an air of gaiety, no doubt; and we may be sure it made a better head-covering for a march of 250 miles at that season than would the stiff hat he had lost. Corporal Betts alone was permitted to keep his hat, as insignia of rank, and it is to be hoped he got some comfort out of it.

It would take too long to give all the dismal details of Davy's dreary tramp across the State. Other captivities which I have spoken of had incidents of more dire misery and greater horror than befel the party to which Ogden belonged; and this is one reason why I have chosen to dwell upon his adventures, because my aim is, by a personal narrative, to illustrate the average experience of the time.

There were hundreds of American prisoners brought to Fort Niagara during the period we are studying, but it would be far from just to their captors, and would throw our historical perspective out of focus, to take the extreme cases as types for the whole.

Yet, put it mildly as we can, the experience persists in being serious. At Oneida Castle Brant, evidently fearing pursuit, roused his party in the middle of the night, and a forced march was begun through the heavy timber and up and down the long hills to the westward. When the moon went down they halted, but at the first streak of daylight they pushed on, not waiting even to boil their samp. An occasional handful of parched corn, pounded fine and taken with a swallow of water, was all the food any of the party had that day.

The next encampment was on the Onondaga River, south of the lake; and here occurred an incident as characteristic of Indian character as was the row of shoe-buckles in the road. Some Indians found a small cannon, which had probably been abandoned by one of the detachments sent out by Sullivan on his retreat from the Genesee in '79. Brant, who had plenty of powder, ordered his American prisoners to load and fire this gun a number of times, the Indians meanwhile yelling in delight and the Tories and British enjoying the chagrin of the helpless Americans. Then the march was resumed; over the watershed to Cayuga Lake, which they crossed on the ice near the outlet, a long train, each man far from his fellow, for the ice was rotten and full of air-holes; then along the old trail to Seneca River, which they forded; thence the route was west by north, one camp being somewhere between the present villages of Waterloo and Lyons. Brant on this expedition appears to have kept to the north of Kanadasaga.[1] A day later they came to the outlet of Canandaigua Lake, where the Indians, finding a human head which they said was the head of a Yankee, had an improvised game of football with it, with taunts and threats for the edification of their prisoners. The next day they crossed the Genesee River, at or near the old Genesee Castle. And still, as throughout all this march, unsalted, often uncooked, samp was their only food.

On the march Davy and each of his fellows had worn about their necks a rope of some fourteen or sixteen feet in length. In the daytime these ropes were wound about their necks and tied. At night they were unwound, each prisoner placed between two captors, and one end of the rope was fastened to each of the double guard. Under the circumstances it is no reflection upon our hero's courage that he had not made his escape.

---

[1] Perhaps more correctly, according to eminent authority (Lewis H. Morgan), "Ga-nun-da-sa-ga." It was one of the most important of the Seneca towns, situated near the site of the present town of Geneva. Gen. Sullivan destroyed it in September, 1779, and no attempt was ever made to rebuild it.

West of the Genesee, and beyond the country which had been ravaged by Sullivan, signs of Indian occupancy multiplied; but as yet there was no other food than corn to be had for their ill-conditioned bodies. As they filed along the trail, through the snow and mud of March, they met another large party just setting out from Niagara on a foray for prisoners and scalps. There were noisy greetings and many exultant yells; and as the outbound savages passed the prisoners, they snatched from each one's head the raccoon-skin cap; so that for the rest of the journey Davy and his companions met the weather bare-headed — all save Corporal Betts, to whom again was still spared the old three-cornered hat. The incident bespeaks either the lack of control or the negligent good nature of Brant, for fifteen raccoon-skins at Fort Niagara would surely have been worth at least fifteen quarts of rum. Corporal Betts, however, must have got little comfort out of his hat; for seeing him look so soldierly in it, the whim seized upon Brant to compel the unlucky corporal to review his woebegone troops.

"Drill your men," said the fun-loving chief, "and let us see if these Yankees can go through the tactics of Baron Steuben."

And so poor Betts, but with a broken spirit, mustered his forlorn guard, dressed them in a straight line, and put them through the manual according to Steuben. I doubt if the history of Western New York can show a stranger military function than this reluctant muster of patriot prisoners under compulsion of a playful tiger of an Indian, jeered at meanwhile by British soldiers from Fort Niagara. When these latter went too far in their ridicule Brant stopped them. "The Yankees," he said angrily, "do it a damned sight better than you can."

This affair took place, as nearly as I can make out, somewhere between Batavia and Lockport; probably not far from the old Indian village of Tonawanda.

Being now in the valley of the Tonawanda, Brant seems to have sent ahead a runner to announce his approach; for the second or third day after crossing the Genesee they were met by a party from the fort, bringing pork and flour, whereupon there was a camp and a feast; with the not strange result that many of them had to return to the astringent parched corn as a corrective.

From this point on Davy and his friends were subjected to a new experience; for, as they passed through the Indian villages, the old women and children exercised their accustomed privilege of beating and abusing the prisoners. On one occasion, as Davy was plodding along the path, a squaw ran up to him, and, all unawares, hit him a terrific blow on the side of the head, whereupon the boy came near getting into trouble by making a vigorous effort to kick the lady. At another time, as David marched near Brant, he saw a young Indian raise a pole, intending to give the prisoner a whack over the head. Davy dodged, and the blow fell on Brant's back. The chief, though undoubtedly hurt, paid no attention to the Indian lad, but advised Davy to run, and Davy, knowing perfectly well that to run away meant torture and death, wisely ran towards the fort, which was but a few miles distant. A companion named Hawkins, who had marched with him, ran by his side. And, as they ran, they came upon still another village of the Senecas, from which two young savages took after them. Believing that their pursuers would tomahawk them, the boys let out a link or two of their speed, and coming to a creek where logs made a bridge, Hawkins hid under the bridge, while Davy ran behind a great buttonwood tree. The young Indians, however, had seen them, and on coming up, one of them promptly went under the bridge, and the other around the tree for Davy. This Indian held out his hand in friendship, and said: "Brother, stop." And the boys, seeing that the Indians had no tomahawks and could do them no harm, were reassured, and they all went on together toward Fort Niagara.

Soon they met a detail of soldiers from the fort, who detained them until the rest of the party came up, when Davy saw that some of his friends had been so badly wounded by the assaults of these village Indians that they were now being carried. As the party went on together, the path was continually lined with Indians, whose camps were on the open plains about the fort; and the clubbing and beating of the prisoners became incessant. This was all a regular part of a triumphal return to Fort Niagara of a party of British and Indians with American prisoners, and was the mild preliminary of that dread ordeal known as running the gauntlet.

When Davy, well to the front of the procession, had been marched some distance farther through the wood, he looked out upon a clearing, across which extended a long line of fallen trees, which lay piled with the butts inward, so that the sharpened points of the forked branches all pointed outwards, making a *chevaux-de-frise* upon which one might impale himself, but which could scarcely be scaled. Beyond this barrier, as Davy looked, he saw, first, the wagon road which ran between this *chevaux-de-frise* and the palisades or pickets of the fort beyond. Within the palisades he could see the outlines of the fortification, the upper part of the old castle which still stands there, and other buildings, and over all the red flag of Great Britain. But while he noted these things, his chief regard must have fallen upon the great crowd of Indians who were ranged along on either side of the road between the outwork of fallen trees and the palisades — two close ranks of painted savages in front, and behind them on either side a dense mass of yelling, gesticulating bucks, squaws, old men and children, impatient for the passing of the prisoners. Beyond, the British sentries, officers and other inmates of the fort, awaited the sport, like spectators at a play.

Davy knew the gravity and the chances of the situation. He knew the Indian custom, which does not seem to have been at all interfered with by the officers

What Befel David Ogden.

in command at Niagara,[1] which allowed the spectator to assault or wound the prisoner who should run between the ranks, in any way which his ingenuity could suggest, except with hatchets and knives; these could be used only on prisoners whose faces were painted black, by which sign wretches doomed to death were known; yet any prisoner, even the black-painted ones, who lived through the gauntlet and gained the gate of the fort, was safe from Indian judgment, and could rest his case upon the mercies of the British.

I do not know whether or not Davy's heart stood still for a second, but I am bound to say there was not a drop of craven blood in his veins. He was not exactly in training, as we would say of a sprinter today — his diet, the reader will remember, had been somewhat deficient. But if he hesitated or trembled it was not for long. We can see him as he stands between the soldiers from the fort — bareheaded, ragged, dirty; a blanket pinned about his shoulders and still with the rope about his neck by which he was secured at night. And now, as his guards look back to see the others come up, Davy tightens the leather strap at his waist, takes a deep breath, bends low, darts forward, and is half way down the line before the waiting Indians know he is coming.

How he does run! And how the yells and execrations follow! There is a flight of stones and clubs, but

---

[1] Except perhaps in the case of Capt. Alexander Harper and his party, for whom the ordeal was made light, most of the Indians having been enticed away from the vicinity of the fort; but this was apparently due to Brant, rather than to the British.—*See* Ketchum's "History of Buffalo," Vol. I., pp. 374, 375.

not one touches the boy. One huge savage steps forward, to throw the runner backward — he clutches only the blanket, which is left in his hands, and Davy runs freer than before. The twenty rods of this race for life are passed, and as the boy dashes upon the bridge by which the road into the fort crosses the outer ditch, he is confronted by an evil-looking squaw, who aims a blow with her fist square at his face. Davy knocks up her arm with such force that she sprawls heavily to the ground, striking her head on one of the great spikes that held the planking. And straight on runs Davy, not down the road along the wall to the place set for prisoners, but through the inner gate, under the guard-house; and so, panting and spent, out upon the old parade-ground.

Thus came the boy-soldier of the Revolution, David Ogden, to Fort Niagara, 118 years ago.

The sentries hailed him with laughter and jeers, and asked him what he was doing there. "Go back," they said, "under the guard-house and down the road outside the wall, to the bottom."

This was where Guy Johnson's house stood, and there the prisoners were to report. But when Davy looked forth he concluded that discretion was the better part of valor, for the angry Indians had closed upon his fellows who followed, and were clubbing them, knocking them down and kicking them; so that of the whole party taken prisoners near Fort Stanwix, Davy Ogden was the only one who reached Fort Niagara without serious harm. Turning back upon the parade ground he flatly refused to go out again, whereupon the officer of the guard was called, who questioned him, took pity on him, and sheltered him in his own quarters for three days.

Now, if this were a mere story, we would expect, right here, a happy turn in Davy's fortunes. As matter of fact, the most dismal days in Davy's life were just to begin. He had hoped that the worst would be detention at the fort, and a speedy shipment down the lake to Montreal, for exchange. But after some days he was summoned to Guy Johnson's house, where were many Indians, and here he was handed over to a squaw to be her son, in place of one she had lost in the war. David was powerless; and after what, many years later, he described as a powwow had been held over him, he was led away by the squaw and her husband. A British soldier, named Hank Haff, added to his grief by telling him that he was adopted by the Indians and would have to live with them forever; and, as he was led off across the plain, away from his friends and even from communication with the British, who were at least of his own blood, it was small consolation to know that his adopted father's name was Skun-nun-do, that the hideous old hag, his mother, was Gunna-go-let, that there was a daughter in the wigwam named Au-lee-zer-quot, or that his own name was henceforth to be Chee-chee-le-coo, or "Chipping-bird"—a good deal, I submit, for a soldier of the Revolution to bear, even if he were only a boy.[1]

---

[1] I have followed the old narrative in the spelling of these Indian names, which, no doubt, students of Indian linguistics will discover are not wholly in accord with the genius of the Seneca tongue.

David lived with this fine family for over two years, being virtually their slave, and always under circumstances which made escape impossible. He dressed in Indian fashion, and learned their language, their yells and signal whoops. During the first months of his adoption, their wigwam was about four miles from the fort — presumably east or southeast of it; and one of David's first duties was to go with Gunna-go-let out on to the treeless plain overlooking Lake Ontario, where the old squaw had found a prize in the shape of a horse which had died of starvation. David helped her cut up the carcass and "tote" it home — and he was glad to eat of the soup which she made of it. They were always hungry. Skun-nun-do being a warrior, the burden of providing for the family fell upon Gunna-go-let. Her principal recourse was to cut faggots in the woods and carry them to the fort. Many a time did she and Davy Ogden carry their loads of firewood on their backs up to the fort, glad to receive in exchange cast-off meat, stale bread or rum. So much of this work did Davy do during the two years that he was kept with these Indians that his back became sore, then calloused.

When he had lived with Gunna-go-let three months, she packed up and moved her wigwam to the carrying-place, now Lewiston. Here there was cleared land, and some 200 huts or wigwams were pitched, while the Indians planted, hoed and gathered a crop of corn. Davy was kept hard at work in the field, or in carrying brooms, baskets and other things to the fort for sale.

What Befel David Ogden. 133

When he had been at the carrying-place about a year and a half, he saw a large party of captives brought in from the settlements. Among them was a young woman who had been at Fort Stanwix when Ogden was on duty there. As she sat in the camp, Davy being present, she began to observe him carefully. Although our hero was dressed as an Indian — Indian gaiters, a short frock belted at the waist, and with his hair cut close to the scalp over the whole head except a long tuft on the crown — yet this poor girl saw his real condition and soon learned who he was. There was no chance for confidences. What little they said had to be spoken freely, without feeling, as if casually between strangers indifferent to each other. She told David that she was gathering cowslip greens in a field, when an Indian rushed upon her and carried her away. What she endured while being brought to the Niagara I leave to the imagination. Davy saw her carried away by her captors across the river into Canada; and thus vanishes Hannah Armstrong, for I find no mention of her except in this reminiscence of her drawn from Ogden's own lips.

About this time David was taken to the fort, old Gunna-go-let having heard that the British would give her a present for the lad. Davy trudged the nine miles from their hut to the fort with a good heart, for to him the news meant a chance of exchange. At Guy Johnson's house he and his mother sat expectant on the steps. Presently out came Capt. Powell, who had married Jane Moore — who had herself been brought to the fort a captive from Cherry Valley. This fine couple, from whom the lad had some right to expect kindness, paraded up and down the "stoop" or verandah of the house for a while, the wife hanging on her captain's arm and both ignoring the boy. At length they paused, and Capt. Powell said:

"You are one of the squaw boys? Do you want to quit the Indians?"

"Yes," said Davy, heart in mouth.

"What for?" quizzed the captain.

"To be exchanged — to get back home, to my own country."

"Well," said Powell, "if you really want to get free from the Indians come up and enlist in Butler's Rangers. Then we can ransom you from this old squaw — will you do it?"

"No, I won't!" blazed Davy, fiercely.

Capt. Powell turned on his heel. "Go back with the Indians again and be damned!" and with that he vanished into the house; and we have no means of knowing whether Jane, his wife, had by this time become so "Tory" that she made no protest; but it is pleasanter to think of her as remembering her own captivity, and, still loyal at heart, as interceding for the boy.[1] But that was the end of it for this time, and

---

[1] Ketchum gives Capt. Powell a better character than this incident would indicate; and says that he "visited the prisoners among the Senecas, at Buffalo Creek, several times during the time they remained there, not only to encourage them by his counsel and sympathy, but to administer to their necessities, and to procure their release; which was ultimately accomplished, mainly through his efforts, assisted by other officers at the fort, which [sic] the example and interest of Jane Moore, the Cherry Valley captive had influenced to coöperate in this work of mercy." ["History of Buffalo," Vol. I., p. 376.] I have adhered to the spirit and in part, to the language, of Ogden's own narrative.

back Davy went, with an angry squaw, to continue his ignoble servitude until the next spring. Then word spread all through the region that the prisoners must be brought into Fort Niagara, and this time Davy was not disappointed, for with many others he was hurried on board the schooner Seneca and carried to Oswego. Obviously the news of the preparations for a peace had reached Niagara. Although the Treaty of Paris was not signed until September 3d of that year (1783), yet the preliminary articles had been agreed upon in January. The order from the British Ministry to cease hostilities reached Sir Guy Carleton about the 1st of April, and a week or so would suffice for its transmission to Niagara. Captives who had been detained and claimed by the Indians continued to be brought in during that summer, but we hear no more of returning war parties arriving with new prisoners. The War of the Revolution was over, even at remote Niagara, although for one pretext and another — and for some good reasons — the British held on to Fort Niagara and kept up its garrison for thirteen years more.

With the sailing of the Seneca the connection of Davy Ogden with Fort Niagara ended; but no one who has followed his fortunes thus far can wish to drop him, as it were, in the middle of Lake Ontario. That is where Davy came near going, for a gale came up which not only made him and the throng of others who were fastened below decks desperately sick, but came near wrecking the schooner. She was compelled to put in at Buck's Island, and after some days reached Oswego, then strongly garrisoned. Here Davy stayed, still a prisoner, but living with the British Indians, through the winter. In the spring, with a companion named Danforth, who stole a loaf of bread for their sustenance, he made his escape. He ran through the woods, twenty-four miles in four hours; swam the Oswego River, and on reaching the far side, and fearing pursuit, did not stop to dress, but ran on naked through the woods until he and his companion hoped they had distanced their pursuers. A party had been sent after them from the fort, but on reaching the point where the boys had plunged into the river, gave up the chase. Ogden and Danforth pressed on, around Oneida Lake — having an adventure with a bear by the way, and another with rattlesnakes — and finally, following old trails, reached Fort Herkimer, having finished their loaf of bread and run seventy miles on the last day of their flight. Here Davy was among friends. The officers promptly clothed him, gave him passports, and in a few days he found his parents at Warrensburg, in Schoharie County.

When the War of 1812 broke out, David took his gun again. He fought at the Battle of Queenston, where forty men in his own company were killed or wounded. Two bullets passed through his clothes, but he was unharmed. We can imagine the interest with which he viewed the Lewiston plateau where he had lived with Gunna-go-let more than thirty years before. After the war he returned East, and in 1840 was living in the town of Franklin, Delaware Co., being then seventy-six years old. The story of his adventures was gathered from his own lips, but I do not think it has ever been told before as a part of the history of the Niagara frontier.

A Fort Niagara Centennial.

A FORT NIAGARA CENTENNIAL.

With Especial Reference to the British Retention of that Post for Thirteen Years after the Treaty of 1783.[1]

THE PART assigned to me in these exercises is to review the history of Fort Niagara; to summon from the shades and rehabilitate the figures whose ambitions or whose patriotism are web and woof of the fabric which Time has woven here. It is a long procession, led by the disciples of St. Francis and Loyola — first the Cross, then the scalping-knife, the sword and musket. These came with adventurers of France, under sanction of Louis the Magnificent, who first builded our Fort Niagara and with varying fortunes kept here a feeble footing for four score years, until, one July day, Great Britain's wave of continental conquest passed up the Niagara; and here, as on all the frontier from Duquesne to Quebec,

"The lilies withered where the Lion trod." [2]

The fragile emblem of France vanished from these shores, and the triple cross waved over Fort Niagara until, 100 years ago to-day, it gave way to a fairer

---

[1] Address delivered at Fort Niagara, N. Y., at the celebration of the centennial of British evacuation, August 11, 1896. Amplification on some points, not possible in the brief time allotted for the spoken address on that occasion, is here made in foot-notes.

[2] See Oliver Wendell Holmes's beautiful poem, "Francis Parkman," read at the meeting of the Massachusetts Historical Society in memory of the historian, who died November 8, 1893.

flag. This is the event we celebrate, this, with the succeeding years, the period we review: a period embracing three great wars between three great nations; covering our Nation's birth, growth, assertion and maintenance of independence. The story of Fort Niagara is peculiarly the story of the fur trade and the strife for commercial monopoly; and it is, too, in considerable measure, the story of our neighbor, the magnificent colony of Canada, herself worthy of full sisterhood among the nations. It is a story replete with incident of battle and siege, of Indian cruelty, of patriot captivity, of white man's duplicity, of famine, disease and death,—of all the varied forms of misery and wretchedness of a frontier post, which we in days of ease are wont to call picturesque and romantic. It is a story without a dull page, and it is two and a half centuries long.

Obviously something must be here omitted, for your committee have allotted me fifteen minutes in which to tell it!

Let us note, then, in briefest way, the essential data of the spot where we stand.

A French exploratory expedition headed by Robert Cavelier, called La Salle, attempted the first fortification here in 1679.[1] There was a temporary Indian

---

[1] The first official step towards such fortification was taken by Frontenac. On Nov. 14, 1674, he wrote to the Minister, Colbert: "Sieur Joliet . . . has returned three months ago, and discovered some very fine Countries, and a navigation so easy through the beautiful rivers he has found, that a person can go from Lake Ontario and Fort Frontenac in a bark to the Gulf of Mexico, there being only one carrying place, half a league in length, where Lake Ontario communicates with Lake Erie. A settlement could be made at this point and another bark built on Lake Erie. These are projects which it will be possible to effect when Peace will be

A Fort Niagara Centennial. 143

village on the west side of the river, but no settlement here, neither were there trees on this point. Here, under the direction of La Motte de Lussiere, were built two timber redoubts, joined by a palisade. This structure, called Fort Conty, burned the same year, and the site of Fort Niagara was unfortified until the summer of 1687, when the Marquis de Denonville, Governor General of Canada, after his expedition against the Senecas, made rendezvous on this point, and (metaphorically) shaking his fist at his rival Dongan, the Governor of the English Colony of New York, built here a fort which was called Fort Denonville. It was a timber stockade, of four bastions; was built in three days, occupied for eleven months by a garrison which dwindled from 100 men to a dozen, and would no doubt entirely have succumbed to the scurvy and the besieging Iroquois but for the timely arrival of friendly Miamis. It was finally abandoned September 15, 1688, the palisades being torn down, but the little huts which had sheltered the garrison left standing. How long they endured is not recorded. All traces of them had evidently vanished by 1721, when in May of that year Charlevoix rounded yonder point in his canoe and came up the Niagara. His Journal gives no account of any structure here. Four years more elapsed before the French ventured to take

---

firmly established, and whenever it will please the King to prosecute these discoveries." [Paris Docs. I., N. Y. Colonial MSS.] Joliet, it must be remembered, was never on the Niagara; whatever representations he made to Frontenac regarding it were based on hearsay, very likely on reports made to him by La Salle at their meeting in 1669; so that priority in promoting the Niagara route reverts after all to that gallant adventurer.

decided stand on this ground. In 1725 Governor De Vaudreuil deputed the General De Longueil to erect a fort here. The work was entrusted to the royal engineer Chaussegros de Léry — the elder of the two distinguished engineers bearing that name. He came to this spot, got his stone from Lewiston Heights and his timber from the forest west of the river, and built the "castle." Some of the cut stone was apparently brought from the vicinity of Fort Frontenac, now Kingston, across the lake. The oldest part of this familiar pile, and more or less of the superstructure, is therefore 171 years old.[1] There is, however, probably but little suggestion of the original building in the present construction, which has been several times altered and enlarged. But from 1725 to the present hour Fort Niagara has existed and, with one brief interim, has been continuously and successively garrisoned by the troops of France, England, and the United States.

By 1727 De Léry had completed the fortification of the "castle," and the French held the post until 1759, when it surrendered to the English under Sir William Johnson. It was in its last defence by the French that the famous Capt. Pouchot first established the fortification to the eastward, with two bastions and a curtain-wall, apparently on about the same lines as those since maintained. The story of the siege, the battle, and the surrender is an eventful one; it is also one of the most familiar episodes in the history of the place, and may not be dwelt upon here.

---
[1] In 1896.

A Fort Niagara Centennial. 145

July 25, 1759, marks the end of the French period in the history of Fort Niagara. The real significance of that period was even less in its military than in its commercial aspect. During the first century and more of our story the possession of the Niagara was coveted for the sake of the fur trade which it controlled. I cannot better tell the story of that hundred years in less than a hundred words, than to symbolize Fort Niagara as a beaver skin, held by an Indian, a Frenchman, an Englishman and a Dutchman, each of the last three trying to pull it away from the others (the poor Dutchman being early bowled over in the scuffle), and each European equally eager to placate the Indian with fine words, with prayers or with brandy, or to stick a knife into his white brother's back.

This vicinity also has peculiar precedence in the religious records of our State. It was near here[1] that Father Melithon Watteaux, the first Catholic priest to minister to whites in what is now New York State, set up his altar.[2] It has been claimed, too, by eminent authority, that on this bank of the Niagara, was acquired by the Catholic Church its first title to property in this State[3]; and here at Fort Niagara, under

---

[1] In the palisaded cabin on the site of Lewiston.

[2] Father Watteaux (also spelled "Watteau," "Vatteaux," etc.) was first only in the sense of being assigned to a located mission. "Father Gabriel [de la Ribourde] was named Superior. . . . Father Melithon was to remain at Niagara and make it his mission." (Le Clercq, Shea's translation, Vol. I., p. 112.) "Father Melithon remained in the house at Niagara with some laborers and clerks." (*Ib.*, p. 113.) This was in the summer of 1679; but six months earlier mass had been celebrated on the New York side of the Niagara by Father Hennepin.

[3] This statement, which I have elsewhere accepted (*See* "The Cross-Bearers," p. 28 of this volume), is on the usually unimpeachable authority of Dr. John Gilmary Shea, the historian of the Catholic Church in Amer-

the French *régime*, ministered Fathers Lamberville and Milet, Crespel and others of shining memory. But the capture of Fort Niagara by Sir William Johnson overthrew the last altar raised by the French on the east bank of the Niagara.

The first period of British possession of this point extends from 1759 to 1796. This includes the Revolutionary period, with sixteen years before war was begun, and thirteen years after peace was declared. When yielded up by the French, most of the buildings were of wood. Exceptions were the castle, the old barracks and magazine, the two latter, probably, dating from 1756, when the French engineer, Capt. Pouchot, practically rebuilt the fort. The southwest blockhouse may also be of French construction. A tablet on the wall of yonder bake-house says it was erected in 1762. There were constant repairs and alterations under the English, and several periods of important construction. They rebuilt the bastions and waged constant warfare against the encroaching lake. In 1789 Capt. Gother Mann, Royal Engineer, made report on the needs of the place, and his recommendations were followed the succeeding year. In his report for 1790 he enumerates various works which have been accomplished on the fortifications, and says: "The blockhouse [has

---

ica. (*See* "The Catholic Church in Colonial Days," p. 322.) I find, however, on referring to the authorities on which Dr. Shea rests his statement that the particular grant made on the date named — May 27, 1679 — was not at Niagara but at Fort Frontenac. (Hennepin, "Nouvelle Découverte," p. 108.) At Frontenac La Salle had seigniorial rights, and could pass title as he wished; but on the Niagara he had no right to confer title, for he held no delegated power beyond the letters patent from the King, which permitted him to explore and build forts, under certain restrictions.

been] moved to the gorge of the ravelin so as to form a guard-house for the same, and to flank the line of picketts. . . . A blockhouse has been built on the lake side." This obviously refers to the solid old structure still standing there.[1]

The real life of the place during the pre-Revolutionary days can only be hinted at here. It was the scene of Sir William Johnson's activities, the rendezvous and recruiting post for Western expeditions. Here was held the great treaty of 1764; and here England made that alliance with the tribes which turned their tomahawks against the "American rebels." It may not be too much to say that the greatest horrors of the Revolutionary War had their source in this spot. Without Fort Niagara there would have been no massacre of Wyoming,[2] no Cherry Valley and Bowman's Creek outrages. Here it was that the cunning of Montour and of Brant joined with the zeal of the But-

---

[1] This would seem to fix the date of the northeast blockhouse at 1790; but on examination of other sources of information I discover strong evidence that the original construction was earlier. The Duke de la Rochefoucault Liancourt, who visited Fort Niagara in June, 1795, wrote: "All the buildings, within the precincts of the fort, are of stone, and were built by the French." ("Travels," etc., London ed., 1799, Vol. I., p. 257.) This would make them antedate July, 1759, which is not true of the bakehouse. The Duke may therefore have erred regarding other buildings, the northeast blockhouse among them; yet had it been but four or five years old, he would not be likely to attribute it to the French. Pouchot's plan of the fort (1759) does not show it. I have seen the original sketch of a plan in the British Museum, dated Niagara, 1773, which shows, with several buildings long since destroyed, two constructions where the blockhouses now stand, with this note: "Two stone redoubts built in 1770 and 1771." An accompanying sketch of the southwest redoubt shows a striking similarity to the southwest blockhouse as it now stands, although a roadway ran through it and a gun was mounted on top. These redoubts may have been remodeled by Gother Mann.

[2] Although I am aware that some American writers, and probably all Canadian writers who touch the subject, are offering evidence that there was no "massacre" at Wyoming, I still find in the details of that affair what I regard as abundant warrant for the designation of "massacre."

lers and Guy Johnson, and all were directed and sanctioned by the able and merciless Haldimand, then Governor General of Canada. When Sullivan, the avenger, approached in 1779, Fort Niagara trembled; had he but known the weakness of the garrison then, one page of our history would have been altered. The British breathed easier when he turned back, but another avenger was in the camp; for the 5,000 inflocking Indians created a scarcity of provisions; and starvation, disease and death, as had been the case more than once before on this point, became the real commanders of the garrison at Fort Niagara.

I hurry over the Revolutionary period in order to dwell, briefly, on the time following the treaty of 1783. By that treaty Great Britain acknowledged the independence of this country. When it was signed the British held the posts of Point au Fer and Dutchmen's Point on Lake Champlain, Oswegatchie on the St. Lawrence, Oswego, Niagara, Detroit and Mackinac. The last three were important depots for the fur trade and were remote from the settled sections of the country. The British alleged that they held on to these posts because of the non-fulfillment of certain clauses in the treaty by the American Government. But Congress was impotent; it could only recommend action on the part of the States, and the impoverished States were at loggerheads with each other. England waited to see the new Nation succumb to its own domestic difficulties. It is exceedingly interesting to note at this juncture the attitude of Gov. Haldimand.

In November, 1784, more than a year after the signing of the treaty, he wrote to Brig.-Gen. St. Leger: "Different attempts having been made by the American States to get possession of the posts in the Upper Country, I have thought it my duty uniformly to oppose the same until His Majesty's orders for that purpose shall be received, and my conduct upon that occasion having been approved, as you will see by enclosed extract of a letter from His Majesty's Minister of State, I have only to recommend to you a strict attention to the same, which will be more than ever necessary as uncommon returns of furs from the Upper Country this year have increased the anxiety of the Americans to become masters of it, and have prompted them to make sacrifices to the Indians for that purpose"; and he adds, after more in this vein, that should evacuation be ordered, "on no account whatever are any stores or provisions to be left in the forts" for the use of the Americans.

Not only did Haldimand, during the years immediately following the treaty, refuse to consider any overtures made by the Americans looking to a transfer of the posts, but he was especially solicitous in maintaining the garrisons, keeping them provisioned, and the fortifications in good repair. There were over 2,000, troops, Loyalists and Indians, at Fort Niagara, October 1, 1783. A year later it was much the best-equipped post west of Montreal ; and ten years later it was not only well garrisoned and armed, mounting twelve 24-pounders, ten 12-pounders, two howitzers and five mortars, with large store of shell and powder, but it had become such an important depot of supply to the impoverished Loyalists that a great scandal had arisen over the matter of feeding them with King's stores; and the last spring of the Britishers' sojourn here was enlivened by the proceedings of a court of inquiry, with a possible court-martial in prospect, over a wholesale embezzlement of the King's flour.

Haldimand prized Niagara at its true value. In October, 1782, several months before peace was declared, with admirable forethought and diplomacy, he wrote to the Minister: "In case a peace or truce should take place during the winter . . . great care should be taken that Niagara and Oswego should be annexed to Canada, or comprehended in the general words, that each of the contending parties in North America should retain what they possessed at the time. The possession of these two forts is essentially necessary to the security as well as trade of the country."[1] He ordered the commandant at Fort Niagara to be very much on his guard against surprise by the wily Americans, and at the same time to "be very industrious in giving every satisfaction to our Indian allies."[2]

---

[1] Haldimand to T. Townshend, October 25, 1782.

[2] Haldimand to Lord North, June 2, 1782. In the same letter he wrote "I have lately received a letter from Brig.-Gen. Maclean who commands at Niagara. . . . Affairs with the Indians are in a very critical state I have ordered and insisted upon Sir John Johnson's immediate departure for Niagara in hopes that his influence may be of use in preventing the bad consequences which may be apprehended. I have been assured by the officers who brought me the accounts of the cessation of arms, via New York, that Gen. Schuyler and the American officers made no secret of their hostile intentions against the Indians and such Royalists as had served amongst them. It is to be hoped that the American Congress will adopt a line of conduct more consonant to humanity as well as Policy."

A Fort Niagara Centennial.

On the 2d of May, 1783, an express messenger from Gen. Washington arrived at Fort Niagara, bringing the terms of the treaty. The news gave great uneasiness to Indian-Supt. Butler. "Strict attention to the Indians," he wrote next day to Capt. Mathews, "has hitherto kept them in good humor, but now I am fearful of a sudden and disagreeable change in their conduct. The Indians, finding that their lands are ceded to the Americans, will greatly sour their tempers and make them very troublesome." The British, with good reason, were constantly considering the effect of evacuation upon the Indians.

The Americans made an ineffectual effort to get early possession of the posts. New York State made a proposition for garrisoning Oswego and Niagara, but Congress did not accede. On January 21, 1784, Gov. Clinton advised the New York State Senate and Assembly on the subject. The British commander [Haldimand], he said, had treated the Provisional Articles as a suspension of hostilities only, "declined to withdraw his garrison and refused us even to visit those posts."[1] The Legislature agreed with the Governor

---

[1] The full story of the efforts of the United States Government to obtain possession of Fort Niagara and the other posts on the northern frontier would make a long chapter. I have barely touched a few features of it. One episode was the mission of the Baron Steuben to Haldimand, to claim the delivery of the posts. Washington selected Steuben because of his appreciation of that general's tact and soundness of judgment in military matters. The President's instructions under date of July 12, 1783, were characteristically precise and judicious. Steuben was to procure from General Haldimand, if possible, immediate cession of the posts ; failing in that, he was to get a pledge of an early cession ; "but if this cannot be done," wrote Washington, "you will endeavor to procure from him positive and definite assurances, that he will as soon as possible give information of the time that shall be fixed on for the evacuation of these posts, and that the troops of his Britannic Majesty shall not be drawn therefrom until sufficient previous notice shall be given of that event ; that the troops of

that nothing could be done until spring.¹ Spring found them equally impotent. In March Gov. Clinton sent a copy of the proclamation announcing the ratification of the treaty to Gen. Haldimand: "Having no doubt that Your Excellency will, as soon as the season admits, withdraw the British garrisons under your command from the places they now hold in the United States, agreeable to the 7th Article of the Treaty, it becomes a

the United States may be ready to occupy the fortresses as soon as they shall be abandoned by those of his Britannic Majesty." An exchange of artillery and stores was also to be proposed. Having made these arrangements with Haldimand, Steuben was to go to Oswego, thence to Niagara, and after viewing the situation, and noting the strength and all the military and strategic conditions, was to pass on to Detroit. Armed with these instructions from the Commander-in-Chief, Steuben went to Canada, and on the 8th of August met Gen. Haldimand at Sorel. For once, the man who had disciplined the American Army met his match. His report to Washington indicates an uncommonly positive reception.

"To the first proposition which I had in charge to make," he wrote to Washington, Aug. 23, 1783 ["Correspondence of the Revolution," IV., 41, 42], "Gen. Haldimand replied that he had not received any orders for making the least arrangement for the evacuation of a single post; that he had only received orders to cease hostilities; those he had strictly complied with, not only by restraining the British troops, but also the savages, from committing the least hostile act; but that, until he should receive positive orders for that purpose, he would not evacuate an inch of ground. I informed him that I was not instructed to insist on an immediate evacuation of the posts in question, but that I was ordered to demand a safe conduct to, and a liberty of visiting the posts on our frontiers, and now occupied by the British, that I might judge of the arrangements necessary to be made for securing the interests of the United States. To this he answered that the precaution was premature; that the peace was not yet signed; that he was only authorized to cease hostilities; and that, in this point of view, he could not permit that I should visit a single post occupied by the British. Neither would he agree that any kind of negotiation should take place between the United States and the Indians, if in his power to prevent it, and that the door of communication should, on his part, be shut, until he received positive orders from his court to open it. My last proposal was that he should enter into an agreement to advise Congress of the evacuation of the posts, three months previous to their abandonment. This, for the reason before mentioned, he refused, declaring that until the definite treaty should be signed, he would not enter into any kind of agreement or negotiation whatever."

¹ The inability of the New York State Government to accomplish anything in the matter at this time is illustrated by the following extract from Gov. Clinton's speech to the Senate and Assembly, January 21, 1784: "You will perceive from the communication which relates to the subject that I have not been inattentive to the circumstances of the western posts within this State. They are undoubtedly of great importance for the protection of our trade and frontier settlements, and it was with concern I learnt

part of my duty to make the necessary provisions for receiving the Post of Niagara and the other posts within the limits of this State, and it is for this purpose I have now to request that Your Excellency would give me every possible information of the time when these posts are to be delivered up."

Lieut.-Col. Fish, who carried Gov. Clinton's letter to Quebec, received no satisfaction. Gen. Haldimand evaded anything like a direct reply, saying that he would obey the instructions of His Majesty's Ministers — whom he was meanwhile urging to hold on to the posts — but he gave the American officer the gratuitous information that in his [Haldimand's] private opinion " the posts should not be evacuated until such time as the American States should carry into execution the articles of the treaty in favor of the Loyalists; that in conformity to that article [I quote from Haldimand's report of the interview to Lord North], I had given liberty to many of the unhappy people to go into the States in order to solicit the recovery of their

---

that the propositions made by the State for governing those posts were not acceded to by Congress. It affords me, however, some satisfaction to find that the Commander-in-Chief was in pursuit of measures for that purpose, but my expostulations proved fruitless. The British commander in that Department treating the Provisional Articles as a suspension of hostilities only, declined to withdraw his garrisons and refused us even to visit these posts. It is necessary for me to add that it will now be impracticable to take possession of them until spring, and that I have no reason to believe that Congress have, or are likely to make any provision for the expense which will necessarily occur, it therefore remains for you to take this interesting subject into your further consideration."

To this the Senate made answer: "The circumstances of our western posts excite our anxiety. We shall make no comment on the conduct of the British officer in Canada as explained by your Excellency's communication. It would be in vain. Convinced that our frontier settlements, slowly emerging from the utter ruin with which they were so lately overwhelmed, and our fur trade which constitutes a valuable branch in our remittances, will be protected by these posts, we shall adopt the best measures in our power for their reëstablishment."

estates and effects, but that they were glad to return, without effecting anything after having been insulted in the grossest manner; that although in compliance with His Majesty's order, and [to] shun everything which might tend to prevent a reconciliation between the two countries, I had make no public representation on that head. I could not be insensible to the sufferings of those who had a right to look up to me for protection, and that such conduct towards the Loyalists was not a likely means to engage Great Britain to evacuate the posts; for in all my transactions," he adds, "I never used the words either of my 'delivering' or their 'receiving' the posts, for reasons mentioned in one of my former letters to Your Lordship." And with this poor satisfaction Col. Fish was sent back to Gov. Clinton.[1]

In June, Maj.-Gen. Knox, Secretary of War, sent Lieut.-Col. Hull to Quebec on the same errand. In a most courteous letter he asked to be notified of the time of evacuation, and proposed, "as a matter of mutual convenience, an exchange of certain cannon and stores now at these posts for others to be delivered at West Point upon Hudson's River, New York, or some other convenient place," and he added that Lieut.-Col. Hull was fully authorized to make final arrangements, "so that there may remain no impediment to the march of the American troops destined for this ser-

---

[1] "Lt.-Col. Fish," the Governor General's report continues, "gave me the strongest assurances that the proceedings against the Loyalists were disapproved by the leading men in the different States, and gave me a recent instance of Gov. Clinton having [? saving] Capt. Moore [?] of the 53d Regiment from the insolence of the mob in New York."

vice." Holdfast Haldimand sent him back with no satisfaction whatever, and again exulted, in his report to Lord Sydney, over his success in withstanding the Americans.[1] It was with great reluctance that in the summer of 1784 he reduced the number of British vessels by one on each of the lakes Erie and Ontario. "It appears to be an object of National advantage," he wrote to an official of the British Treasury, "to prevent the fur trade from being diverted to the American States, and no measure is so likely to have effect as the disallowing, as long as it shall be in our power, the navigation of the lakes by vessels or small crafts of any kind belonging to individuals; hence I was the more inclined to indulge the merchants, though in opposition to the plan of economy which I had laid down."[2]

In October, 1784, Congress ordered 700 men to be raised for garrisoning the posts; but the season was late, the States impotent or indifferent, and nothing came of the order. Congress faithfully exercised all the power it possessed in the matter. In 1783, and again in 1787, it unanimously recommended to the States (and the British commissioner was aware, when the treaty was made, that Congress could do no more than recommend) to comply speedily and exactly with

---

[1] " Lt.-Col. Hull in the American service, arrived here on the 10th inst. with a letter from Major Gen. Knox, dated New York the 13th June. . . I did not think myself, from the tenor of Yr Lordship's letter of the 8th of April, authorized to give publicly, any reason for delaying the evacuation of the Posts, tho' perhaps it might have had some effect in quickening the efforts of Congress to produce the execution of the Article of the Definitive Treaty in favor of the Royalists, tho' I held the same private conversation to Lt.-Col. Hull as I had to Lt.-Col. Fish." — Haldimand to Lord Sydney Quebec, July 16, 1784.

[2] Haldimand to Thos. Steile, Esq., of the Treasury; Quebec, Sept. 1, 1784.

that portion of the treaty that concerned creditors and Royalists. The States were unable to act in concert, and alleged infractions of the compact by the British, as, indeed, there were. There was a sporadic show of indignation in various quarters over the continued retention of the posts; but in view of more vital matters, and consciousness that the British claim of unfulfilled conditions was not wholly unfounded, the agitation slumbered for long periods, and matters remained *in statu quo.*

The establishment of the Federal Constitution in 1789 gave the States a new and firmer union; and the success of Wayne's expedition materially loosened the British hold on the Indians and the trade of the lake region; so that Great Britain readily agreed to the express stipulation in the commercial treaty of 1794, that the posts should be evacuated "on or before the 1st of June, 1796." This treaty, commonly called Jay's, was signed in London, November 19, 1794, but not ratified until October 28, 1795. No transfer of troops was then reasonably to be expected during the winter. Indeed, it was not until April 25, 1796, that Lord Dorchester officially informed his council at Castle St. Louis that he had received a copy of the treaty. Even then the transfer was postponed until assurances could be had that English traders among the Indians should not be unduly dealt with.[1] There was

---

[1] At the risk of overloading my pages with citations from this old correspondence, I venture to give the following letter from Lord Dorchester to Lt.-Gov. Simcoe, so admirably does it illustrate the British apprehensions at the time. It is dated Quebec, Apr. 3, 1796:

"Circumstances have arisen, which will probably, for a time, delay the evacuation of the Upper Posts, among which some relating to the interests

much highly-interesting correspondence between Lord Dorchester and the commandant at Niagara on this point; with James McHenry, our Secretary of War; with Robert Liston, the British Minister at Philadelphia; and, of course, with the Duke of Portland and others of the Ministry. Capt. Lewis, representing the United States, was sent to Quebec for definite information of British intention. He fared better than the American emissaries had twelve years before. He was cordially received and supplied with a copy of the official order commanding evacuation of the posts. Whereupon, having received the assurance which his Government had so long sought, he immediately requested that the posts should not be evacuated until the troops of the United States should be at hand to pro-

---

of the Indians do not appear the least important. By the 8th article of the treaty entered into the 3d August last, between Mr. Wayne and them, it is stipulated that no person shall be allowed to reside among or to trade with these Indian tribes, unless they be furnished with a license from the Government of the United States, and that every person so trading shall be delivered up by the Indians to an American Superintendent, to be dealt with according to law, which is inconsistent with the third article of the Treaty of Amity, Commerce and Navigation, previously concluded between His Majesty and the United States by which it is agreed that 'it shall at all times be free to His Majesty's subjects and to the citizens of the United States and also to the Indians, dwelling on either side of the Boundary Line, freely to *pass and repass*, by land or inland navigation, into the respective territories and countries of the two parties on the Continent of America (the country within the limits of the Hudson Bay Co. only excepted), and to navigate the lakes, rivers and waters thereof, and freely to carry on trade and commerce *with each other*.'

"Previously therefore to the actual execution of the treaty on our part, it is requisite that we should be convinced that the stipulations entered into by the United States will also be fulfilled by them; and on a point so interesting to His Majesty's subjects and more especially to the Indians, it is indispensably necessary that all doubts and misconceptions should be removed. His Majesty's Minister at Philadelphia is accordingly instructed to require an explanation on this subject. Till therefore the same shall be satisfactorily terminated I shall delay the surrender of the Posts. These matters you will be pleased to explain to the Indians, pointing out to them at the same time the benevolent care and regard always manifested towards them by the King their Father, and particularly the attention that has been shown to their interests on the present occasion."

tect the works and public buildings. "Being desirous," wrote Lord Dorchester, "to meet the wishes of the President, I have qualified my orders in a manner that I think will answer this purpose."[1] Thus it happened that the evacuation occurred at several different dates. It not being thought necessary to await the coming of American forces at the small posts on Lake Champlain and at Oswegatchie, the British withdrew from those points without ceremony about July 1st. Detroit followed, July 11th; then Oswego, July 15th. Most of the garrison appears to have left Fort Niagara early in July, but an officer's guard remained until August 11th,[2] when American troops arrived from Oswego, and the Stars and Stripes went to the masthead.

I have dwelt upon this period in the history of Fort Niagara at some length, partly because it is the exact period marked by our celebration today, partly because most of the data just related are gleaned from unpublished official MSS., of which but scant use appears to have been made by writers on the subject.

[1] Dorchester to Robert Liston (British Minister at Philadelphia), June 6, 1796.

[2] Under date of Niagara, August 6, 1796, Peter Russell wrote to the Duke of Portland: "All the posts we held on the American side of the line in the vicinity of this province, are given up to the United States agreeable to the treaty, excepting that of Niagara, which remains occupied by a small detachment from the 5th Regiment, until the garrison they have ordered thither may arrive from Oswego. And I understand that they have not yet taken possession of Michillimackinac from the want of provisions. I have directed the officers commanding his Majesty's troops in this Province to make me a return of the effective number that may remain after the departure of the 5th and 24th Regiments, and of their distribution." On August 20th he wrote: "The Fort of Niagara was delivered up to a detachment of troops belonging to the United States of America on the 11th inst. and the guard left in it by the 5th Regiment has sailed for Lower Canada." Mackinac, the last of the posts to be surrendered, did not pass into the hands of the Americans until the following October

A Fort Niagara Centennial.

Of Fort Niagara under the American flag I shall be very brief. No loyal American can take pride in telling of its surrender to the British, December 19, 1813. There was neither a gallant defense nor a generous enemy. Cowardice on the one hand and retaliation on the other sum up the episode. The place was restored to the United States March 27, 1815, and with the exception of one brief interim has been maintained as a garrison to this day. The Morgan affair of 1826 need only be alluded to. The last defensive work of consequence — the brick facing of the bastions, fronting east — dates from 1861.

In the continental view, Fort Niagara was never of paramount importance. Before the British conquest, Niagara was the key to the inner door, but Quebec was the master-lock. The French Niagara need never have been attacked; after the fall of Quebec it would inevitably have become Great Britain's without a blow. In English hands its importance was great, its expense enormous. Without it, Detroit and Mackinac could not have existed; yet England's struggle with the rebellious colonies would have been inevitable, and would have terminated exactly as it did, had she never possessed a post in the lake region. And of Fort Niagara as an American possession, the American historian can say nothing more true than this: that it is a striking exemplification of the fact that his beloved country is ill prepared upon her frontiers for anything save a state of international amity and undisturbed peace.

The Journals and Journeys of an Early Buffalo Merchant.

THE JOURNALS AND JOURNEYS OF AN EARLY BUFFALO MERCHANT.

ON THE frosty morning of February 5, 1822, a strange equipage turned out of Erie Street into Willink Avenue, Buffalo, drove down that steep and ungraded highway for a short distance, then crossed to Onondaga Street, and turning into Crow, was soon lost to sight among the snowdrifts that lined the road running round the south shore of Lake Erie. At least, such I take to have been the route, through streets now familiar as Main, Washington and Exchange, which a traveler would choose who was bound up the south shore of Lake Erie.

The equipage, as I have said, was a strange one, and a good many people came out to see it; not so much to look at the vehicle as to bid good-bye to its solitary passenger. The conveyance itself was nothing more nor less than a good-sized crockery-crate, set upon runners. Thills were attached, in which was harnessed a well-conditioned horse. The baggage, snugly stowed, included a saddle and saddle-bags, and a sack of oats for the horse. Sitting among his effects, the passenger, though raised but a few inches above the snow, looked snug and comfortable. With a chorus of well-wishes following him, he left the village and by nightfall had traveled many miles to the westward, taking his course on the ice that covered Lake Erie.

This was John Lay, a merchant of the early Buffalo, whom even yet it is only necessary to introduce to the young people and to new-comers. The older generation remembers well the enterprising and successful merchant who shared fortunes with Buffalo in her most romantic days. Before going after him, up the ice-covered lake, let us make his closer acquaintance.

Mr. Lay, who was of good New-England stock, came to Buffalo in 1810 to clerk in the general store of his brother-in-law, Eli Hart. Mr. Hart had built his store on Main near the corner of Erie Street, the site now occupied by the American Express Co.'s building. His dwelling was on Erie Street, adjoining, and between the house and store was an ample garden. The space now occupied by St. Paul's Church and the Erie County Savings Bank was a rough common; native timber still stood thick along the east side of Main, above South Division Street; the town had been laid out in streets and lots for four years, and the population, exceeding at that time 400, was rapidly increasing. There was a turnpike road to the eastward, with a stage route. Buffalo Creek flowed lazily into the lake; no harbor had been begun; and on quiet days in summer the bees could still be heard humming among the basswoods by its waters.

This was the Buffalo to which young Lay had come. Looking back to those times, even more novel than the condition of the frontier village, was the character of the frontier trade carried on by Mr. Hart. The trade of the villagers was less important than that which was held with the Canadians or English who were in office under the Government. To them they sold India goods, silks and muslins. Side by side with these the shelves were stocked with hardware, crockery, cottonades, jeans and flannels, Indian supplies, groceries and liquors. The young New Englander soon found that with such customers as Red Jacket and other representative red-men his usefulness was impaired unless he could speak Indian. With characteristic energy he set himself at the task, and in three months had mastered the Seneca. New goods came from the East by the old Mohawk River and Lewiston route, were poled up the Niagara from Schlosser's, above the falls, on flatboats, and were stored in a log house at the foot of Main Street.

Up to 1810 the growth of Buffalo had been exceedingly slow, even for a remote frontier point. But about the time Mr. Lay came here new life was shown. Ohio and Michigan were filling up, and the tide of migration strengthened. Mr. Hart's market extended yearly farther west and southwest, and for a time the firm did a profitable business.

Then came the war, paralysis of trade, and destruction of property. Mr. Lay was enrolled as a private in Butts's Company, for defense. The night the village was burned he with his brother-in-law, Eli Hart, were in their store. The people were in terror, fearing massacre by the Indians, hesitating to fly, not knowing in which direction safety lay.

"John," said Mr. Hart, "there's all that liquor in the cellar — the redskins mustn't get at that."

Together they went down and knocked in the heads of all the casks until, as Mr. Lay said afterwards, they stood up to their knees in liquor. As he was coming up from the work he encountered a villainous-looking Onondaga chief, who was knocking off the iron shutters from the store windows. They had been none too quick in letting the whisky run into the ground. Mr. Lay said to the Indian:

"You no hurt friend?"

Just then a soldier jumped from his horse before the door. Mr. Lay caught up a pair of saddle-bags, filled with silver and valuable papers, threw them across the horse, and cried out to his brother-in-law:

"Here, jump on and strike out for the woods."

Mr. Hart took this advice and started. The horse was shot from under him, but the rider fell unharmed, and, catching up the saddle-bags, made his way on foot to the house of another brother-in-law, Mr. Comstock. Later that day they came back to the town, and with others they picked up thirty dead bodies and put them into Rees's blacksmith shop, where the next day they were burned with the shop.

After starting his relatives toward safety, Mr. Lay thought of himself. The Onondaga had disappeared, and Mr. Lay went into the house, took a long surtout that hung on the wall and put it on. As he stepped

An Early Buffalo Merchant.   167

out of the door he was taken prisoner, and that night, with many others, soldiers and civilians, was carried across the river to Canada.

And here begins an episode over which I am tempted to linger; for the details of his captivity, as they were related to me by his widow, the late Mrs. Frances Lay, are worthy of consideration. I will only rehearse, as briefly as possible, the chief events of this captivity in Canada, which, although not recorded in Mr. Lay's journals, resulted in one of his most arduous and adventurous journeys.

The night of December 30, 1813, was bitterly cold. The captured and the captors made a hard march from Fort Erie to Newark — or, as we know it now, Niagara, Ont., on Lake Ontario. The town was full of Indians, and many of the Indians were full of whisky. Under the escort of a body-guard Mr. Lay was allowed to go to the house of a Mrs. Secord, whom he knew. While there, the enemy surrounded the house and demanded Lay, but Mrs. Secord hid him in a closet, and kept him concealed until Mr. Hart, who had followed with a flag of truce, had learned of his safety. Then came the long, hard march through Canadian snows to Montreal. The prisoners were put on short rations, were grudgingly given water to drink, and were treated with such unnecessary harshness that Mr. Lay boldly told the officer in charge of the expedition that on reaching Montreal he should report him to the Government for violating the laws of civilized warfare.

In March he was exchanged at Greenbush, opposite Albany. There he got some bounty and footed it across the country to Oneida, where his father lived. As he walked through the village he saw his father's sleigh in front of the postoffice, where his parents had gone, hoping for news from him. They burned his war-rags, and he rested for a time at his father's home, sick of the horrors of war and fearful lest his constitution had been wrecked by the hardships he had undergone. It will be noted that this enforced journey from Buffalo through Canada to Montreal and thence south and west to Oneida had been made in the dead of winter and chiefly, if not wholly, on foot. Instead of killing him, as his anxious parents feared it might, the experience seems to have taught him the pleasures of pedestrianism, for it is on foot and alone that we are to see him undertaking some of his most extended journeys.

I cannot even pause to call attention to the slow recovery of Buffalo from her absolute prostration. The first house rebuilt here after the burning was that of Mrs. Mary Atkins, a young widow, whose husband, Lieut. Asael Atkins, had died of an epidemic only ten days before the village was destroyed. The young widow had fled with the rest, finding shelter at Williamsville, until her new house was raised on the foundation of the old. It stood on the corner of Church and Pearl streets, where the Stafford Building now is.

The reader is perhaps wondering what all this has to do with John Lay. Merely this: that when, at Mr. Hart's solicitation, Mr. Lay once more returned to

Buffalo, he boarded across the common from the rebuilt store, with the Widow Atkins, and later on married her daughter Frances, who, many years his junior, long survived him, and to whose vigorous memory and kind graciousness we are indebted for these pictures of the past.

The years that followed the War of 1812 were devoted by Messrs. Hart & Lay to a new upbuilding of their business. Mr. Hart, who had ample capital, went to New York to do the buying for the firm, and continued to reside there, establishing as many as five general stores in different parts of Western New York. He had discerned in his young relative a rare combination of business talents, made him a partner, and entrusted him with the entire conduct of the business at Buffalo. After peace was declared the commercial opportunities of a well-equipped firm here were great. Each season brought in larger demands from the western country. Much of the money that accrued from the sale of lands of the Holland Purchase flowed in the course of trade into their hands. The pioneer families of towns to the west of Buffalo came hither to trade, and personal friendships were cemented among residents scattered through a large section. I find no period of our local history so full of activities. From Western New York to Illinois it was a time of foundation-laying. Let me quote a few paragraphs from memoranda which Mrs. Lay made relating to this period :

> The war had brought men of strong character, able to cope with pioneer life ; among others, professional men, surgeons,

doctors and lawyers: Trowbridge, Marshall, Johnson, and many others. Elliot of Erie was a young lawyer, of whom Mr. Lay had often said, "His word is as good as his bond." Another friend was Hamot of Erie, who had married Mr. Hart's niece. He made frequent visits to his countryman, Louis Le Couteulx. [At whose house, by the way, John Lay and Frances Atkins were married, Red Jacket being among the guests.] At Erie, then a naval station, were the families of Dickinson, Brown, Kelso, Reed, Col. Christy, and many others, all numbered among Mr. Lay's patrons. Albert H. Tracy came here about that time; he brought a letter from his brother Phineas, who had married Mr. Lay's sister. He requested Mr. Lay to do for him what he could in the way of business. Mr. Lay gave him a room over his store, and candles and wood for five years. Even in those days Mr. Tracy used to declare that he should make public life his business.

Hart & Lay became consignees for the Astors in the fur business. I well remember that one vessel-load of furs from the West got wet. To dry them Mr. Lay spread them on the grass, filling the green where the churches now are. The wet skins tainted the air so strongly that Mr. Lay was threatened with indictment — but he saved the Astors a large sum of money.

Hart & Lay acquired tracts of land in Canada, Ohio and Michigan. To look after these and other interests Mr. Lay made several adventurous journeys to the West — such journeys as deserve to be chronicled with minutest details, which are not known to have been preserved. On one occasion, to look after Detroit interests, he went up the lake on the ice with Maj. Barton and his wife; the party slept in the wigwams of Indians, and Mr. Lay has left on record his admiration of Mrs. Barton's ability to make even such rough traveling agreeable.

An Early Buffalo Merchant.

A still wilder journey took him to Chicago. He went alone, save for his Indian guides, and somewhere in the Western wilderness they came to him and told him they had lost the trail. Before it was regained their provisions were exhausted, and they lived for a time on a few kernels of corn, a little mutton tallow, and a sip of whisky. Fort Dearborn — or Chicago — at that date had but one house, a fur-trading post. When Mr. Lay and his guides reached there they were so near starvation that the people dared give them only a teaspoonful of pigeon soup at a time. Nor had starvation been the only peril on this journey. An attempt to rob him, if not to murder him, lent a grim spice to the experience. Mr. Lay discovered that he was followed, and kept his big horse-pistols in readiness. One night, as he lay in a log-house, he suddenly felt a hand moving along the belt which he wore at his waist. Instantly he raised his pistol and fired. The robber dashed through the window, and he was molested no more.

Such adventurous journeyings as these formed no inconsiderable part of the work of this pushing Buffalo merchant during the half dozen years that followed the burning of the town. Business grew so that half a dozen clerks were employed, and there were frequently crowds of people waiting to be served. The store became a favorite rendezvous of prominent men of the place.

Many a war episode was told over there. Albert Gallatin and Henry Clay, Jackson and the United

States banks — the great men and measures of the day — were hotly discussed there; and many a time did the group listen as Mr. Lay read from *Niles' Register*, of which he was a constant subscriber. There were sometimes lively scrimmages there, as the following incident, narrated by Mrs. Lay, will illustrate:

There was a family in New York City whose son was about to form a misalliance. His friends put him under Mr. Hart's care, and he brought the youth to Buffalo. Here, however, an undreamed-of difficulty was encountered. A young Seneca squaw, well known in town as Suse, saw the youth from New York and fell desperately in love with him. Mr. Lay, not caring to take the responsibility of such a match-making, shipped the young man back to New York. The forest maiden was disconsolate; but, unlike *Viola*, she told her love, nor "let concealment, like the worm i' the bud, feed on her damask cheek." Not a bit of it. On the contrary, whenever Suse saw Mr. Lay she would ask him where her friend was. One day she went into the store, and, going up to the counter behind which Mr. Lay was busy, drew a club from under her blanket and "let him have it" over the shoulders. The attack was sudden, but just as suddenly did he jump over the counter and tackle her. Suse was a love-lorn maid, but she was strong as a wildcat and as savage. Albert H. Tracy, who was in the store, afterwards described the trouble to Mrs. Lay.

"I never saw a fight," he said, "where both parties came so near being killed; but Lay got the better of her, and yanked her out into the street with her clothes torn off from her."

"I should think you would have helped John," said the gentle lady, as Mr. Tracy told her this.

By the close of the year 1821, although still a young man, the subject of this sketch had made a considerable fortune. Feeling the need of rest, and anxious to extend his horizon beyond the frontier scenes to which he was accustomed, he decided to go to Europe. Telling Mr. Hart to get another partner, the business was temporarily left in other hands; and on February 5, 1822, as narrated at the opening of this paper, Mr. Lay drove out of town in a crockery-crate, and took his course up the ice-covered lake, bound for Europe.

Recall, if you please, something of the conditions of those times. No modern journeyings that we can conceive of, short of actual exploration in unknown regions, are quite comparable to such an undertaking as Mr. Lay proposed. Partly, perhaps, because it was a truly extraordinary thing for a frontier merchant to stop work and set off for an indefinite period of sightseeing; and partly, too, because he was a man whose love for the accumulation of knowledge was regulated by precise habits, we are now able to follow him in the closely-written, faded pages of half a dozen fat journals, written by his own hand day by day during the two years of his wanderings. No portion of these journals has ever been published; yet they are full of interesting pictures of the past, and show Mr. Lay to have been a close observer and a receptive student of nature and of men.

The reason for his crockery-crate outfit may have been divined. He wanted a sleigh which he could leave behind without loss when the snow disappeared.

Business took him first to Cleveland, which he reached in six days, driving much of the distance on the lake. Returning, at Erie he headed south and followed the old French Creek route to the Allegheny. Presently the snow disappeared. The crockery-crate sleigh was abandoned, and the journey lightly continued in the saddle; among the few *impedimenta* which were carried in the saddle-bags being "a fine picture of Niagara Falls, painted on satin, and many Indian curiosities to present to friends on the other side."

Pittsburg was reached March 2d; and, after a delay of four days, during which he sold his horse for $30, we find our traveler embarked on the new steamer Gen. Neville, carrying $120,000 worth of freight and fifty passengers.

Those were the palmy days of river travel. There were no railroads to cut freight rates, or to divert the passenger traffic. The steamers were the great transporters of the middle West. The Ohio country was just emerging from the famous period which made the name "river-man" synonymous with all that was disreputable. It was still the day of poor taverns, poor food, much bad liquor, fighting, and every manifestation of the early American vulgarity, ignorance and boastfulness which amazed every foreigner who ven-

An Early Buffalo Merchant. 175

tured to travel in that part of the United States, and sent him home to magnify his bad impressions in a book. But with all its discomforts, the great Southern river route of 1822 proved infinitely enjoyable to our Buffalonian. At Louisville, where the falls intercepted travel, he reëmbarked on the boat Frankfort for a fourteen-days' journey to New Orleans. Her cargo included barrels of whisky, hogsheads of tobacco, some flour and cotton, packs of furs, and two barrels of bear's oil — how many years, I wonder, since that last item has been found in a bill of lading on an Ohio steamer!

I must hurry our traveler on to New Orleans, where, on a Sunday, he witnessed a Congo dance, attended by 5,000 people, and at a theater saw "The Battle of Chippewa" enacted. There are antiquarians of the Niagara Frontier today who would start for New Orleans by first train if they thought they could see that play.

April 27th, Mr. Lay sailed from New Orleans, the only passenger on the ship Triton, 310 tons, cotton-laden, for Liverpool. It was ten days before they passed the bar of the Mississippi and entered the Gulf, and it was not until June 28th that they anchored in the Mersey. The chronicle of this sixty days' voyage, as is apt to be the case with journals kept at sea, is exceedingly minute in detail. Day after day it is recorded that "we sailed thirty miles to-day," "sailed forty miles to-day," etc. There's travel for you — thirty miles on long tacks, in twenty-four hours! The ocean greyhound was as yet unborn. The chief diversion of the passage was a gale which blew them along 195 miles in twenty-four hours; and an encounter with a whaleship that had not heard a word from the United States in three years. "I tossed into their boat," Mr. Lay writes, "a package of newspapers. The captain clutched them with the avidity of a starving man."

Ashore in Liverpool, the first sight he saw was a cripple being carried through the streets — the only survivor from the wreck of the President, just lost on the Irish coast.[1]

He hastened to London just too late to witness the coronation of George IV., but followed the multitude to Scotland, where, as he writes, "the outlay of attentions to this bad man was beyond belief. Many of the nobility were nearly ruined thereby." He was in Edinburgh on the night of August 15, 1822, when that city paid homage to the new King; saw the whole coast of Fife illuminated "with bonfires composed of thirty tons of coal and nearly 1,000 gallons of tar and other combustibles"; and the next day, wearing a badge of Edinburgh University, was thereby enabled to gain a good place to view the guests as they passed on their way to a royal levee. To the nobility our Buffalonian gave little heed; but when Sir Walter Scott's carriage drove slowly by he gazed his fill. "He

---

[1] This must not be confounded with the wreck of the steamer President, which was never heard from after the storm of March 13, 1841. The President of which Mr. Lay wrote was obviously a bark, ship, or other sailing craft.

has gray thin hair and a thoughtful look," Mr. Lay wrote. "The Heart of Midlothian" had just been published, and Mr. Lay went on foot over all the ground mentioned in that historical romance. He stayed in pleasant private lodgings in Edinburgh for six months, making pedestrian excursions to various parts of Scotland. In twenty-eight days of these wanderings he walked 260 miles.

Instead of following him closely in these rambles, my readers are asked to recall, for a moment, the time of this visit. Great Britain was as yet, to all intents and purposes, in the eighteenth century. She had few canals and no railroads, no applied uses of steam and electricity. True, Stephenson had experimented on the Killingworth Railway in 1814; but Parliament had passed the first railway act only a few months before Mr. Lay reached England, and the railway era did not actually set in until eight years later. There is no reference in the Lay journals to steam locomotives or railways. Liverpool, which was built up by the African slave trade, was still carrying it on; the Reform Bill was not born in Parliament; it was still the old *régime*.

Our traveler was much struck by the general bad opinion which prevailed regarding America. On meeting him, people often could not conceal their surprise that so intelligent and well-read a man should be an American, and a frontier tradesman at that. They quizzed him about the workings of popular government.

I told them [writes this true-hearted democrat] that as long as we demanded from our public men honesty and upright dealings, our institutions would be safe, but when men could be bought or sold I feared the influence would operate ruinously, as all former republics had failed for lack of integrity and honesty.

His political talks brought to him these definitions, which I copy from his journal :

Tory was originally a name given to the wild Irish robbers who favored the massacre of the Protestants in 1641. It was afterward applied to all highflyers of the Church. Whig was a name first given to the country field-elevation meetings, their ordinary drink being whig, or whey, or coagulated sour milk. Those against the Court interest during the reigns of Charles II. and James II. and for the Court in the reigns of William and George I. were called Whigs. A Yankee is thus defined by an Englishman, who gives me what is most likely the correct derivation of the epithet : The Cherokee word eanker [?] signifies coward or slave. The Virginians gave the New Englanders this name for not assisting in a war with the Cherokees in the early settlement of their country, but after the affair of Bunker Hill the New Englanders gloried in the name, and in retaliation called the Virginians Buckskins, in allusion to their ancestors being hunters, and selling as well as wearing buckskins in place of cloth.

In Edinburgh he saw and heard much of some of Scotia's chief literary folk. Burns had been dead twenty-six years, but he was still much spoken of, much read, and admired far more than when he lived. With Mr. Stenhouse, who for years was an intimate of Burns, Mr. Lay formed a close acquaintance:

Mr. Stenhouse has in his possession [says the journal] the mss. of all of Burns's writings. I have had the pleasure of perusing them, which I think a great treat. In the last of Burns's letters which I read he speaks of his approaching dissolution with sorrow, of the last events in his life in the most touching and delicate language.

The journal relates some original Burns anecdotes, which Mr. Lay had from the former companions of the bard, but which have probably never been made public, possibly because — in characteristic contrast to the letter referred to above — they are touching but *not* delicate.

Our Buffalonian encountered numerous literary lions, and writes entertainingly of them. He speaks often of Scott, who he says "is quite the theme. He is constantly writing — something from his pen is shortly expected. I saw him walking on the day of the grand procession. He is very lame, has been lame from his youth, a fact I did not know before." James Hogg, author of the "Winter Evening Tales," lived near Edinburgh. Mr. Lay described him as "a singular rustic sort of a genius, but withal clever — very little is said about him."

I have touched upon Mr. Lay's achievements in pedestrianism, a mode of travel which he doubtless adopted partly because of the vigorous pleasure it afforded, partly because it was the only way in which to visit some sections of the country. A man who had walked from Fort Erie to Montreal, to say nothing of hundreds of miles done under pleasanter circumstances, would naturally take an interest in the pedestrian achievements of others. Whoever cares for this "sport" will find in the Lay journals unexpected revelations on the diversions and contests of three-quarters of a century ago. Have we not regarded the walking-match as a modern mania, certainly not antedating Weston's achievements? Yet listen to this page of the old journal, dated Edinburgh, Aug. 27, 1822:

I went to see a pedestrian named Russell, from the north of England, who had undertaken to walk 102 miles in twenty-four successive hours. He commenced his task yesterday at 1.15 o'clock. The spot chosen was in the vale between the Mound and the North Bridge, which gave an opportunity for a great number of spectators to see him to advantage; yet the numbers were so great and so much interested that there were persons constantly employed to clear his way. The ground he walked over measured one eighth of a mile. I saw him walk the last mile, which he did in twelve minutes. He finished his task with eleven minutes to spare, and was raised on the shoulders of men and borne away to be put into a carriage from which the horses were taken. The multitude then drew him through many principal streets of the city in triumph. The Earl of Fyfe agreed to give him £30 if he finished his work within the given time. He also got donations from others. Large bets were depending, one of 500 guineas. He carried a small blue flag toward the last and was loudly cheered by the spectators at intervals.

Nor was the "sport" confined to Scotland. August 4, 1823, being in London, Mr. Lay writes:

To-day a girl of eight years of age undertook to walk thirty miles in eight consecutive hours. She accomplished her task in seven hours and forty-nine minutes without being distressed. A wager of 100 sovereigns was laid. This great pedestrian feat took place at Chelsea.

A few weeks later he writes again:

This is truly the age of pedestrianism. A man has just accomplished 1,250 miles in twenty successive days. He is now to walk backward forty miles a day for three successive days. Mr. Irvine, the pedestrian, who attempted to walk from London to York and back, 394 miles, in five days and eight hours, accomplished it in five days seven and one-half hours.

An Early Buffalo Merchant. 181

With men walking backwards and eight-years-old girls on the track, these Britons of three-quarters of a century ago still deserve the palm. But Mr. Lay's own achievements are not to be lightly passed over. Before leaving London he wrote: "The whole length of my perambulations in London and vicinity exceeds 1,200 miles."

The journals, especially during the months of his residence in Scotland, abound in descriptions of people and of customs now pleasant to recall because for the most part obsolete. He heard much rugged theology from Scotland's greatest preachers; had an encounter with robbers in the dark and poorly-policed streets of Edinburgh; had his pockets picked while watching the King; and saw a boy hanged in public for housebreaking. With friends he went to a Scotch wedding, the description of which is so long that I can only give parts of it:

About forty had assembled. The priest, a Protestant, united them with much ceremony, giving them a long lecture, after which dinner was served up and whisky toddy. At six, dancing commenced and was kept up with spirit until eleven, when we had tea, after which dancing continued until three in the morning. The Scotch dances differ from the American, and the dancers hold out longer. The girls particularly do not tire so early as ours at home. We retired to the house where the bride and groom were to be bedded. The females of the party first put the bride to bed, and the bridegroom was then led in by the men. After both were in bed liquor was served. The groom threw his left-leg hose. Whoever it lights upon is next to be married. The stocking lighted on my head, which caused a universal shout. We reached home at half past six in the morning, on foot.

I have been much too long in getting Mr. Lay to London, to go about much with him there. And yet the temptation is great, for to an American of Mr. Lay's intelligence and inquiring mind the great city was beyond doubt the most diverting spot on earth. One of the first sights he saw — a May-day procession of chimney-sweeps, their clothes covered with gilt paper — belonged more to the seventeenth century than to the nineteenth. Peel and Wilberforce, Brougham and Lord Gower, were celebrities whom he lost no time in seeing. On the Thames he saw the grand annual rowing match for the Othello wherry prize, given by Edmund Kean in commemoration of Garrick's last public appearance on June 10, 1776. Mr. Lay's description of the race, and of Kean himself, who "witnessed the whole in an eight-oared cutter," is full of color and appreciative spirit. He saw a man brought before the Lord Mayor who " on a wager had eaten two pounds of candles and drank seven glasses of rum," and who at another time had eaten at one meal "nine pounds of ox hearts and taken drink proportionately"; and he went to Bartholomew's Fair, that most audacious of English orgies, against which even the public sentiment of that loose day was beginning to protest. As American visitors at Quebec feel to-day a flush of patriotic resentment when the orderly in the citadel shows them the little cannon captured at Bunker Hill, so our loyal friend, with more interest than pleasure, saw in the chapel at Whitehall, "on each side and over the altar eight or ten eagles, taken from the

French, and flags of different nations; the eagle of the United States is among them, two taken at New Orleans, one at Fort Niagara, one at Queenston, and three at Detroit"; but like the American at Quebec, who, the familiar story has it, on being taunted with the captured Bunker Hill trophy, promptly replied, "Yes, you got the cannon, but we kept the hill," Mr. Lay, we may be sure, found consolation in the thought that though we lost a few eagle-crested standards, we kept the Bird o' Freedom's nest.

On July 5, 1823, he crossed London Bridge on foot, and set out on an exploration of rural England; tourings in which I can not take space to follow him. When he first went abroad he had contemplated a trip on the continent. This, however, he found it advisable to abandon, and on October 5, 1823, on board the Galatea, he was beating down the channel, bound for Boston. The journey homeward was full of grim adventure. A tempest attended them across the Atlantic. In one night of terror, "which I can never forget," he writes, "the ship went twice entirely around the compass, and in very short space, with continual seas breaking over her." The sailors mutinied and tried to throw the first mate into the sea. Swords, pistols and muskets were made ready by the captain. Mr. Lay armed himself and helped put down the rebellion. When the captain was once more sure of his command, "Jack, a Swede, was taken from his confinement, lashed up, and whipped with a cat-o'-nine-tails, then sent to duty." The dose of cat was afterwards administered to the others. It is no wonder that the traveler's heart was cheered when, on November 13th, the storm-tossed Galatea passed under the guns of Forts Warren and Independence and he stepped ashore at Boston.

He did not hurry away, but explored that city and vicinity thoroughly, going everywhere on foot, as he had, for the most part, in England. He visited the theaters and saw the celebrities of the day, both of the stage and the pulpit. At the old Boston Theater, Cooper was playing *Marc Antony*, with Mr. Finn as *Brutus*, and Mr. Barrett as *Cassius*.

On November 20th he pictures a New-England Thanksgiving:

> This is Thanksgiving Day throughout the State of Massachusetts. It is most strictly observed in this city; no business whatever is transacted — all shops remained shut throughout the day. All the churches in the city were open, divine service performed, and everything wore the appearance of Sunday. Great dinners are prepared and eaten on this occasion, and in the evening the theaters and ball-rooms tremble with delight and carriages fill the streets. . . . A drunken, riotous gang of fellows got under our windows yelping and making a great tumult.

A week later, sending his baggage ahead by stagecoach, he passed over Cambridge Bridge, on foot for Buffalo, by way of New York, Philadelphia, Washington, Pittsburg and Erie.

Once more I must regret that reasonable demands on the reader's patience will not let me dwell with much detail on the incidents and observations of this unusual journey. No man could take such a grand walk and fail to see and learn much of interest. But here was a practical, shrewd, observant gentleman who, just returned from two years in Great Britain, was studying his own countrymen and weighing their condition and ideas by most intelligent standards. The result is that the pages of the journals reflect with unaccustomed fidelity the spirit of those days, and form a series of historical pictures not unworthy our careful attention. Just a glimpse or two by the way, and I am through.

The long-settled towns of Massachusetts and Connecticut appeared to him in the main thrifty and growing. Hartford he found a place of 7,000 inhabitants, "completely but irregularly built, the streets crooked and dirty, with sidewalks but no pavements." He passed through Wethersfield, "famous for its quantities of onions. A church was built here, and its bell purchased," he records, "with this vegetable." New Haven struck him as "elegant, but not very flourishing, with 300 students in Yale." Walking from twenty-five to thirty-five miles a day, he reached Rye, just over the New York State line, on the ninth day from Boston, and found people burning turf or peat for fuel, the first of this that he had noticed in the United States.

At Harlem Bridge, which crosses to New York Island, he found some fine houses, "the summer residences of opulent New Yorkers"; and the next day "set out for New York, seven miles distant, over a perfectly straight and broad road, through a rough, rocky and unpleasing region." In New York, where he rested a few days, he reviewed his New England walk of 212 miles :

> The general aspect of the country is pleasing ; inns are provided with the best, the people are kind and attentive. I think I have never seen tables better spread. I passed through thirty-six towns on the journey, which are of no mean appearance. I never had a more pleasant or satisfactory excursion. There are a great number of coaches for public conveyance plying on this great road. The fare is $12 for the whole distance. Formerly it was 254 miles between Boston and New York, but the roads are now straightened, which has shortened the distance to 212 miles.

He had experienced a Boston Thanksgiving. In New York, on Thursday, December 18th, he had another one. Thanksgiving then was a matter of State proclamation, as now, but the day had not been given its National character, and in many of the States was not observed at all. We have seen what it was like in Boston. In New York, "business appears as brisk as on any other laboring day." The churches, however, were open for service, and our traveler went to hear the Rev. Mr. Cummings in Vanderventer Street, and to contribute to a collection in behalf of the Greeks.

Four days before Christmas he crossed to Hoboken, and trudged his way through New Jersey snow and mud to Philadelphia, which he reached on Christmas. At the theater that night he attended —

> a benefit for Mr. Booth of Covent Garden, London, and was filled with admiration for Mr. Booth, but the dancing by Miss Hathwell was shocking in the extreme. The house was for a long time in great uproar, and nothing would quiet them but an assurance from the manager of Mr. Booth's reappearance.

This of course was Junius Brutus Booth. Here is Mr. Lay's pen-picture of Philadelphia seventy-six years ago :

> The streets of Philadelphia cross at right angles; are perfectly straight, well-paved but miserably lighted. The sidewalks break with wooden bars on which various things are suspended, and in the lower streets these bars are appropriated for drying the washwomen's clothes. Carpets are shaken in the streets at all hours, and to the annoyance of the passer-by. Mr. Peale of the old Philadelphia Museum was lecturing three nights a week on galvanism, and entertaining the populace with a magic lantern.

It is much the same Philadelphia yet.

January 8th, Mr. Lay took his way south to Baltimore, making slow progress because of muddy roads; but he had set out to walk, and so he pushed ahead on to Washington, although there were eight coaches daily for the conveyance of passengers between the two cities, the fare being $4. The road for part of the way lay through a wilderness. "The inns generally were bad and the attention to travelers indifferent."

In Washington, which he reached on January 14th, he lost no time in going to the House of Representatives, where he was soon greeted by Albert H. Tracy, whose career in Congress I assume to be familiar to the reader.

> On the day named, the House was crowded to excess with spectators, a great number of whom were ladies, in consequence of Mr. Clay's taking the floor. He spoke for two hours on the subject of internal improvements, and the next day the question of erecting a statue to Washington somewhere about the Capitol, was debated warmly.

On his return North, in passing through Baltimore, he called on Henry Niles, who as editor of *Niles' Weekly*

Register, was to thousands of Americans of that day what Horace Greeley became later on — an oracle; and on January 18th struck out over a fine turnpike road for Pittsburg.

The Pittsburg pike was then the greatest highway to the West. The Erie Canal was nearing completion, and the stage-routes across New York State saw much traffic. Yet the South-Pennsylvania route led more directly to the Ohio region, and it had more traffic from the West to the East than the more northern highways had for years to come. In the eastern part of the State it extends through one of the most fertile and best-settled parts of the United States. Farther west it climbs a forest-clad mountain, winds through picturesque valleys, and from one end of the great State to the other is yet a pleasant path for the modern tourist. The great Conestoga wagons in endless trains, which our pedestrian seldom lost sight of, have now disappeared. The wayside inns are gone or have lost their early character, and the locomotive has everywhere set a new pace for progress.

When Mr. Lay entered the Blue Ridge section, beyond Chambersburg, he found Dutch almost the only language spoken. The season was at first mild, and as he tramped along the Juniata, it seemed to him like May. "Land," he notes, "is to be had at from $1 to $3 per acre." It took him seventeen days to walk to Pittsburg. Of the journey as a whole he says:

> At Chambersburg the great stage route from Philadelphia unites with the Baltimore road. Taverns on these roads are fre-

quent and nearly in sight of each other. The gates for the collection of tolls differ in distance — some five, others ten, and others twenty-five miles asunder. Notwithstanding the travel is great the stock yields no profit, but, on the contrary, it is a sinking concern on some parts, and several of the companies are in debt for opening the road. About $100 per mile are annually expended in repairs. It cost a great sum to open the road, particularly that portion leading over the mountains and across the valleys.

Taverns are very cheap in their charges; meals are a fourth of a dollar, beds 6¼ cents, liquors remarkably cheap. Their tables are loaded with food in variety, well prepared and cleanly served up with the kindest attention and smiling cheerfulness. The women are foremost in kind abilities. Beer is made at Chambersburg of an excellent quality and at other places. A good deal of this beverage is used and becoming quite common; it is found at most of the good taverns. Whisky is universally drank and it is most prevalent. Places for divine service are rarely to be met with immediately on the road. The inhabitants, however, are provided with them not far distant in the back settlements, for almost the whole distance. The weather has been so cold that for the two last days before reaching Pittsburg I could not keep myself comfortable in walking; indeed, I thought several times I might perish.

In Pittsburg he lodged at the old Spread Eagle Tavern, and afterwards at Conrad Upperman's inn on Front Street at $2 a week. He found the city dull and depressed:

The streets are almost deserted, a great number of the houses not tenanted, shops shut, merchants and mechanics failed; the rivers are both banked by ice, and many other things wearing the aspect of decayed trade and stagnation of commerce. Money I find purchases things very low. Flour from this city is sent over the mountains to Philadelphia for $1 per barrel, which will little more than half pay the wagoner's expenses for the 280 miles. Superfine flour was $4.12½ in Philadelphia, and coal three cents per bushel. Coal for cooking is getting in use in this city — probably two-thirds the cooking is with coal.

He had had no trouble up to this point in sending his baggage ahead. It was some days before the stage left for Erie. All was at length dispatched, however, and on February 14th he crossed over to Allegheny — I think there was no bridge there then — and marched along, day after day, through Harmony, Mercer and Meadville, his progress much impeded by heavy snow; at Waterford he met his old friend G. A. Elliott, and went to a country dance; and, finally, on February 20th found himself at Mr. Hamot's dinner-table in Erie, surrounded by old friends. They held him for two days; then, in spite of heavy snow, he set out on foot for Buffalo. Even the faded pages of the old journal which hold the record of these last few days bespeak the eager nervousness which one long absent feels as his wanderings bring him near home. With undaunted spirit, our walker pushed on eastward to the house of Col. N. Bird, two miles beyond Westfield; and the next day, with Col. Bird, drove through a violent snowstorm to Mayville to visit Mr. William Peacock — the first ride he had taken since landing in Boston in November of the previous year. But he was known throughout the neighborhood, and his friends seem to have taken possession of him. From Mr. Bird's he went in a stage-sleigh to Fredonia to visit the Burtons. Snow two feet deep detained him in Hanover town, where friends showed him "some tea-seed bought of a New-England peddler, who left written directions for its cultivation." "It's all an imposition," is Mr. Lay's comment — but what a horde of smooth-tongued tricksters New England has to answer for!

The stage made its way through the drifts with difficulty to the Cattaraugus, where Mr. Lay left it, and stoutly set out on foot once more. For the closing stages of this great journey let me quote direct from the journal:

> I proceeded over banks of drifted snow until I reached James Marks's, who served breakfast. The stage wagon came up again, when we went on through the Four-mile woods, stopping to see friends and spending the night with Russell Goodrich. On February 29th [two years and twenty-four days from the date of setting out] I drove into Buffalo on Goodrich's sleigh and went straight to Rathbun's, where I met a great number of friends, and was invited to take a ride in Rathbun's fine sleigh with four beautiful greys. We drove down the Niagara as far as Mrs. Seely's and upset once.

What happier climax could there have been for this happy home-coming!

Misadventures of Robert Marsh.

MISADVENTURES OF ROBERT MARSH.

ROBERT MARSH claimed American citizenship, but the eventful year of 1837 found him on the Canadian side of the Niagara River. His brother was a baker at Chippewa, and Robert drove a cart, laden with the bakery products, back and forth between the neighboring villages. From St. Catharines to Fort Erie he dispensed bread and crackers and the other perhaps not wholly harmless ammunition that was moulded in that Chippewa bakery; and he naturally absorbed the ideas and the sentiments of the men he met. The Niagara district was at fever heat. Mackenzie had sown his Patriot literature broadcast, and what with real and imaginary wrongs the majority of the community sentiment seemed ripe for rebellion.

It is easy enough now, as one reads the story of that uprising, to see that the rebels never had a ghost of a chance. The grip of the Government never was in real danger of being thrown off in the upper province; but a very little rebellion looks great in the eyes of the rebel who hazards his neck thereby; and it is no wonder that Robert Marsh came to the conclusion that the colonial government of Canada was about to be overthrown, or that he decided to cast in his lot with those who should win glory in the cause of freedom. As an American citizen he had a right to do this. History was full of high precedents. Did not Byron espouse the cause of the Greeks? Did not Lafayette make his name immortal in the ranks of American rebels? One part of America had lately thrown off the hated yoke of Great Britain; why should not another part? So our cracker peddler reasoned; and reasoning thus, began the train of adventures for the narration of which I draw in brief upon his own obscure narrative. It is a story that leads us over some strange old trails, and its value lies chiefly in the fact that it illustrates, by means of a personal experience, a well-defined period in the history of the Niagara region. Robert Marsh is hardly an ideal hero, but he is a fair type of a class who contrived greatly to delude themselves, and to pay roundly for their experience. He thought as many others thought; what he adventured was also adventured by many other men of spirit; and what he endured before he got through with it was the unhappy lot of many of his fellows.

It was a time of great discontent and discouragement on both sides of the border. Throughout the Holland Purchase the difficulties over land titles had reached a climax, and the sheriff and his deputies enforced the law at the risk of their lives. This year of 1837 also brought the financial panic which is still a high-water mark of hard times in our history. Buffalo suffered keenly, and it is not strange that such of her young men as had a drop of adventurous blood in their veins were ready to turn "Patriot" for the time being; though as a matter of sober fact it must be recorded that the enthusiasm of the majority did not blind their judgment to the hopelessness of the rebellion. On the Canadian side the case was different. Unlike their American brethren, many of the residents there felt that they had not a representative government. It is not necessary now, nor is it essential to our story, to rehearse the grievances which the Canadian Patriots undertook to correct by taking up arms against the established authority. They are presented with great elaboration in many histories; they are detailed with curious ardor in the Declaration of Rights, a document ostentatiously patterned after the Declaration of Independence. William Lyon Mackenzie was a long way from being a Thomas Jefferson; yet he and his associates undertook a reform which — taking it at their valuation — was as truly in behalf of liberty as was the work of the Signers of the Declaration of Independence. They made the same appeal to justice; argued from the same point of view for man's inalienable rights; they were temperate, too, in their demands, and sought liberty without bloodshed. Yet while the American patriots were enabled to persist and win their cause, though after two bitter and exhausting wars, their Canadian imitators were ignominiously obliterated in a few weeks. In the one case the cause of Liberty won her brightest star. In the other, there is complete defeat, without a monument save the derision of posterity.

It was in November of this year of rebellion 1837 that Marsh, being at Chippewa, decided to cast in his lot with the Patriots. "I began to think," he says, "that I must soon become an actor on one side or the other." He saw the Government troops patrolling every inch of the Canadian bank of the Niagara, and concentrating in the vicinity of Chippewa. "Boats of every description were brought from different parts; at the same time they were mustering all their cannon and mortars intending to drive them [the Patriots] off; one would think by their talk, that they would not only kill them all, but with their cannon mow down all the trees, and what the balls failed in hitting the trees would fall upon, and thus demolish the whole Patriot army." Our hero's observations have this peculiar value: they are on the common level. He heard the boasts and braggadocio of the common soldier; the diplomatic or guarded speech of officers and officials he did not record. He heard all about the plot to seize the Caroline, and could not believe it at first. But, he says, "when I beheld the men get in the boats and shove off and the beacon lights kindled on the shore, that they might the more safely find the way back, my eyes were on the stretch, towards where the ill-fated boat lay." When he saw the party return and heard them boast of what they had done, he thought it high time for him to leave the place. "Judge my feelings," he says, "on beholding this boat on fire, perhaps some on board, within two short miles of the Falls of Niagara, going at the rate of twelve miles an hour.'"[1]

The Caroline was burned on the 29th of December. On the next day our hero and a friend set out to join the Patriots. Let me quote in condensed fashion from his narrative, which is a tolerably graphic contribution to the history of this famous episode:

"We succeeded in reaching the river six miles above Chippewa about 11 o'clock in the evening, after a tedious and dangerous journey through an extensive swamp. There is a small settlement in a part of this swamp which has been called Sodom. There were many Indians prowling about. We managed to evade them but with much difficulty. There were sentinels every few rods along the line." A friendly woman at a farmhouse let them take a boat. They offered her $5 for its use, but she declined; "she said she would not take anything . . . as she knew our situation and felt anxious to do all in her power to help us across the river; she also told us that her husband had taken Mackenzie across a few nights previous. 'Leave the boat in the mouth of the creek,' said she, pointing

---

[1] In one Canadian work, John Charles Dent's "Story of the Upper Canadian Rebellion," statements are printed to show that the Caroline did not go over the falls, but that her hull sank in shallow water not far below the Schlosser landing. There is however a mass of evidence to other effect. It is striking that so sensational an episode, happening within the memory of many men yet living, should be thus befogged. The contemporary accounts which were published in American newspapers were wildly exaggerated, one report making the loss of life exceed ninety. (There was but one man killed.) Mackenzie himself is said to have spread these extravagant reports. He had a gift for the sort of journalism which in this later day is called "yellow," a chief iniquity of which is its wanton perversion of contemporary record, and the ultimate confusion of history.

across the river towards Grand Island, . . . 'there is a man there that will fetch it back, you have only to fasten it, say nothing and go your way.' We were convinced that we were not the only ones assisted by this patriotic lady."

Marsh and his companion, whose surname was Thomas, launched the boat with much difficulty, and with muffled oars they rowed across to Grand Island. "It was about 1 o'clock in the morning and we had to go eight or nine miles through the woods and no road. There had been a light fall of snow, and in places [was] ice that would bear a man, but oftener would not; once or twice in crossing streams the ice gave way and we found ourselves nearly to the middle in water." Our patriot's path, the reader will note, was hard from the outset, but he kept on, expecting to be with his friends again in a few days, and little dreaming of what lay ahead of him. "We at near daylight succeeded in reaching White Haven, a small village, where we were hailed by one of our militia sentinels: 'Who comes there?' 'Friends.' 'Advance and give the countersign.' Of course we advanced, but we could not give the countersign; a guard was immediately dispatched with us to headquarters, where we underwent a strict examination."

He was sent across to Tonawanda, where he took the cars for Schlosser. There the blood-stains on the dock where Durfee had been killed sealed his resolution; he crossed to Navy Island and presented himself at the headquarters of William Lyon Mackenzie, the peppery little Scotchman who was the prime organizer of the Provisional Government, and of General Van Rensselaer, commander-in-chief of the Patriot Army. "The General produced the list and asked me the length of time I wished to enlist. I was so confident of success that I unhesitatingly replied, 'Seven years or during the war.' The General remarked, 'I wish I had 2,000 such men, we have about 1,000 already,' and I think this Caroline affair will soon swell our force to 2,000, and then I shall make an attack at some point where they least expect, . . . and as you are well acquainted there I want you to be by my side.'" Here was preferment indeed, for Marsh believed that Van Rensselaer was brave and able ; history has a different verdict ; but we must assume that our hero entered upon the campaign with high hopes and who knows what visions of glory.

Now, at the risk of tiresomeness, I venture to dwell a little longer on this occupancy of Navy Island ; I promise to get over ground faster farther along in the story. It is assumed that the reader knows the principal facts of this familiar episode ; but in Marsh's journal I find graphic details of the affair not elsewhere given, to my knowledge. Let me quote from his obscure record :

After my informing the General of their preparations and intention of attacking the Island, breastworks were hastily thrown up,

---

[1] By the end of December, 1837, about 600 men had resorted to Navy Island in the guise of "Patriots." Although this number was later somewhat increased, the entire "army" at that point probably never numbered 1,000.

and all necessary arrangements made to give them a warm reception. There were twenty-five cannon, mostly well mounted, which could easily be concentrated at any point required; and manned by men that knew how to handle them. Besides other preparations, tops of trees and underbrush were thrown over the bank at different places to prevent them landing. I know there were various opinions respecting the strength of the Island, but from close observation, during these days of my enlistment, it is my candid opinion that if they had attacked the Island, as was expected, they would mostly or all have found a watery grave. The tories were fearful of this, for when the attempt was made men could not be found to hazard their lives in so rash an attempt. . . .

It was hoped and much regretted by all on the Island that the attempt was not made; for if they had done so it would have thinned their ranks and made it the more easy for us to have entered Canada at that place. They finally concluded to bring all their artillery to bear upon us, and thus exterminate all within their reach. They were accordingly arranged in martial pomp, opposite the Island, the distance of about three-quarters of a mile. Now the work of destruction commences; the balls and bombs fly in all directions. The tops of the trees appear to be a great eye-sore to them. I suppose they thought by commencing an attack upon them, their falling would aid materially in the destruction of lives below.

Robert, the reader will have observed, had a fine gift of sarcasm. The thundering of artillery was heard, by times, he says, for twenty and thirty miles around, for a week, "[the enemy] being obliged to cease firing at times for her cannons to cool. They were very lavish with Her Gracious Majesty's powder and balls." He continues:

I recollect a man standing behind the breastwork where were four of us sitting as the balls were whistling through the trees.

"Well," says he, "if this is the way to kill the timber on this island, it certainly is a very expensive way as well as somewhat comical; I should think it would be cheaper to come over with axes, and if they are not in too big a hurry, girdle the trees and they will die the sooner." I remarked: "They did not know how to use an axe, but understood girdling in a different way." An old gentleman from Canada taking the hint quickly responded, "Yes. Canada can testify to the fact of their having other ways of girdling besides with the axe, and unless there is a speedy stop put to it, there will not be a green tree left." There was another gentleman about to say something of their manner of swindling in other parts of the world, he had just commenced about Ireland when I felt a sudden jar at my back, and the other three that set near me did the same; we rose up and discovered that a cannon ball had found its way through our breastwork, but was kind enough to stop after just stirring the dirt at our backs. I had only moved about an inch of dirt when I picked up a six-pound ball.

As it happened, our gun was a six-pounder. We concluded, as that was the only ball that had as yet been willing to pay us a visit, we would send it back as quick as it come. We immediately put it into our gun and wheeled around the corner of the breastwork. "Hold," said I, "there is Queen Ann's Pocket Piece, as it is called, it will soon be opposite, and then we'll show them what we can do." It was not mounted, but swung under the ex [axle] of a cart, such as are used for drawing saw-logs, with very large wheels. I had seen it previous to my leaving Chippewa. I think there was six horses attached to the cart, for it was very heavy, it being a twenty-four-pounder. I suppose it was their intention to split the Island in two with it, hoping by so doing it might loosen at the roots and move off with the current and go over the falls, and thus accomplish their great work of destruction at once. As they were opposite, the words "ready, fire," were given; we had the satisfaction of seeing the horses leave the battleground with all possible speed. The gun was forsaken in no time, and in less than five minutes there was scarcely a man to be seen. The ball had gone about three feet further to the left than had been intended; it was intended to lop the wheels, but it severed the tongue from the ex and the horses took the liberty to move off as fast as possible.

We were about to give them another shot, when the officer of the day came up and told us the orders from headquarters were not to fire unless it was absolutely necessary, that we must be saving of our ammunition. I told him that it was their own ball that we had just sent back. When he saw the execution it had done he smiled and went on, remarking, "They begin to fire a little lower." "Yes," said I, "and as that was the first, we thought we would send it back and let them know we did not want it, that we had balls of our own."

This incident was the beginning of more active operations. For the next nine days and nights there was a great deal of firing, with one killed and three wounded. The Patriot army held on to its absurd stronghold for four weeks, causing, as Marsh quaintly puts it, "much noise and confusion on both sides"; and he at least was keenly disappointed when it was evacuated, Jan. 12, 1838. The handful of Patriots scattered and Chippewa composed herself to the repose which, but for one ripple of disturbance in 1866, continues to the present day.

Up to the end of this abortive campaign Robert Marsh's chief misadventure had been to cut himself off, practically, from a safe return to the community where his best interests lay. But he had a stout heart if a perverse head. "I was born of Patriot parentage," he boasted; "I am not a Patriot today and tomorrow the reverse"; and being fairly identified with the rebels, he determined to woo the fortunes of war wherever opportunity offered. His ardor must have been considerable, for he made his way in the dead of winter from Buffalo to Detroit; just how I do not know; but he speaks of arriving at Sandusky "after a tedious walk of five days." Here he joined a party for an attack on Malden, but the Patriots were themselves attacked by some 300 Canadian troops who came across the lake in sleighs; there was a lively fight on the ice, with some loss of life, when each party was glad to retire. Next he tried it with a band of rebels on Fighting Island, below Detroit; treachery and "the power of British gold" seem to have kept Canada from falling into their hands; and presently, "being sick of island fighting," as he puts it, he made his way to Detroit, where, all through that troubled summer of '38, he appears to have been one of the most active and ardent of the plotters. Certain it is that he was promptly to the front for the battle of Windsor, and was with the invaders on Dec. 4, 1838, when a band of 164 misguided men crossed the Detroit River to take Canada. He was "Lieutenant" Marsh on this expedition, but it was the emptiest of honors. At four in the morning they attacked the barracks on the river banks above Windsor, and, as often happens with the most fatuous enterprises, met at the outset with success. They burned the barracks and took thirty-eight prisoners (whom they could not hold), looking meanwhile across the river for help which never came. "We were about planting our standard," wrote Marsh afterward; "the flag was a splendid one, with two stars for

Upper and Lower Canada. We had just succeeded in getting a long spar and was in the act of raising it, as the cry was heard, — ''There comes the Red-coats! There are the dragoons!''' Our Patriot, it will be observed, made no nice distinctions between British and Canadian troops; that distinction will not fail to be made for him, in a province which has always claimed the honor — to which it is fully entitled — of putting down this troublesome uprising without having to call for help upon the British regulars. But the invaders did not raise nice points then. They hastily formed and withstood the attack for a little; but it was a hopeless stand, for numbers and discipline were all on the other side. According to Marsh, the regulars numbered 600. There was sharp firing, eleven Patriots and forty-four Canadians were killed; and seeing this, and learning, later than his friends across the river, that discretion is the better part of valor, he did the only thing that remained to do — he took to the woods.

The woods were full just then of discreet Patriots, and several of them held a breathless council of war. Here is Marsh's account of it:

> It was finally concluded for every man to do the best he could for himself. We accordingly separated and I found myself pursued by a man hollowing at the top of his voice, "Stop there, stop, you damned rebel, or I'll shoot you! stop, stop!" I was near a fence at that time crossing a field. I proceeded to the fence, dropped on one knee, put my rifle through the fence, took deliberate aim. He had a gun and was gaining on me. I had a cannister of powder, pouch of balls, two pistols and an overcoat on, which prevented me from attempting to run. I saw all hopes

of escape was useless; I discharged my rifle, but cannot say whether it hit the mark or not, for I did not look, but immediately rose and walked off. At any rate I heard no more "Stop there, you damned rebel."

Marsh's narrative is too diffuse, not to mention other faults, for me to follow it *verbatim et (il-)literatim*. I give the events of the next few days as simply as possible. After he fired his gun through the fence at the red-coat who followed no more — his last shot, be it remarked, for the relief of Canada — he found that he was very tired. It was late in the day of the battle and he had eaten nothing for nearly forty-eight hours. Pushing on through the woods he came to a barn, but had scarcely entered when it was surrounded by ten or twelve "dragoons," as he calls them. He scrambled up a ladder to the hay-mow, dug a hole in the hay, crawled in and smoothed it over himself, and, he says, "had just got a pistol in each hand as the door flew open; in they rushed, crying, 'Come out, you damned rebel, we'll shoot you, we'll not take you before the Colonel to be shot, come out, come out, we'll hang you.' Said another, 'We'll quarter you and feed you to the hogs as we've just served one!' They thrust their swords into the hay, and threatened to burn the barn; but as it belonged to one of their sort, they thought better of it and went off. They soon came back, and saying they would place a sentry, disappeared again." Marsh tore up certain papers which he feared would be troublesome if found on him and then slept. It was dark when he awoke. He crept out of the barn and wandered through the woods until daylight, narrowly escaping some Indians. He applied at the house of a French settler for something to eat; frankly admitting, what it obviously was folly to deny, that he was a fugitive. Three "large bony Frenchmen" came to the door, made him their prisoner and marched him off through the woods to Sandwich, where he was stripped of his valuables and locked up with several others, his captors cheerfully assuring them that they would have a fine shooting-match tomorrow. Marsh stoutly maintained that, as he owed the Queen no allegiance, he was not a rebel; but his protests did him no good. He was not shot on the morrow, although others of the captives were summarily executed, without a pretext of trial or even a chance to say their prayers.

And now begins an imprisonment of ten months full of such distress and atrocity that I should not please, however much I might edify, by its recital. We read today of the horrors of Spanish and Turkish massacres or of Siberian prisons, and every page of history has its record of inhumanity — its Black Hole, its Dartmoor, its Andersonville. In this dishonor roll of official outrages surely may be included the backwoods prisons of Upper Canada in 1838 and '39. Our misadventurer was shifted from one to another. At Fort Malden, on the shore of Lake Erie, he was kept for seven weeks in a small room with twenty-eight other men. It was the dead of winter, but they had no warmth save from their emaciated and vermin-infested bodies. They were ironed two and two, day and night. They were so crowded that there was not floor-room for all to sleep at once. According to Marsh, who afterwards wrote a minute record of this imprisonment, their feeding and care would have been fatal to a herd of hogs. The acme of the miseries of the prison at Fort Malden I cannot even hint at with propriety. When transferred from Sandwich to Malden, and later from Malden to London, Marsh, like many of his fellow sufferers, had his feet frozen; and when his limbs swelled so that life itself was threatened, it was not the surgeon but a clumsy blacksmith who cut off the irons and supplied new ones.

In London the treatment of Malden was repeated. Here the trials began. The gallows was erected close to the jail wall; day by day the doomed ones walked out of a door in the second story to the death platform; and day by day Marsh and the other wretches in the cells heard the drop as it swung, in falling, against the jail wall. Marsh lived in hourly expectation of the summons, but before his turn came there was a stay in the work which had been going on under the warrants signed by Sir George Arthur — as great a tyrant, probably, as ever held power on the American continent. A far more philosophic writer than Robert Marsh has called him the Robespierre of Canada. Whatever may be held as to the illegality of the trials which sent some twenty-five men to the gallows at this time, certain it is that the hangings stopped before our hero's neck was stretched. Fate still had her quiver full of evil days for him; and fortune, like a gleam of sun between clouds, moved him on to the prison at Toronto, where his mother came to see him.

It was in the early spring of 1839 that he was transferred to Toronto. In June following, with a boat-load of companions, he was shipped down to Fort Henry at Kingston. Here, for three months, he was deluded with the constant expectation of release; but he must have had some foreshadowings of his fate when, after three months of wretched existence at Fort Henry, he was again sent on, down the river to Quebec; and there, on September 28, 1839, he and 137 companions in irons were put aboard the British prison-ship Buffalo, commanded by Capt. Wood. They were stowed on the third deck, below the water line; 140 sailors were placed over them; and the Buffalo took her course down the widening gulf. The dismal departure was lightened by a touch of human nature. There were several of the convicts who, like Marsh, claimed American citizenship, and American blood will show itself.[1] As the prisoners were marched down with clanking chains from Fort Henry for the shipment to Quebec, many of them thought that it was their last shift before release. "There were three or four

---

[1] There were about 150 Patriots, claiming to be citizens of the United States, who were taken prisoners in Upper Canada, and transported to Van Dieman's Land. Among those taken near Windsor, besides Marsh, were Ezra Horton, Joseph Horton and John Simons of Buffalo, John W. Simmons and Truman Woodbury of Lockport. Taken at Windmill Point, near Prescott, was Asa M. Richardson of Buffalo. Taken at Short Hills, Welland Co., was Linus W. Miller of Chautauqua Co., who afterwards wrote a book on the rebellion and his exile; and Benjamin Waite, whose "Letters from Van Dieman's Land" were published in Buffalo in 1843. Waite died at Grand Rapids, Mich., Nov. 9, 1895, aged eighty-two. It is not unlikely that some Americans who underwent that exile are still living. I have seen no list of Americans captured during the outbreak in Lower Canada.

very good singers amongst us," says Marsh, "which made the fort ring with the 'American Star,' 'Hunters of Kentucky' and other similar songs, which caused many to flock to our windows. Some of them remarked, 'You will not feel like singing in Botany Bay.' 'Give us "Botany Bay,"' said one, and it was done in good style."

If the reader will permit the digression, it may afford a little entertainment to consider for a moment these old songs. The literature of every war includes its patriotic songs — seldom the work of great poets, and most popular when they appeal to the quick sympathies and sense of humor of the common people. Every people has such songs, sometimes cherished and sung for generations. England has them without number, Canada has hers, the United States has hers; and among the most popular for many years, strange as it now may seem, were "The American Star" and "The Hunters of Kentucky," which were sung by these none-too-worthy representatives of the United States, through Canadian prison bars, this autumn morning sixty years ago. Both songs had their origin, I believe, at the time of the War of 1812. That such barren and bombastic lines as "The American Star" should have remained popular a quarter of a century seems incredible, and appears to indicate that the youth of the country were very hard up for patriotic songs worth singing. Here follows "The American Star":

> Come, strike the bold anthem, the war dogs are howling,
> Already they eagerly snuff up their prey,

The red clouds of war o'er our forests are scowling,
    Soft peace spreads her wings and flies weeping away ;
The infants, affrighted, cling close to their mothers,
    The youths grasp their swords, for the combat prepare,
While beauty weeps fathers, and lovers and brothers,
    Who rush to display the American Star.

Come blow the shrill bugle, the loud drum awaken,
    The dread rifle seize, let the cannon deep roar ;
No heart with pale fear, or faint doubtings be shaken,
    No slave's hostile foot leave a print on our shore.
Shall mothers, wives, daughters and sisters left weeping,
    Insulted by ruffians, be dragged to despair !
Oh no ! from her hills the proud eagle comes sweeping
    And waves to the brave the American Star.

The spirits of Washington, Warren, Montgomery,
    Look down from the clouds with bright aspect serene ;
Come, soldiers, a tear and a toast to their memory,
    Rejoicing they'll see us as they once have been.
To us the high boon by the gods has been granted,
    To speed the glad tidings of liberty far ;
Let millions invade us, we'll meet them undaunted,
    And vanquish them by the American Star.

Your hands, then, dear comrades, round Liberty's altar,
    United we swear by the souls of the brave
Not one from the strong resolution shall falter,
    To live independent, or sink to the grave !
Then, freemen, fill up — Lo, the striped banner's flying,
    The high bird of liberty screams through the air ;
Beneath her oppression and tyranny dying —
    Success to the beaming American Star.

Every one of its turgid and wordy lines bespeaks the struggling infancy of a National literature. "The Hunters of Kentucky" is a little better, because it has humor—though of the primitive backwoods type—in it.

If the reader has not heard it lately, perhaps he can stand a little of it. It was inspired by the battle of New Orleans:

> Ye gentlemen and ladies fair,
>   Who grace this famous city,
> Just listen, if you've time to spare,
>   While I rehearse a ditty;
> And for the opportunity
>   Conceive yourselves quite lucky,
> For 'tis not often that you see
>   A hunter from Kentucky;
>   O! Kentucky,
>   The hunters of Kentucky.
>
> We are a hardy free-born race,
>   Each man to fear a stranger;
> Whate'er the game, we join in chase,
>   Despising toil and danger;
> And if a daring foe annoys,
>   Whate'er his strength or force is,
> We'll show him that Kentucky boys
>   Are alligators,—horses:
>   O! Kentucky, etc.
>
> I s'pose you've read it in the prints,
>   How Packenham attempted
> To make Old Hickory Jackson wince,
>   But soon his schemes repented;
> For we, with rifles ready cock'd,
>   Thought such occasion lucky,
> And soon around the general flock'd
>   The hunters of Kentucky:
>   O! Kentucky, etc.
>
> I s'pose you've heard how New Orleans
>   Is famed for wealth and beauty;

There's gals of every hue, it seems,
  From snowy white to sooty :
So, Packenham he made his brags
  If he in fight was lucky,
He'd have their gals and cotton bags,
  In spite of Old Kentucky :
    O ! Kentucky, etc.

But Jackson he was wide awake,
  And wasn't scared at trifles,
For well he knew what aim we take
  With our Kentucky rifles ;
So, he led us down to Cypress Swamp,
  The ground was low and mucky ;
There stood John Bull in martial pomp —
  But here was Old Kentucky :
    O ! Kentucky, etc.

We raised a bank to hide our breasts,
  Not that we thought of dying,
But then we always like to rest,
  Unless the game is flying ;
Behind it stood our little force
  None wish'd it to be greater,
For every man was half a horse
  And half an alligator :
    O ! Kentucky, etc.

They didn't let our patience tire
  Before they show'd their faces ;
We didn't choose to waste our fire,
  But simply kept our places ;
And when so near we saw them wink,
  We thought it time to stop 'em,
It would have done you good, I think,
  To see Kentuckians drop 'em :
    O ! Kentucky, etc.

> They found, at length, 'twas vain to fight,
>   When lead was all their booty,
> And so, they wisely took to flight,
>   And left us all the beauty.
> And now, if danger e'er annoys,
>   Remember what our trade is;
> Just send for us Kentucky boys,
>   And we'll protect you, ladies:
>   O! Kentucky, etc.

At least it has a gallant ending, which was not altogether apposite to the situation of Marsh and his fellow-prisoners at Kingston. "Botany Bay" was more in their line just then; but, at any rate, it was just as philosophic to go into exile singing as mourning or cursing.

Were I a Herman Melville or a Clark Russell I should be tempted to dwell on this dreary voyage of the prison-ship Buffalo. Even Marsh's humble chronicle of it is graphic with unstudied incidents. They ran into rough weather at once; so that to the wretchedness of their imprisonment was added the misery of seasickness. No one had told them of their destination, and many of them, like Marsh, stoutly maintained from first to last that they were transported without a sentence. Their daily life in this dark and crowded 'tween-decks, practically the hold of a staggering old sailer, could not be detailed without offense; and if it could be, I have no desire to heap up the horrors. In mid-voyage there was an attempted mutiny; the convicts tried to seize the ship; but the only result was heavier irons, closer confinement, and a stricter guard.

After two months of the stormy Atlantic the Buffalo put into Rio Janeiro, where she lay three tantalizing days. "It happened to be the Emperor's birthday," says Marsh, "and although we were not allowed to go on shore, we could discover through a skylight the flags on the pinnacles of houses and hills apparently reaching to the clouds." A little fruit was had aboard to allay the scurvy which was making havoc, and the Buffalo lumbered away again and ran straight into a savage gale, in which she sprung a bad leak. She was an old ship, and had formerly been a man-of-war, but for some years now had been employed as a convict transport between England and New South Wales. From Rio around the Cape of Good Hope the log kept by Robert Marsh is a story of sickness and death. Those who had had their limbs frozen in Canada now found the skin and flesh coming away and the sea water on their bare feet gave them excruciating agony. The shotted sack slid into the shark-patrolled waters of the Indian Ocean, and the wretches who still lived were envious of the dead. And on the 13th of February, 1840, four months and a half from Quebec, the Buffalo anchored in Hobart Town harbor, Van Dieman's Land.

And now a word about this antipodean land on which our unlucky hero looked out from the prison-ship. We are wont to regard it, perhaps, as a new and well-nigh unknown part of the world; possibly some of us would have to think twice if asked offhand, Where is Van Dieman's Land? Of course we remember, when we glance at the map, that it is a good-sized island just south of Australia. From extreme north to extreme south it is about as far as from Buffalo to Philadelphia, and east and west not quite so far as from Buffalo to Albany. And here is a coincidence: Hobart Town, in the harbor of which the prison-ship Buffalo dropped anchor with her load of misery, is exactly as far south of the equator as Buffalo is north of it. Other parallel data may perhaps be helpful: It was in 1642 that the navigator Tasman discovered the island, naming it after his Dutch patron, Van Dieman. The explorer's name has now been substituted, as it should be, and Tasmania, not Van Dieman's Land, appears on modern maps. The history of that land dates from 1642. It was in 1641 that those adventurous missioners, Brébeuf and Chaumonot, first carried their portable altar across the Niagara; and from the Relations of their order for that year the world gained the first actual glimpse of the Niagara region. In the world's annals, therefore, this far-away island and our own Niagara and lake region are of the same age. One other parallel may be ventured. The first permanent settlement in Van Dieman's Land was made in 1803. In 1804 Buffalo had fifteen actual settlers and a few squatters. But here our parallels end, for when, on that February morning of 1840, the unhappy Marsh was put ashore, he found a community unlike any that has ever existed in this happier part of the world. For over thirty years England had been sending thither her worst criminals. Shipload after shipload, year after year, of the most depraved and vicious of mankind, had been sent out. England had made of it and of Botany Bay a dumping-ground for whatever manner of evil men and women she could scrape from her London slums. There was some free colonization, but it went on slowly. Honest men hesitated to go where society was so handicapped. The treatment of the convicts varied according to the Governors, but for years before Marsh arrived it seems to have been as harsh and brutalizing as imperiousness and cruelty could devise. In 1836 Sir John Franklin was sent out to the station. He was an exceptionally humane and generous man, according to most accounts. Marsh does not complain of any severity from him, but calls him an old granny, a glutton and a temporizer in his promises to convicts. It is something foreign to our purpose to dwell upon this point, nor is it a gracious thing to seek any imputation against a character which history delights to hold as the embodiment of the gallant and heroic. We must remember that Robert Marsh's point of view was not likely to bring him to favorable estimates of those in authority over him and through whom his very real oppression came. Years after, when the great explorer's bones lay whitening in the unknown North, this far-away colony raised to his memory a noble bronze statue, which stands to-day in Franklin Square, Hobart, not far from the old Government House, the scene of his uncongenial administration.

And now behold our hero marched ashore with his fellows; reeling like a drunken man, the strange effect of firm earth under foot after months of heaving seaway; examined, ticketed and numbered, clad in Her Majesty's livery, and sent to a near-by country station, where he is put to work under savage overseers at carrying stone for road-building; and thus began five years of unmitigated suffering for Robert Marsh in that detestable land. There were about 43,000 convicts on the island at the time, 25,000 of whom were driven to daily work in chain gangs, on the roads, in the wet mines or the forest. The rest were ex-convicts; had served their sentences and counted themselves among the free population, which all told did not then exceed 60,000. Conceive of a free community, nearly one half of whom, men and women, were former convicts, but not regenerate. For years the brothels of London, Glasgow, Edinburgh, were emptied into Van Dieman's Land. A reputable writer has said that at this time female virtue was unknown in the island. The wealthy land-owners, under government patronage, were autocrats in their own domain. The whipping-post, the triangle — a refinement of cruelty — and the gallows were familiar sights. The slightest failure at his daily task sent the convict to the whipping-post or to solitary confinement.

Official iniquity flourished under Sir George Arthur's reign of eleven years. He was Franklin's predecessor, and his minions were still in control when Marsh came under their power. He was shifted from station to station; fed like a dog, lodged in the meanest huts and worked well nigh to death. The worst characters were his overseers, and the day began with the lash. A convict's strength would give out under his load; he would lag behind, or stop to rest. At once he would be taken to the station, stripped to the waist — if he chanced to have anything on — strung up to the post or triangle, and flogged. As an additional measure of reform, brine was thrown into the gashes which the lash had made. These were the milder forms of daily punishment. Sir George Arthur's prouder record comes from the executions. Travelers to-day tell us that Tasmania is really a second England; in its settled portions it is a land of pleasant vales and gentle rivers, rich in harvests of the temperate zone. "Appleland," some have called it, from its fruitful orchards; but no tree transplanted from Merrie England ever flourished more than the black stock from Tyburn Hill. Sir George hanged 1,500 during his stay. Marsh tells of a compassionate clergyman who was watching with interest the erection of a gallows. "Yes," he said, "I suppose it will do, but it is not as large as we need. I think ten will hang comfortable, but twelve will be rather crowded."

It is small wonder that our hero tried to escape. He took to the bush — which means the unexplored and inhospitable forest — with a band of friends; was captured, punished, and thereafter dressed in magpie — trousers and frock one half black, one half yellow; and in this garb, which advertised to all that he had been a bush-ranger, he worked on until the spring of 1842, when Sir John Franklin made him a ticket-of-leave man. This relieved him from the overseers, and gave him permission to work, for whatever wages he could get, in an assigned district.

And now again, of this new phase of his misadventures, a long story could be made. At that time the best circumstanced ticket-of-leave men got about a shilling a day and boarded themselves. But there was little work and many seekers. They roamed over the country, turned away from plantation after plantation, and in many cases became the boldest of outlaws. Escape from the island was well nigh impossible; but after many hardships, utterly unable to get honest work, Marsh was one of a party that determined to try it. Making their way eighty miles to the seashore, they hid in the woods, where for a week or so they gathered firewood, buried potatoes and snared kangaroo. One of their number reached a settlement and returned with the word that an American whaler was coming to take them off. After six days more of waiting the vessel hove in sight. As she tried to draw near and send boats ashore a storm came up and she narrowly escaped the breakers. At this critical moment a British armed patrol schooner rounded a point down the coast and the American made her escape with great difficulty, leaving the score of runaway convicts at their precarious lookout, hopeless and despondent.

They were soon arrested, Marsh among them. He was tried for breaking his patrol, and sent to an inland district, 100 miles through the bush and swamps. "It was all punishment," he says pathetically, in describing this journey on which he nearly perished. So down-hearted and distressed were they, so appalled by the war of nature and man against them, that one of Marsh's companions, with fagged-out brain, came to the conclusion that they were really in hell and that the devil himself was in charge of them. But there is always a turn to the tide. They trapped a kangaroo and did not starve. Marsh reached his district and this time found work, which had to be light, for he was weak, emaciated and troubled day and night with a pain in his chest. And finally the glad word came that he was gazetted for pardon and could go to Hobart. There, on January 27, 1845, after ten months in Canada prisons, four and a half months in a transport ship, and five years in a convict colony, he went on board the American whaler Steiglitz of Sag Harbor, Selah Young, master, a free man.

The Steiglitz was bound out on a whaling voyage. No matter, she would take Marsh away from that hell. She cruised for whale off New Zealand, then made north, and in April anchored off Honolulu. King Hamehameha III., on hearing the story of the convict Americans, welcomed them ashore, and there Marsh stayed for four months, exploring the islands and waiting for a chance to get home. At last it came in the welcome shape of the whaler Samuel Robertson, Capt. Warner, bound for New Bedford. She touched at the Society Islands and Pernambuco, and on March 13, 1846, after seven years four and a half months absence, Marsh stepped ashore in his own country again. The people of New Bedford helped him and a few others as far as Utica. There one of his comrades in exile left him for his home in Watertown, and others went their several ways. Marsh was helped as far as Canandaigua, where his brother met him and took him to his home in Avon; and after a time of recuperation there, they came on to Buffalo, where he met his father, his mother and sister. He soon crossed the river, visited Toronto, and probably looked over the scenes of his early cracker-peddling and subsequent campaigning, up and down the Niagara. He had traveled 77,000 miles, but here his journey ended; and here the Patriot exile told his story, which I have drawn on in an imperfect way, for this true chronicle of old trails.

Underground Trails.

UNDERGROUND TRAILS.

IT WAS Dame Nature who decreed that the Niagara region should be peculiarly a place of trails. When she set the great cataract midway between two lakes, she thereby ordained that in days to come the Indian should go around the falls, on foot. The Indian trail was a footpath; nothing more. Here it followed the margin of a stream; there, well nigh indiscernable, it crossed a rocky plateau; again, worn deep in yielding loam, it led through thick woods, twisting and turning around trees and boulders, with detours for swamps or bad ground, and long stretches along favorable slopes or sightly ridges. Who can hazard a guess as to the time when, or by what manner of men, these trails were first established in our region? Immemorial in their source — akin in natural origins to the path the deer makes in going to the salt-lick or to drink — they were old, established, when our history begins. And when the white man came he followed the old trails. Traveling like the Indian, by water when he could; when lakes and rivers did not serve, he found the footpaths ready made for him in the forest. Armies came, cutting military roads. Settlers followed to banish forests, drain swamps, and make new highways. And yet the horseman, the military train, the wagon of the pioneer, the early stage-coach, the railroad, each in its day, along many of the most direct and important thoroughfares, has but followed the ancient ways. The thing is axiomatic. Nature for the most part decrees where men shall walk. Her lakes and rivers and her hills may be strewn by whim; but there are plain reasons enough for our road-building. We go where we can, with safety and expedition. So ran the red man. We still follow the old trails.

Other aspects of our frontier are worthy of a thought. Two nations look across the Niagara, so that, even though its flow were placid from lake to lake, it would still be a political barrier, a halting-place. This fact has filled it full of trails in history. Again, as the gateway of the West, the paths of immigration and of commerce for a century have here converged. The early settlers of Michigan and Wisconsin went by the old Lewiston ferry. From Buffalo by boat, and from old Suspension Bridge by rail, who can estimate the thousands who have gone on to create the New West? From the earliest Iroquois raid upon the Neuters, down to yesterday's excursion, the Niagara frontier has been peculiarly a region of passing, of coming and going, along old trails.

Now of all the paths that have led hitherward, none has greater significance in American history than that known as the Underground Railroad. Other paths, touching here, have led to war, to wealth, to pleasure; but this led to Liberty. Thousands of negro slaves, gaining after infinite hardships these shores of the lake or river, have looked across the smiling expanse to such an elysium as only a slave can dream of. Once the passage made, no matter how poor the passenger, freedom became his possession and the heritage of his children. The chattel became a man. I can never sail upon the blue lake, or down the pleasant river, without seeing in fancy this throng of famished, frightened, blindly hopeful blacks, for whom these waters were the gateway to new life. The most vital part of the Underground Railroad was the over-water ferry. Bark canoe and great steamer alike leave no lasting trail; but to him who reads the history of our region, this fair waterway at our door is thronged as a street; and every secret traveler thereby is worthy of his attention. Much has been recorded of these refugees, who came, singly or in small parties, for more than thirty years preceding the Civil War. Indeed, runaway slaves passed this way to Canada soon after the War of 1812. The tales of soldiers returning to Kentucky from the Niagara frontier and other campaigns of that war, first planted in the minds of Southern slaves the idea that Canada was a land of freedom. By 1830 many earnest people who disapproved of slavery, the Quakers prominent among them, were giving organized aid to the escaping blacks. In many secret ways the refugees were passed on from one friend to another. Hiding-places were established, and routes which were found advantageous were regularly followed.

It is no part of my present plan to enter upon a general sketch of the Underground Railroad. That task has already been admirably performed, at voluminous length, by careful students. My aim in this paper is to bring together a number of incidents and narratives, particularly illustrative of its work at the eastern end of Lake Erie and along the Niagara frontier, in order that the student may the better appreciate how vital this phase of the slavery issue was, even in this region, for more than a generation preceding the Civil War. There were established routes for the passage of fugitive slaves: From the seaboard States to the North, by water from Newberne, S. C., and Portsmouth, Va.; or by land routes from Washington and Philadelphia, to and through New England and so into Quebec. There was "John Brown's route" through Eastern Kansas and Nebraska; and there were many routes through Iowa and Illinois, most of them leading to Chicago and other Lake Michigan ports, whence the refugees came by boat to Canadian points, chiefly along the north shore of Lake Erie; or even, in some cases, by water to Collingwood on Georgian Bay, where a considerable number of runaway slaves were carried prior to the Civil War. But the travel by these extreme East and West routes was insignificant as compared with the number that came through Western Pennsylvania, Ohio and Indiana, to points on the south shore of Lake Erie and the Detroit and Niagara rivers at either end. The region bounded by the Ohio, the Allegheny, and the western border of Indiana was a vast plexus of Underground routes. The negroes were taken across to Canada in great numbers from Detroit and other points on that river; from Sandusky to Point

Pelee; from Ashtabula to Port Stanley; from Conneaut to Port Burwell; from Erie to Long Point; and from all south-shore points on Lake Erie they were brought by steamer to Buffalo. Often, the vessel captains would put the refugees ashore between Long Point and Buffalo. At other times, the fugitives were sent to stations at Black Rock or Niagara Falls, whence they were soon set across the river and were free. There were some long routes across New York State, the chief one being up the Hudson and Mohawk valleys to Lake Ontario ports. There was some crossing to Kingston, and some from Rochester to Port Dalhousie or Toronto. Another route led from Harrisburg up the Susquehanna to Williamsport, thence to Elmira, and northwesterly, avoiding large towns, to Niagara Falls. But the most active part in the Underground Railroad operations in New York State was borne by the western counties. There were numerous routes through Allegany, Chautauqua and Cattaraugus counties, along which the negroes were helped; all converging at Buffalo or on the Niagara. In the old towns of this section are still many houses and other buildings which are pointed out to the visitor as having been former stations on the Underground. The Pettit house at Fredonia is a distinguished example.

It is impossible to state even approximately the number of refugee negroes who crossed by these routes to Upper Canada, now Ontario. In 1844 the number was estimated at 40,000;[1] in 1852 the Anti-Slavery

---

[1] *See* "Reminiscences of Levi Coffin," p. 253.

Society of Canada stated in its annual report that there were about 30,000 blacks in Canada West; in 1858 the number was estimated as high as 75,000.[1] This figure is probably excessive; but since the negroes continued to come, up to the hour of the Emancipation Proclamation, it is probably within the fact to say that more than 50,000 crossed to Upper Canada, nearly all from points on Lake Erie, the Detroit and Niagara rivers.

Runaway slaves appeared in Buffalo at least as early as the '30's. "Professor Edward Orton recalls that in 1838, soon after his father moved to Buffalo, two sleigh-loads of negroes from the Western Reserve were brought to the house in the night-time; and Mr. Frederick Nicholson of Warsaw, N. Y., states that the Underground work in his vicinity began in 1840. From this time on there was apparently no cessation of migrations of fugitives into Canada at Black Rock, Buffalo and other points."[2] Those too were the days of much passenger travel on Lake Erie, and certain boats came to be known as friendly to the Underground cause. One boat which ran between Cleveland and Buffalo gave employment to the fugitive William Wells Brown. It became known at Cleveland that Brown would take escaped slaves under his protection without charge, hence he rarely failed to find a little company ready to sail when he started out from Cleveland. "In the year 1842," he says, "I conveyed from the 1st of May to the 1st of December, sixty-nine fugitives over

---

[1] *See* "John Brown and His Men," p. 171.
[2] *See* Siebert's "The Underground Railroad," pp. 35, 36.

Lake Erie to Canada."[1] Many anecdotes are told of the search for runaways on the lake steamers. Lake travel in the *ante-bellum* days was ever liable to be enlivened by an exciting episode in a "nigger-chase"; but usually, it would seem, the negroes could rely upon the friendliness of the captains for concealment or other assistance.

There are chronicled, too, many little histories of flights which brought the fugitive to Buffalo. I pass over those which are readily accessible elsewhere to the student of this phase of our home history.[2] It is well, however, to devote a paragraph or two to one famous affair which most if not all American writers on the Underground Railroad appear to have overlooked.

One day in 1836 an intelligent negro, riding a thoroughbred but jaded horse, appeared on the streets of Buffalo. His appearance must have advertised him to all as a runaway slave. I do not know that he made any attempt to conceal the fact. His chief concern was to sell the horse as quickly as possible, and get across to Canada. And there, presently, we find him, settled at historic old Niagara, near the mouth of the river. Here, even at that date, so many negroes had

---

[1] "Narrative of William W. Brown," 1848, pp. 107, 108. Quoted by Siebert.

[2] There is a considerable literature on the specific subject of the Underground Railroad, and a great deal more relating to it is to be found in works dealing more broadly with slavery, and the political history of our country. Of especial local interest is Eber M. Pettit's "Sketches in the History of the Underground Railroad," etc., Fredonia, 1879. The author, "for many years a conductor on the Underground Railroad line from slavery to freedom," has recorded many episodes in which the fugitives were brought to Buffalo, Black Rock, or Niagara Falls, and gives valuable and interesting data regarding the routes and men who operated them in Western New York and Western Pennsylvania.

made their way from the South, that more than 400 occupied a quarter known as Negro Town. The newcomer, whose name was Moseby, admitted that he had run away from a plantation in Kentucky, and had used a horse that formerly belonged to his master to make his way North. A Kentucky grand jury soon found a true bill against him for horse-stealing, and civil officers traced him to Niagara, and made requisition for his arrest and extradition. The year before, Sir Francis Bond Head had succeeded Sir John Colborne as Governor of Canada West, and before him the case was laid. Sir Francis regarded the charge as lawful, notwithstanding the avowal of Moseby's owners that if they could get him back to Kentucky they would "make an example of him"; in plainer words, would whip him to death as a warning to all slaves who dared to dream of seeking freedom in Canada.

Moseby was arrested and locked up in the Niagara jail; whereupon great excitement arose, the blacks and many sympathizing whites declaring that he should never be carried back South. The Governor, Sir Francis, was petitioned not to surrender Moseby; he replied that his duty was to give him up as a felon, "although he would have armed the province to protect a slave." For more than a week crowds of negroes, men and women, camped before the jail, day and night. Under the leadership of a mulatto schoolmaster named Holmes, and of Mrs. Carter, a negress with a gift for making fiery speeches, the mob were kept worked up to a high pitch of excitement, although, as a contemporary writer avers, they were unarmed, showed "good sense, forbearance and resolution," and declared their intention not to commit any violence against the English law. They even agreed that Moseby should remain in jail until they could raise the price of the horse, but threatened, "if any attempt were made to take him from the prison, and send him across to Lewiston, they would resist it at the hazard of their lives." The order, however, came for Moseby's delivery to the slave-hunters, and the sheriff and a party of constables attempted to execute it. Moseby was brought out from the jail, handcuffed and placed in a cart; whereupon the mob attacked the officers. The military was called out to help the civil force and ordered to fire on the assailants. Two negroes were killed, two or three wounded, and Moseby ran off and was not pursued. The negro women played a curiously-prominent part in the affair. "They had been most active in the fray, throwing themselves fearlessly between the black men and the whites, who, of course, shrank from injuring them. One woman had seized the sheriff, and held him pinioned in her arms; another, on one of the artillery-men presenting his piece, and swearing that he would shoot her if she did not get out of his way, gave him only one glance of unutterable contempt, and with one hand knocking up his piece, and collaring him with the other, held him in such a manner as to prevent his firing."[1]

---

[1] I have drawn these facts from Mrs. Jameson's "Winter Studies and Summer Rambles in Canada," published in London in 1838. Mrs. Jameson was at Niagara in 1837, apparently during or soon after the riot. She

Soon after, in the same year, the Governor of Kentucky made requisition on the Governor of the province of Canada West for the surrender of Jesse Happy, another runaway slave, also on a charge of horse-stealing. Sir Francis held him in confinement in Hamilton jail, but refused to deliver him up until he had laid the case before the Home Government. In a most interesting report to the Colonial Secretary, under date of Toronto, Oct. 8, 1837, he asked for instructions "as a matter of general policy," and reviewed the Moseby case in a fair and broad spirit, highly creditable to him alike as an administrator and a friend of the oppressed. "I am by no means desirous," he wrote, "that this province should become an asylum for the guilty of any color; at the same time the documents submitted with this dispatch will I conceive show that the subject of giving up fugitive slaves to the authorities of the adjoining republican States is one respecting which it is highly desirable I should receive from Her Majesty's Government specific instructions. . . . . It may be argued that the slave escaping from bondage on his master's horse is a vicious struggle between two guilty parties, of which the slave-owner is not only the aggressor, but the blackest criminal

---

called on one of the negro women who had been foremost in the fray. This woman was "apparently about five-and-twenty," had been a slave in Virginia, but had run away at sixteen. This would indicate that she may have come a refugee to the Niagara as early as 1828. William Kirby, in his "Annals of Niagara," has told Moseby's story, with more detail than Mrs. Jameson; he reports only one as killed in the *mêlée* — the schoolmaster Holmes — and adds that " Moseby lived quietly the rest of his life in St. Catharines and Niagara." Sir Francis Bond Head's official communication to the Home Government regarding the matter reports two as killed.

of the two. It is a case of the dealer in human flesh *versus* the stealer of horse-flesh ; and it may be argued that, if the British Government does not feel itself authorized to pass judgment on the plaintiff, neither should it on the defendant." Sir Francis continues in this ingenious strain, observing that "it is as much a theft in the slave walking from slavery to liberty in his master's shoes as riding on his master's horse." To give up a slave for trial to the American laws, he argued, was in fact giving him back to his former master; and he held that, until the State authorities could separate trial from unjust punishment, however willing the Government of Canada might be to deliver up a man for trial, it was justified in refusing to deliver him up for punishment, "unless sufficient security be entered into in this province, that the person delivered up for trial shall be brought back to Upper Canada as soon as his trial or the punishment awarded by it shall be concluded." And he added this final argument, begging that instructions should be sent to him at once :

> It is argued, that the republican states have no right, under the pretext of any human treaty, to claim from the British Government, which does not recognize slavery, beings who by slave-law are not recognized as *men* and who actually existed as brute beasts in moral darkness, until on reaching British soil they suddenly heard, for the first time in their lives, the sacred words, "Let there be light ; and there was light !" From that moment it is argued they were created *men*, and if this be true, it is said they cannot be held responsible for conduct prior to their existence.[1]

---

[1] *See* "A Narrative," by Sir Francis Bond Head, Bart., 2d ed., London, 1839, pp. 200-204.

Sir Francis left the Home Government in no doubt as to his own feelings in the matter; and although I have seen no further report regarding Jesse Happy, neither do I know of any case in which a refugee in Canada for whom requisition was thus made was permitted to go back to slavery. It did sometimes happen, however, that refugees were enticed across the river on one pretext or another, or grew careless and took their chances on the American side, only to fall into the clutches of the ever-watchful slave-hunters.

British love of fair play could be counted on to stand up for the rights of the negro on British soil; but that by no means implies that this inpouring of ignorant blacks, unfitted for many kinds of pioneer work and ill able to withstand the climate, was welcomed by the communities in which they settled. At best, they were tolerated. Very different from the spirit shown in Sir Francis Bond Head's plea, is the tone of much tourist comment, especially during the later years of the Abolition movement. Thus, in 1854, the Hon. Amelia M. Murray wrote, just after her Niagara visit:

"One of the evils consequent upon Southern Slavery, is the ignorant and miserable set of coloured people who throw themselves into Canada. . . . I must regret that the well-meant enthusiasm of the Abolitionists has been without judgment."[1] Another particularly unamiable critic, W. Howard Russell, a much-exploited English war correspondent who wrote volum-

---

[1] "Letters from the United States, Cuba and Canada," London, 1856, p. 118.

inously of the United States during the Civil War, and who showed less good will to this country than any other man who ever wrote so much, came to Niagara in the winter of 1862, and in sourly recording his unpleasant impressions wrote: "There are too many free negroes and too many Irish located in the immediate neighborhood of the American town, to cause the doctrines of the Abolitionists to be received with much favor by the American population; and the Irish of course are opposed to free negroes, where they are attracted by paper mills, hotel service, bricklaying, plastering, housebuilding, and the like — the Americans monopolizing the higher branches of labor and money-making, including the guide business.[1] A few pages farther on, however, describing his sight-seeing on the Canadian side, he speaks of "our guide, a strapping specimen of negro or mulatto." Quotations of like purport from English writers during the years immediately preceding the Civil War, might be multiplied. One rarely will find any opinion at all favorable to the refugee black, and never any expression of sympathy with the Abolitionists by English tourists who wrote books, or endorsal of the work accomplished by the Underground Railroad.

From its importance as a terminal of the Underground, one would look to Buffalo for a wealth of reminiscence on this subject. On the contrary, comparatively little seems to have been gathered up

---

[1] "Canada, Its Defences, Condition and Resources," by W. Howard Russell, LL. D., London, 1865, pp. 33, 34.

regarding Buffalo stations and workers. The Buffalo of *ante-bellum* days was not a large place, and many "personally-escorted" refugees were taken direct from country stations to the river ferries, without having to be hid away in the city. Certain houses there were, however, which served as stations. One of these, on Ferry Street near Niagara, long since disappeared. When the "Morris Butler house," at the corner of Utica Street and Linwood Avenue, built about 1857, was taken down a few years ago, hiding-places were found on either side of the front door, accessible only from the cellar. Old residents then recalled that Mr. Butler was reputed to keep the last station on the Underground route to Canada.[1]

Many years before Mr. Butler's time runaway slaves used to appear in Buffalo, eagerly asking the way to Canada. Those days were recalled by the death, on Aug. 2, 1899, in the Kent County House of Refuge, Chatham, Ont., of "Mammy" Chadwick, reputed to be over 100 years old. She was born a slave in Virginia; was many times sold, once at auction in New Orleans, and later taken to Kentucky. She escaped and made her way by the Underground to Buffalo in 1837. She always fixed her arrival at Fort Erie as "in de year dat de Queen was crowned." She mar-

---

[1] Mr. Butler's name does not appear in Siebert's history, "The Underground Railroad." The "operators" for Erie County named therein (p. 414) are Gideon Barker, the Hon. Wm. Haywood, Geo. W. Johnson, Deacon Henry Moore, and Messrs. Aldrich and Williams. For Niagara County he names Thomas Binmore, W. H. Childs, M. C. Richardson, Lyman Spaulding. Chautauqua and Wyoming counties present longer lists, and thirty-six are named for Monroe County. As appears from my text, the Erie County list could be extended.

ried in Fort Erie, but after a few years went to Chatham, in the midst of a district full of refugee blacks, and there she lived for sixty years, rejoicing in the distinction of having nursed in their infancy many who became Chatham's oldest and most prominent citizens.

There still lives at Fort Erie an active old woman who came to Buffalo, a refugee from slavery, some time prior to 1837; she herself says, "a good while before the Canadian Rebellion," and her memory is so clear and vigorous in general that there appears no warrant for mistrusting it on this point. This interesting woman is Mrs. Betsy Robinson, known throughout the neighborhood as "Aunt Betsy." She lately told her story to me at length. Robbed of all the picturesque detail with which she invested it, the bare facts are here recorded. Her father, mother, and their seven children were slaves on a plantation in Rockingham County, Virginia. There came a change of ownership, and Baker (her father) heard he was to be sold to New Orleans — the fate which the Virginia slave most dreaded; "and yet," says Aunt Betsy, "I've seen dem slaves, in gangs bein' sent off to New Orleans, singin' and playin' on jewsharps, lettin' on to be that careless an' happy." But not so Baker. He made ready to escape. For a week beforehand his wife hid food in the woods. On a dark night the whole family stole away from the plantation, crossed a river, probably the north fork of the Shenandoah, and pushed northward. The father had procured three "passes," which commended them for assistance to friends along the way. According to Aunt Betsy, there were a good many white people in the South in those days who helped the runaway. She was a little girl then, and she now recalls the child's vivid impressions of the weeks they spent traveling and hiding in the mountains, which she says were full of rattlesnakes, wolves and deer. It was a wild country that they crossed, for they came out near Washington, Pa. Here the Quakers helped them; and her father and brothers worked in the coal mines for a time. Then they came on to Pittsburg. From that city north there was no lack of help. "We walked all the way," she says. "There was no railroads in them days, an' I don't remember's we got any wagon-rides. You see, we was so many, nine in all. I remember we went to Erie, and came through Fredonia. We walked through Buffalo — it was little then, you know — and down the river road. My father missed the Black Rock ferry an' we went away down where the bridge is now. I remember we had to walk back up the river, and then we got brought across to Fort Erie. That was a good while before the Canadian Rebellion."[1]

Samuel Murray, a free-born negro, came to Buffalo from Reading, Pa., in 1852. For a time he was employed at the American Hotel, and went to work

---

[1] No doubt an investigator could find a number of former slaves, rich in reminiscences of Underground days, still living in the villages and towns of the Niagara Peninsula, though they would not be very numerous, for, as Aunt Betsy says, "the old heads are 'bout all gone now." Between Fort Erie and Ridgeway lives Daniel Woods, a former slave, who came by the Underground. Harriet Black, a sister-in-law of Mrs. Robinson, still living near Ridgeway, was also a "passenger." Probably others live at St. Catharines, Niagara and other points of former negro settlement, who could tell thrilling tales of their escape from the South. There are many

very early in the morning. It was, he has said, a common occurrence to meet strange negroes, who would ask him the way to Canada. "Many a time," said Murray, "I have gone into the hotel and taken food for them. Then I would walk out Niagara Street to the ferry and see them on the boat bound for Canada." Mr. Murray has related the following incidents:

"There was a free black man living in Buffalo in the '50's who made a business of going to the South after the wives of former slaves who had found comfortable homes, either in the Northern States or in Canada. They paid him well for his work, and he rarely failed to accomplish his mission.

"While connected with the Underground Railroad in Buffalo word was sent us that a colored man from Detroit, a traitor to his color, was coming to Buffalo. This man made a business of informing Southerners of the whereabouts of their slaves, and was paid a good sum per head for those that they recovered. When we heard that he was coming a meeting was held and a committee appointed to arrange for his reception. After being here a few days, not thinking that he was known, he was met by the committee and taken out in the woods where the Parade House now stands. Here he was tied to a tree, stripped and cow-hided until he

---

survivors on the Canada side of the Niagara, of another class; men or women who were born in slavery but were "freed by the bayonet," and came North with no fear of the slave-catchers. Of this class at Fort Erie are Melford Harris and Thomas Banks. Mr. Banks was sold from Virginia to go "down the river"; got his freedom at Natchez, joined the 102d Michigan Infantry, and fought for the Union until the end of the war. His case is probably typical of many, but does not belong to the records of the Underground Railroad.

was almost dead. He lay for a time insensible in a pool of his own blood. Finally regaining consciousness, he made his way back into Buffalo and as soon as he was able complained to the city authorities. His assailants were indentified, arrested, and locked up in the old jail to await the result of his injuries. After a time the excitement caused by the affair subsided and the men were let out one day without having been tried." The sympathy of the sheriff, and probably that of the community as a whole, was plainly not with the renegade who got flogged.

Another celebrated Underground case was the arrest at Niagara Falls of a slave named Sneedon, on a charge of murder, undoubtedly trumped up to procure his return South. Sneedon is described as a fine-looking man, with a complexion almost white. He was brought to trial in Buffalo, when Eli Cook pleaded his case so successfully that he was acquitted. No sooner was he released than he was spirited away *via* the Underground Railroad.

Niagara Falls, far more than Buffalo, was the scene of interesting episodes in the Underground days. Not only did many refugee negroes find employment in the vicinity, especially on the Canada side, but many Southern planters used to visit there, bringing their retinue of blacks. Many a time the trusted body-servant, or slave-girl, would leave master or mistress in the discharge of some errand, and never come back. Instances are related, too, of sudden meetings, at the Falls hotels, between negro waiters and the former masters they had run away from. It is recorded that when Gen. Peter B. Porter brought his Kentucky wife home with him to Niagara Falls, she was attended by a numerous retinue of negro servants, but that one by one they "scented freedom in the air" and ran away, though probably not to any immediate betterment of their condition.

Henry Clay visited Buffalo in September, 1849. When he left for Cleveland his black servant Levi was missing, but whether he had gone voluntarily or against his wishes Mr. Clay was uncertain. "There are circumstances having a tendency both ways," he wrote to Lewis L. Hodges of Buffalo, in his effort to trace the lost property. "If voluntarily, I will take no trouble about him, as it is probable that in a reversal of our conditions I would have done the same thing."[1] The absentee had merely been left in Buffalo — probably he missed the boat — and reported in due time to his master at Ashland. The incident, however, suggests the hazards of Northern travel which in those years awaited wealthy Southerners, who were fond of making long sojourns at Niagara Falls, accompanied by many servants.

An "old resident of Buffalo" is to be credited with the following reminiscence:

"I remember one attempt that was made to capture a runaway slave. It was right up here on Niagara Street. The negro ventured out in daytime and was seized by a couple of men who had been on the watch

---

[1] H. Clay to Lewis L. Hodges; original letter in possession of the Buffalo Historical Society.

for him. The slave was a muscular fellow, and fought desperately for his liberty; but his captors began beating him over the head with their whips, and he would have been overpowered and carried off if his cries had not attracted the attention of two Abolitionists, who ran up and joined in the scuffle. It was just above Ferry Street, and they pulled and hauled at that slave and pounded him and each other until it looked as though somebody would be killed. At last, however, the slave, with the help of his friends, got away and ran for his life, and the slave-chasers and the Abolitionists dropped from blows to high words, the former threatening prosecutions and vengeance, but I presume nothing came of it.'"[1]

Nowhere were the friends of the fugitive more active or more successful than in the towns along the south shore of Lake Erie, from Erie to Buffalo.[2] Some years ago it was my good fortune to become acquainted with Mr. Frank Henry of Erie, who had been a very active "conductor" on the Underground.[3] From him I had the facts of the following

---

[1] Anonymous reminiscences published in the Buffalo Courier, about 1887.

[2] Apparently the greatest travel, at least over these particular routes, was during 1840-41. It was a justifiable boast of the "conductors" that a "passenger" was never lost. In a journal of notes, which was annually kept for many years by one of the zealous anti-slavery men of that day, I find the following entry in 1841: "Nov. 1.—The week has been cold; some hard freezing and snow; now warm; assisted six fugitives from oppression, from this land of equal rights to the despotic government of Great Britain, where they can enjoy their liberty. Last night put them on board a steamboat and paid their passage to Buffalo."

[3] When I knew Frank Henry, he was light-house keeper at Erie. He died in October, 1889, and his funeral was a memorable one. After the body had been viewed by his friends, while it lay in state in the parlor of his old home in Wesleyville, the casket was lifted to the shoulders of the pall-bearers, who carried it through the streets of the little village to the church, all the friends, which included all the villagers and many from the

Underground Trails.

experiences, which he had not in earlier years thought it prudent to make public. These I now submit, partly in Mr. Henry's own language, as fairly-illustrative episodes in the history of Underground trails at the eastern end of Lake Erie.

In the year 1841 Capt. David Porter Dobbins, afterwards Superintendent of Life Saving Stations in the Ninth U. S. District, including Lakes Erie and Ontario, was a citizen of Erie. In politics he was one of the sturdy, old-time Democrats, not a few of whom, in marked contrast to their "Copperhead" neighbors, secretly sympathized with and aided the runaway slaves. Capt. Dobbins had in his employ a black man named William Mason, his surname being taken, as was the usual, but not invariable, custom among slaves, from that of his first master. Now Mason, some time before he came into the employ of Capt. Dobbins, had apparently become tired of getting only the blows and abuse of an overseer in return for his toil ; so one night he quietly left his "old Kentucky home," determined to gain his freedom or die in the attempt. In good time he succeeded in getting to Detroit, then a small town ; and there he found work, took unto himself a

---

city and the country round about, following in procession on foot. The little church could not hold the assemblage, but the overflow waited until the service was over, content, if near enough the windows or the open door, to hear but a portion of the eulogies his beloved pastor pronounced. Then they all proceeded to the graveyard behind the historic church and laid him away. He was a man of an exceptionally frank and lovable character. Prof. Wilbur H. Siebert mentions him in his history, "The Underground Railroad from Slavery to Freedom"; but nowhere else, I believe, is as much recorded of the work which he did for the refugee slaves as in the incidents told in the following pages ; and these, we may be assured, are but examples of the service in which he was engaged for a good many years.

wife, and essayed to settle down. Instead, however, of settling, he soon found himself more badly stirred up than ever before, for his wife proved to be a veritable she-devil in petticoats, with a tongue keener than his master's lash. They parted, and the unfaithful wife informed against him to the slave-hunters. Mason fled, made his way to Erie, and was given work by Capt. Dobbins. He was a stalwart negro, intelligent above the average, altogether too fine a prize to let slip easily, and the professional slave-hunters lost no time in hunting him out.

For many years prior to the Civil War a large class of men made their living by ferreting out and recapturing fugitive slaves and returning them to their old masters; or, as was often the case, selling them into slavery again. Free black men, peaceful citizens of the Northern States, were sometimes seized, to be sold to unscrupulous men who stood ever ready to buy them. There was but little hope for the negro who found himself carried south of Mason and Dixon's line in the clutches of these hard men, who were generally provided with a minute description of runaways from the border States, and received a large commission for capturing and returning them into bondage.

One day, as Mason was cutting up a quarter of beef in Capt. Dobbins's house, two men came in, making plausible excuses. Mason saw they were watching him closely, and his suspicions were at once aroused.

"Is your name William?" one of them asked.

"No," said Mason curtly, pretending to be busy with his beef.

Then they told him to take off his shoe and let them see if there was a scar on his foot. On his refusing to do so, they produced handcuffs and called on him to surrender. Livid with desperation and fear, Mason rushed upon them with his huge butcher-knive, and the fellows took to their heels to save their heads. They lost no time in getting a warrant from a magistrate on some pretext or other, and placed it in the hands of an officer for execution.

While the little by-play with the butcher-knife was going on, Capt. Dobbins had entered the house, and to him Mason rushed in appeal. Swearing "by de hosts of heaben" that he would never be captured, he piteously begged for help and the protection of his employer. And in Capt. Dobbins he had a friend who was equal to any emergency. Calling Mason from the room his employer hurried with him to Josiah Kellogg's house, then one of the finest places in Erie, with a commanding view from its high bank over lake and bay.[1] To this house Mason was hurried, and Mrs. Kellogg comprehended the situation at a glance. The fugitive was soon so carefully hidden that, to use the Captain's expression, "The Devil himself couldn't have found him, sir!"

Expeditious as they were, they had been none too quick. Capt. Dobbins had scarcely regained his own

---

[1] Afterwards long known as the Lowry Mansion, on Second Street, between French and Holland streets. It is still standing.

door, when the two slave-hunters came back with the sheriff and demanded Mason.

"Search the premises at your pleasure," was the response.

The house was ransacked from cellar to garret, but, needless to say, Mason was not to be found.

There was living in Erie at that time a big burly negro, Lemuel Gates by name, whose strength was only surpassed by his good nature. He was willing enough to lend himself to the cause of humanity. The Captain owned a very fast horse, and while the officer and his disappointed and suspicious companions were still lurking around, just at nightfall, he harnessed his horse into the buggy and seated the Hercules by his side. All this was quietly done in the barn with closed doors. At a given signal, the servant-girl threw open the doors, the Captain cracked his whip, and out they dashed at full speed. He took good care to be seen and recognized by the spies on watch, and then laid his course for Hamlin Russell's house at Belle Valley. Mr. Russell was a noted Abolitionist, and lived on a cross-road between the Wattsburg and Lake Pleasant roads. Just beyond Marvintown, at Davison's, the Lake Pleasant road forks off from the Wattsburg road to the right. The travelers took the Lake road. When Mr. Russell's house was reached, the Captain slipped a half-eagle into the hand of his grinning companion, with the needless advice that it would be well to make tracks for home as fast as possible. Mr. Russell was told of the clever ruse, and then Capt. Dobbins drove leisurely homeward. At the junction of the two roads he met the officer and his comrades in hot pursuit.

"Where is Mason?" they demanded.

"Find out," was the Captain's only answer, as he drove quietly along, chuckling to himself over the success of his strategy; while the slave-hunters worked themselves into a passion over a fruitless search of Mr. Russell's innocent premises.

Early one morning a few days afterward, as Capt. Dobbins was on the bank of the lake, he saw a vessel round the point of the Peninsula, sail up the channel, and cast anchor in Misery Bay, then, and for many years afterwards, a favorite anchorage for wind-bound vessels. Soon a yawl was seen to put off for the shore with the master of the vessel aboard. Capt. Dobbins contrived to see him during the day, and was delighted to find him an old and formerly intimate shipmate. The ship-master heartily entered into the Captain's plans, and it was agreed to put Mason aboard of the vessel at two o'clock the next morning.

At the time of which we write, the steamer docks and lumber-yards which later were built along the shore at that point, were yet undreamed of, and the waters of the bay broke unhindered at the foot of the high bank on which stood Mrs. Kellogg's house, where Mason was hid. It would not do openly to borrow a boat, and Capt. Dobbins had no small difficulty in getting a craft for the conveyance of his *protégé* to the vessel. At last, late at night, a little, leaky old skiff was temporarily confiscated. By this time a strong breeze had sprung up, and it was difficult to approach the shore. A tree had fallen over the bank with its top in the water, and the Captain found precarious anchorage for his leaky tub by clinging to its branches. With a cry like the call of the whip-poor-will the runaway was summoned. In his hurry to get down the bank he slipped and fell headlong into the fallen treetop; while a small avalanche of stones and earth came crashing after and nearly swamped the boat. When the boat had been lightened of its unexpected cargo, the voyage across the bay began. The poor darky, however, was no sooner sure that his neck was not broken by the tumble, than he was nearly dead with the fear of drowning. Their boat, a little skiff just big enough for one person, leaked like a sieve, and soon became water-logged in the seaway. Mason's hat was a stiff "plug," a former gift of charity. It had suffered sorely by the plunge down the bank, but its ruin was made complete by the Captain ordering its owner to fall to and bail out the boat with it. The brim soon vanished, but the upper part did very well as a bucket; and the owner consoled himself that in thus sacrificing his hat he saved his life. It was a close call for safety. The Captain tugged away at the oars as never before, and the shivering negro scooped away for dear life to keep the boat afloat. In after years Capt. Dobbins experienced shipwreck more than once, but he used to say that never had he been in greater peril than when making that memorable trip across Presque Isle

Underground Trails.

Bay in the wild darkness and storm of midnight. The vessel was at length reached. She was loaded with staves, and a great hole was made in the deck load, within which Mason was snugly stowed away, while the staves were piled over him again. Capt. Dobbins reached the mainland in safety before daylight, and during the morning had the satisfaction of seeing the wind haul around off land, when the vessel weighed anchor and sailed away.

Knowing that pursuit was impossible (there were no steam tugs on the bay in those days), Capt. Dobbins quietly told the officer that he was tired of being watched, and that if he would come along, he would show him where Mason was. The Captain had notified some of his friends, and when the bank of the lake was reached, a crowd had gathered, for the affair had created quite a stir in the village.

"Do you see that sail?" said the Captain, pointing to the retreating vessel.

"Well?" was the impatient answer.

"Mason is aboard of her," was the quiet reply. The befooled magistrate of the law, who had taken great care to bring handcuffs for his expected prisoner, acknowledged himself beaten; while the "nigger-chasers" were glad to sneak off, followed by the shouts and jeers of the crowd. "Pretty well done — for a Democrat," said Mr. Russell to the Captain a few days afterwards. "After your conversion to our principles you will make a good Abolitionist."

Some years after the event above narrated, as Capt.

Dobbins'¹ was in the cabin of his vessel as she lay at Buffalo, a respectably-dressed black man was shown into the cabin. It was Mason, who had come to repay his benefactor with thanks and even with proffered money. He had settled somewhere back of Kingston, Ontario, on land which the Canadian Government at that time gave to actual settlers. He had married an amiable woman, and was prosperous and happy.

I give the following incident substantially as it was set down for me by Mr. Frank Henry:

In the summer of 1858 Mr. Jehiel Towner (now deceased) sent me a note from the city of Erie, asking me to call on him that evening. When night came I rode into town from my home in Harborcreek, and saw Mr. Towner. "There are three 'passengers' hidden in town, Henry," said he, "and we must land them somewhere on the Canada shore. You are just the man for this work; will you undertake to get them across?"

You must remember that we never had anything to do with "runaway niggers" in those days, nor even with "fugitive slaves"; we simply "assisted passengers." I knew well enough that there was a big risk in the present case, but I promised to do my part, and so after talking over matters a little I drove home.

---

¹ Capt. D. P. Dobbins was for many years a distinguished resident of Buffalo. As vessel master, Government official, and especially as inventor of the Dobbins life-boat, he acquired a wide reputation; but little has been told of his Underground Railroad work. He died in 1892.

The next night just about dusk a wagon was driven into my yard. The driver, one Hamilton Waters, was a free mulatto, known to everybody around Erie. He had brought a little boy with him as guide, for he was almost as blind as a bat. In his wagon were three of the strangest-looking "passengers" I ever saw; I can remember how oddly they looked as they clambered out of the wagon. There was a man they called Sam, a great strapping negro, who might have been forty years old. He was a loose-jointed fellow, with a head like a pumpkin, and a mouth like a cavern, its vast circumference always stretched in a glorious grin; for no matter how badly Sam might feel, or how frightened, the grin had so grown into his black cheeks that it never vanished. I remember how, a few nights after, when the poor fellow was scared just about out of his wits, his grin, though a little ghastly, was as broad as ever. Sam was one of the queerest characters I ever met. His long arms seemed all wrists, his legs all ankles; and when he walked, his nether limbs had a flail-like flop that made him look like a runaway windmill. The bases upon which rested this fearfully- and wonderfully-made superstructure were abundantly ample. On one foot he wore an old shoe — at least number twelve in size — and on the other a heavy boot; and his trousers-legs, by a grim fatality, were similarly unbalanced, for while the one was tucked into the boot-top, its fellow, from the knee down, had wholly vanished. Sam wore a weather-beaten and brimless "tile" on his head, and in his hand carried an old-fashioned long-barreled rifle. He set great store by his "ole smooth bo'," though he handled it in a gingerly sort of way, that suggested a greater fear of its kicks than confidence in its aim. Sam's companions were an intelligent-looking negro about twenty-five years old, named Martin, and his wife, a pretty quadroon girl, with thin lips and a pleasant voice, for all the world like *Eliza* in "Uncle Tom's Cabin." She carried a plump little piccaninny against her breast, over which a thin shawl was tightly drawn. She was an uncommonly attractive young woman, and I made up my mind then and there that she shouldn't be carried back to slavery if I had any say in the matter.

The only persons besides myself who knew of their arrival were William P. Trimble and Maj. F. L. Fitch. The party was conducted to the old Methodist church in Wesleyville, which had served for a long time as a place of rendezvous and concealment. Except for the regular Sunday services, and a Thursday-night prayer-meeting, the church was never opened, unless for an occasional funeral, and so it was as safe a place as could well have been found. In case of unexpected intruders, the fugitives could crawl up into the attic and remain as safe as if in Liberia.

It was my plan to take the "passengers" from the mouth of Four-Mile Creek across the lake to Long Point light-house, on the Canada shore, but the wind hung in a bad quarter for the next two or three days, and our party had to keep in the dark. One rainy night, however — it was a miserable, drizzling rain, and dark as Egypt — I was suddenly notified that a sailboat was in readiness off the mouth of Four-Mile Creek. At first I was at a loss what to do. I didn't dare go home for provisions, for I had good reason to believe that my house was nightly watched by a cowardly wretch, whose only concern was to secure the $500 offered by Sam's former master for the capture of the slaves. In the vicinity lived a well-to-do farmer, a devoted pro-slavery Democrat. Notwithstanding his politics, I knew the man was the soul of honor, and possessed a great generous heart. So I marshaled my black brigade out of the church, and marched them off, through the rain, single file, to his house. In answer to our knock, our friend threw open the door; then, with a thousand interrogation points frozen into his face, he stood for a minute, one hand holding a candle above his head, the other shading his eyes, as he stared at the wet and shivering group of darkies, the very picture of dumfounded astonishment. In less time than it takes to tell it, however, he grasped the situation, hustled us all into the house and shut the door with a most expressive slam.

"What in —— does all this mean?" was his pious ejaculation.

He saw what it meant, and it needed but few words of explanation on my part. "They are a party of fugitives from slavery," said I, calling our friend by name. "We are about to cross the lake to Canada; the party are destitute and closely pursued; their only crime is a desire for freedom. This young woman and mother has been sold from her husband and child to a dealer in the far South, and if captured, she will be consigned to a life of shame." The story was all too common in those days, and needed no fine words. The young girl's eyes pleaded more forcibly than any words I could have spoken.

"Well — what do you want of me?" demanded our host, trying hard to look fierce and angry.

"Clothing and provisions," I replied.

"Now look here," said he, in his gruffest voice, "this is a bad job — bad job." Then, turning to the negroes: "Better go back. Canada is full of runaway niggers now. They're freezin' and starvin' by thousands. Was over in Canada t'other day. Saw six niggers by the roadside, with their heads cut off. Bones of niggers danglin' in the trees. Crows pickin' their eyes out. *You* better go back, d'ye *hear?*" he added, turning suddenly towards Sam.

Poor Sam shook in his shoes, and his eyes rolled in terror. He fingered his cherished smooth-bore as though uncertain whether to shoot his entertainer, or save all his ammunition for Canada crows, while he cast a helpless look of appeal upon his companions. The young woman, however, with her keener insight, had seen through the sham brusqueness of their host; and although she was evidently appalled by the horrible picture of what lay before them across the lake, her heart told her it was immeasurably to be preferred to a return to the only fate which awaited her in the South. Her thoughts lay in her face, and our friend read them;

and not having a stone in his broad bosom, but a big, warm, thumping old heart, was moved to pity and to aid. He set about getting a basket of provisions. Then he skirmished around and found a blanket and hood for the woman; all the time declaring that *he* never would help runaway niggers, no sir! and drawing (for Sam's especial delectation) the most horrible pictures of Canadian hospitality that he could conjure up. "You'll find 'em on shore waitin' for ye," said he; "they'll catch ye and kill ye and string ye up for a scare-crow." Seeing that Sam was coatless, he stripped off his own coat and bundled it upon the astonished darky with the consoling remark: "When they get hold of *you* they'll tan your black hide, stretch it for drum-heads, and beat 'God Save the Queen' out of ye every day in the year."

All being in readiness, our benefactor plunged his hand into his pocket, and pulling it out full of small change thrust it into the woman's hands, still urging them to go back to the old life. At the door Sam turned back and spoke for the first time:

"Look 'e hyar, Massa, you's good to we uns an' 'fo' de Lo'd I tank yer. Ef enny No'then gemmen hankah fur my chances in de Souf, I' zign in dair favo'. 'Fo' de good Lo'd I tank ye, Massa, I does, *shuah!*"

Here Sam's feelings got the better of him, and we were hurrying off, when our entertainer said:

"See here, now, Henry, remember you were never at my house with a lot of damned niggers in the night. Do you understand?"

"All right, sir. You are the last man who would ever be charged with Abolitionism, and that's the reason why we came here tonight. Mum is the word."

The rain had stopped and the stars were shining in a cheerful way as we all trudged down the wet road to the lake shore. Our boat was found close in shore, and Martin and his wife had waded out to it, while Sam and I stood talking in low tones on the beach. Suddenly a crash like the breaking of fence-boards was heard on the bank near by, and to the westward of us. We looked up quickly and saw the form of a man climb over the fence and then crouch down in the shadow. Up came Sam's rifle, and with a hurried aim he fired at the moving object. His old gun was trusty and his aim true, and had it not been for a lucky blow from my hand, which knocked the gun upwards just as he fired, and sent the ball whistling harmlessly over the bank, there'd have been one less mean man in the world, and we should have had a corpse to dispose of. I scrambled up the bank, with my heart in my mouth, I'll confess, just in time to see the sneak scurry along in the direction of the highway. I watched a long time at the creek after the boat left, and seeing no one astir started for home. By the time I reached the Lake road the moon had come up, and a fresh carriage-track could be plainly seen. I followed it down the road a short distance, when it turned, ran across the sod, and ended at the fence, which had been freshly gnawed by horses. It then turned back into the highway, followed up the crossroad to Wesleyville, and thence came to the city.

The fugitives reached the promised land in safety, and I heard from them several times thereafter. The man Sam subsequently made two or three successful trips back to the old home, once for a wife and afterwards for other friends. He made some money in the Canada oil fields, and some time after sent me $100, $50 for myself to invest in books, and $50 for the fishermen who carried them safely across to Long Point and liberty.

Of all the places which have sheltered the fugitive slave there is none better known, along the southeastern shore of Lake Erie, than the old Methodist church at Wesleyville, Erie Co., Pennsylvania. It stands today much as it stood a half century since; though repairs have been made from time to time, and of late years modern coal stoves have replaced the capacious but fervid old wood-eaters known as box-stoves. Dedicated to God, it has been doubly hallowed by being devoted to the cause of humanity. To more than one wretch, worn out with the toils of a long flight, it has proved a glorious house of refuge; and if safety lay not within the shadow of its sacred altar, it surely did amidst the shadowy gloom of its dingy garret.

In the year 1856 there lived in Caldwell County, in western Kentucky, a well-to-do farmer named Wilson. He owned a large and well-stocked farm, which he had inherited, with several slaves, from his father. Mr. Wilson was an easy-going and indulgent master, and reaped a greater reward of affection from his "people" than he did of pecuniary gain from his plantation. In the autumn of the above-named year he died, and his servants were divided among the heirs, who lived in Daviess County, in the same State. Two of the slaves, Jack and Nannie, a young man and his sister, fell to the lot of a hard master named Watson. The housekeeper dying, Nannie was taken from the field to fill her place. Nothing could have been worse for the poor girl. She was handsome, her young master a brute. Because she defended her honor she was cruelly punished and locked up for many hours. Her brother succeeded in freeing her, and together they fled, only to be recaptured. They were whipped so terribly that the girl Nannie died. Jack survived, heart-broken, quiet for a time, but with a growing resolve in his heart. One night his master came home from a debauch, and ordered Jack to perform some unreasonable and impossible task. Because the poor boy failed, the master flew at him with an open knife. It was death for one of them. The image of poor Nan, beaten to an awful death, rose before Jack's eyes. In a moment he became a tiger. Seizing a cart-stake, he dealt his master a blow that killed him. The blood of his sister was avenged.

Once more Jack fled. The murder of the master had aroused the neighborhood. Blood-hounds, both brute and human, scoured the woods and swamps; flaming handbills offered great rewards for Jack Watson, dead or alive. With incredible cunning, and grown wary as a wild animal, Jack lurked in the vicinity a long time. When the excitement had somewhat abated, he found his way to Salem, Ohio, and was for a time in the employ of a worthy Quaker named Bonsell, whose descendants still live in that locality. It was then a neighborhood of Friends, and Jack's life among them brought him great good. He learned to read and write, and became in heart and conduct a changed man. His life, however, was haunted by two ghastly forms; and as often as the image of his murdered master rose before him, that of Nan came also to justify the deed. These apparitions wore upon him, and made his life unnatural and highly sensitive. On one occasion, while in Pittsburg, he saw what he took to be the ghost of his murdered master coming toward him in the street. He turned and fled in abject terror, much to the astonishment of all passers-by. Long afterward he learned that the supposed apparition was a half-brother of his former master.

Jack now determined to devote his life to freeing his countrymen from bondage. In due time he found his way to the house of Mr. John Young, a noted Abolitionist of Wilmington township, in Mercer County, Pennsylvania. Mr. Young was one of the first men in Mercer County to proclaim his political convictions to the world, and to stand by them, bravely and consistently, and through many a dangerous hour, until slavery was a thing of the past. No man ever asked brave John Young for help and was refused. His house was known among Abolitionists far and wide as a safe station for the Underground Road.

While Jack was at Mr. Young's he fell in with a young minister, himself a former fugitive from Kentucky, and who was at the time an earnest Baptist preacher in Syracuse, N. Y. This friend, named Jarm W. Loguen, promised Jack shelter if he could but reach Syracuse, and so Jack was "forwarded" along the road.

When he reached Erie, the late Mr. Thomas Elliott, of Harborcreek, carried him to Wesleyville. His pursuers were incidentally heard of as being in the vicinity of Meadville, and it was necessary to proceed with great caution; so Jack was hidden away for a few days beneath the shelter of the old church roof.

It so happened that at this time a protracted meeting was in progress in the church. It was a great awakening, well remembered yet in the neighborhood. There were meetings every night, though the church was shut up during the day. During the evening meetings Jack would stay quietly concealed in the garret; but after the congregation dispersed and the key was turned in the door, he would descend, stir up a rousing fire, and make himself as comfortable as possible until the meeting-hour came round again. It is related that Mr. David Chambers generously kept the house supplied with fuel; and his boys, to whose lot fell the manipulation of the wood-pile, were in constant wonder at the disappearance of the wood. "I shan't be very sorry when this revival winds up," said one of them confidentially to the other; "it takes an awful lot of wood to run a red-hot revival." The meanwhile black

Jack toasted his shins by the revival fire, and found, no doubt, a deal of comfort in the sacred atmosphere of the sheltering church.

The meetings grew in interest with every night. Scores were gathered into the fold of the church, and the whole community, young and old, were touched by the mysterious power. The meetings were conducted by the Rev. John McLean, afterwards a venerable superannuate of the East Ohio Conference, yet living (at least a few years ago) in Canfield, Mahoning County, Ohio; by the Rev. B. Marsteller, and others. The interest came to a climax one Sunday night. A most thrilling sermon had been preached. Every heart was on fire with the sacred excitement, and it seemed as if the Holy Spirit were almost tangible in their very midst. The church was full, even to the gallery that surrounds three sides of the interior. Methodists are not — at least were not in those days — afraid to shout; and Jack, hidden above the ceiling, had long been a rapt listener to the earnest exhortations. His murder, his people in bondage, all the sorrows and sins of his eventful life, rose before his eyes. Overcome with contrition, he knelt upon the rickety old boards, and poured out his troubles in prayer. Meanwhile, down below, the excitement grew. The Rev. James Sullivan made an impassioned exhortation, and when he finished, the altar was crowded with penitents. The service resolved itself into a general prayer-meeting. Men embraced each other in the aisles, or knelt in tearful prayer together; while shouts of victory and groans of repentance filled the church. God bless the good old-fashioned shouting Methodists, who shouted all the louder as the Lord drew near! Some of the old revival hymns, sent rolling across winter fields, and throbbing and ringing through the midnight air, would set the very universe rejoicing, and scatter the legions of Satan in dismay. Alas that the religion of lungs — the shouting, noisy, devout, glorious old worship, is passing away! The whispers of the Devil too often drown the modulations of modern prayer, and instead of glorified visions of angels and the saints, the eyes of modern worshipers rest weariedly upon the things of the world.

As the tide of excitement swelled higher and wilder that night, it caught poor Jack, up in the garret. Through narrow cracks he could see the emotions and devotions of the audience; and in his enthusiasm he wholly forgot that he was in concealment and his presence known to only two or three of the worshipers.

"Come up, sinners, come up to the Throne of Grace and cast your heavy burdens down," called the pastor, his face aglow with exercise and emotion, and his heart throbbing with exultation. "Praise be to God on High for this glorious harvest of souls."

"Glory, glory, amen!" rose from all parts of the church.

"Glory, glory, amen!" came back a voice from the unknown above.

The hubbub was at such a pitch down stairs that Jack's unconscious response was scarcely heard; but to those in the gallery it was plainly audible.

"Lord God of Sabbaoth," prayed the minister, "come down upon us tonight. Send Thy Spirit into our midst!"

"Amen! glory! hallelujah!" shouted Jack in the garret.

The people in the gallery were in holy fear. "It is Gabriel," they said.

"We come to Thee, Lord! We come, we come!" cried the repentent sinners down stairs.

"I come, I come, glory to God, hallelujah, amen!" shouted back the Gabriel in the garret, clapping his hands in the fervor of his ecstacy.

All at once his Abolition friends below heard him. They were struck with consternation and looked at each other in dismay. If Jack was discovered, there would be trouble; they must quiet him at any hazard. "The idea of that nigger getting the power in the garret! A stop must be put to that at once. A revival in full blast is an unusual treat for an Underground Railroad traveler; he should take with gratitude what he could hear, and keep still for the safety of his skin." So thought his frightened friends, who at once cast about for means to quiet him.

Now it so happened — how fortunate that there is always a way out of a dilemma! — that the old stovepipe, which connected with the chimney in the attic, frequently became disconnected; and on more than one occasion incipient fires had started among the dry boards of the garret floor. The people were used to seeing the boys go aloft to look after the safety of the house; so, when Dempster M. Chambers, a son of Mr. Stewart Chambers, inspired by a happy thought, scrambled up the ladder and crawled through the trap-door into the gloom, those who noticed it thought only that the old stove-pipe had slipped out, and continued to throw their sins as fuel into the general religious blaze; or thinking of the fires of hell, gave little heed to lesser flames. Jack was soon quieted, and the meeting, having consumed itself with its own fervor, broke up without further incident. There is no doubt, however, that certain worthy people who were seated in the gallery have ever stoutly maintained that the Angel Gabriel actually replied to the prayers of that memorable night.[1]

In due time Jack Watson reached the home of his friend, the Rev. Jarm W. Loguen; and during the dark days of the War he rendered valuable aid to the Union cause along the Kentucky and Virginia borders, and in one guerrilla skirmish he lost his left arm. A few years since he was still living on a preëmpted land-claim in Rice County, Kansas.

The following incident, connected with Watson's career, will not be out of place in closing this sketch:

Some years since the Rev. Glezen Fillmore, a famous pioneer of the Methodist Episcopal Church in

---

[1] I had the facts of this experience from Mr. Frank Henry, and first wrote them out and printed them in the Erie Gazette in 1880. (Ah, Time, why hasten so!) In 1894 H. U. Johnson of Orwell, O., published a book entitled "From Dixie to Canada, Romances and Realities of the Underground Railroad," in which a chapter is devoted to Jack Watson, and this experience at the Wesleyville church is narrated, considerably embellished, but in parts with striking similarity to the version for which Frank Henry and I were responsible. Mr. Johnson gives no credit for his facts to any source.

Buffalo, and for more than half a century an honored member of the Genesee Conference, was engaged in raising funds for the Freedmen's Aid Society. One day his cousin, the late ex-President Millard Fillmore, rode out from Buffalo to visit him. During the conversation the venerable preacher related the story of Watson's escape, as Watson himself had told it while at Fillmore's Underground Railroad depot. The former President was strongly touched by the story, and at its close he drew a check for fifty dollars for the Freedmen. "Thank you, thank you," said the good old parson. "I was praying that the Lord would open your heart to give ten dollars, and here are fifty."

No study of Underground Railroad work in this region, even though, like the present paper, it aims to be chiefly anecdotal, can neglect recognition of the fact that it was a Buffalo man in the Presidential chair who, by signing the Fugitive Slave act of 1850, brought upon his head the maledictions of the Abolitionists, who were so stimulated thereby in their humanitarian law-breaking, that the most active period in Underground Railroad work dates from the stroke of Millard Fillmore's pen which sought to put a stop to it. No passage in American history displays more acrimony than this. Wherever the friends of the negro were at work on Underground lines, Mr. Fillmore was denounced in the most intemperate terms. In his home city of Buffalo, some who had hitherto prided themselves upon his distinguished acquaintance, estranged themselves from him, and on his return to Buffalo he found cold and formal treatment from people whom he had formerly greeted as friends. Insults were offered him; and the changed demeanor of many of his townsmen showed itself even in the church which he attended. Certain ardent souls there were who refused any longer to worship where he did.[1] Mr. Fillmore met all these hostile demonstrations, as he sustained the angry protests and denunciations of the Abolitionists in general, in dignified impurturbability, resting his case upon the constitutionality of his conduct. The act of 1850 reaffirmed the act of 1793, and both rested upon the explicit provision in the Constitution which declares that "no person held to service or labor in one State under the laws thereof, escaping into another, shall, in consequence of any law or regulation therein, be discharged from such service or labor; but shall be delivered up on claim of the party to whom such service or labor may be due." Obviously, so far as this section was concerned, many people of the North were in rebellion against the Constitution of the United States for many years before the Civil War. That the work of the Underground Railroad was justifiable in the humanitarian aspect needs no argument now. But the student of that period cannot overcome the legal stand taken by Mr. Fillmore, his advisers and sym-

---

[1] Such an one was the anti-slavery worker, Sallie Holley, who had formerly taken great pleasure in the sermons of Mr. Fillmore's pastor, the Rev. Dr. Hosmer of the Unitarian Church. When Mr. Fillmore returned to Buffalo and was seen again in his accustomed seat, Miss Holley refused to attend there. "I cannot consent," she wrote, "that my name shall stand on the books of a church that will countenance voting for any pro-slavery presidential candidate. Think of a woman-whipper and a baby-stealer being countenanced as a Christian!" — *See* " A Life for Liberty," edited by John White Chadwick, pp. 60, 69.

pathizers, unless he asserts, as Mr. Seward asserted, that the provision of the Constitution relating to the rendition of slaves was of no binding force. "The law of nations," he declared, "disavows such compacts — the law of nature written on the hearts and consciences of men repudiates them."[1] This was met by the plausible assertion that "the hostility which was directed against the law of 1850 would have been equally violent against any law which effectually carried out the provision of the Constitution."[2] During the years that followed, efforts were made to recover fugitive slaves under this law. Special officers were appointed to execute it, but in most Northern communities they were regarded with odium, and every possible obstacle put in the way of the discharge of their offensive duties. Many tragic affairs occurred; but the organization of the Underground Railroad was too thorough, its operation was in the hands of men too discreet and determined, to be seriously disturbed by a law which found so little moral support in the communities through which its devious trails ran. Thus the work went on, through civil contention and bloody war, until the Emancipator came to loose all shackles, to put an end to property in slaves, and to stop all work, because abolishing all need, of the Underground Railroad.

---

[1] *See* Seward's "Works," Vol. I., p. 65, *et seq.*
[2] *See* Chamberlain's "Biography of Millard Fillmore," p. 136.

Niagara and the Poets.

NIAGARA AND THE POETS.

ON A DAY in July, 1804, a ruddy-faced, handsome young Irishman, whose appearance must have commanded unusual attention in wild frontier surroundings, came out of the woods that overlooked Lake Erie, picking his way among the still-standing stumps, and trudged down the Indian trail, which had not long been made passable for wagons. Presently he came into the better part of the road, named Willink Avenue, passed a dozen scattered houses, and finally stopped at John Crow's log tavern, the principal inn of the infant Buffalo. He was dusty, tired, and disgusted with the fortune that had brought an accident some distance back in the woods, compelling him to finish this stage of his journey, not merely on foot, but disabled. Here, surrounded by more Indians than whites, he lodged for a day or so before continuing his journey to Niagara Falls; and here, according to his own testimony, he wrote a long poem, which was not only, in all probability, the first poem ever composed in Buffalo, and one of the bitterest tirades against America and American institutions to be found in literature; but which contained, so far as I have been able to discover, the first allusion to Niagara Falls, written by one who actually traveled thither, in the poetry of any language.

The poetry of Niagara Falls is contemporary with the first knowledge of the cataract among civilized men. One may make this statement with positiveness, inasmuch as the first book printed in Europe which mentions Niagara Falls contains a poem in which allusion is made to that wonder. This work is the excessively rare "Des Sauvages" of Champlain (Paris, 1604),[1] in which, after the dedication, is a sonnet, inscribed "Le Sievr de la Franchise av discovrs Dv Sievr Champlain." It seems proper, in quoting this first of all Niagara poems, to follow as closely as may be in modern type the archaic spelling of the original:

> Mvses, si vous chantez, vrayment ie vous conseille
>   Que vous louëz Champlain, pour estre courageux :
> Sans crainte des hasards, il a veu tant de lieux,
>   Que ses relations nous contentent l'oreille.
> Il a veu le Perou,[2] Mexique & la Merueille
>   Du Vulcan infernal qui vomit tant de feux,
> Et les saults Mocosans,[3] qui offensent les yeux
>   De ceux qui osent voir leur cheute nonpareille.

---

[1] For the knowledge that the first mention of Niagara Falls is in Champlain's "Des Sauvages," we are indebted to the Hon. Peter A. Porter of Niagara Falls, who recently discovered, by comparison of early texts, that the allusions to the falls in Marc Lescarbot's "Histoire de la Nouvelle France" (1609), heretofore attributed to Jacques Cartier, are really quotations from "Des Sauvages," published some five years before. There is, apparently, no warrant for the oft-repeated statement that Cartier, in 1535, was the first white man to hear of the falls. That distinction passes to Champlain, who heard of them in 1603, and whose first book, printed at the end of that year or early in 1604, gave to the world its first knowledge of the great cataract.— *See* "Champlain not Cartier," by Peter A. Porter, Niagara Falls, N. Y., 1899.

[2] Champlain a bien été jusqu'à Mexico, comme on peut le voir dans son voyage aux Indes Occidentales ; mais il ne s'est pas rendu au Pérou, que nous sachions.— *Note in Quebec reprint, 1870.* Nor had he been to Niagara.

[3] Mocosa est le nom ancien de la Virginie. Cette expression, *saults Mocosans*, semble donner à entendre que, dès 1603 au moins, l'on avait quelque connaissance de la grande chute de Niagara.— *Note in Quebec reprint, 1870.*

> Il nous promet encor de passer plus auant,
> Reduire les Gentils, & trouuer le Leuant,
> Par le Nort, ou le Su, pour aller à la Chine.
> C'est charitablement tout pour l'amour de Dieu.
> Fy des lasches poltrons qui ne bougent d'vn lieu !
> Leur vie, sans mentir, me paroist trop mesquine.

I regret that some research has failed to discover any further information regarding the poet De la Franchise. Obviously, he took rather more than the permissible measure of poet's license in saying that Champlain had seen Peru, a country far beyond the known range of Champlain's travels. But in the phrase "*les saults Mocosans*," the falls of Mocosa, we have the ancient name of the undefined territory afterwards labeled "Virginia." The intent of the allusion is made plainer by Marc Lescarbot, who in 1610 wrote a poem in which he speaks of "great falls which the Indians say they encounter in ascending the St. Lawrence as far as the neighborhood of Virginia."[1] The allusion can only be to Niagara.

It is gratifying to find our incomparable cataract a theme for song, even though known only by aboriginal report, thus at the very dawn of exploration in this part of America. It is fitting, too, that the French should be the first to sing of what they discovered. More than a century after De la Franchise and Lescarbot, a Frenchman who really saw the falls introduced them to the muse, though only by a quotation. This

---

[1] "Lescarbot écrit, en 1610, une pièce de vers dans laquelle il parle des grands sauts que les sauvages disent rencontrer en remontant le Saint-Laurent jusqu'au voisinage de la Virginie."—*Benj. Sulte*, "*Mélanges D'Histoire et de Litterature*," *p. 425*.

was Father Charlevoix, who, writing "From the Fall of Niagara, May 14, 1721," to the Duchess of Lesdiguieres, was moved to aid his description by quoting poetry. "Ovid," the priest wrote to the duchess, "gives us the description of such another cataract, situated according to him in the delightful valley of Tempe. I will not pretend that the country of Niagara is as fine as that, though I believe its cataract much the noblest of the two," and he thereupon quotes these lines from the "Metamorphoses":

> Est nemus Hæmoniæ, præmpta quod undique claudit
> Sylva; vocant Tempe, per quæ Peneus ab imo
> Effusus Pindo spumosis volvitur undis,
> Dejectisque gravi tenues agitantia fumos
> Nubila conducit, summisque aspergine sylvas,
> Impluit, et sonitu plusquam vicina fatigat.

It would be strange if there were not other impressionable Frenchmen who composed or quoted verses expressive of Niagara's grandeur, during the eighty-one years that elapsed between the French discovery of Niagara Falls and the English Conquest — a period of over three-quarters of a century during which earth's most magnificent cataract belonged to France. But if priest or soldier, coureur-de-bois or verse-maker at the court of Louis said aught in meter of Niagara in all that time, I have not found it.

A little thunder by Sir William Johnson's guns at Fort Niagara, a little blood on the Plains of Abraham, and Niagara Falls was handed over to Great Britain. Four years after the Conquest English poetry made its

Niagara and the Poets. 279

first claim to our cataract. In 1764 appeared that ever-delightful work, "The Traveller, or, a Prospect of Society," wherein we read:

> Have we not seen at pleasure's lordly call
> The smiling long-frequented village fall?
> Behold the duteous son, the sire decayed,
> The modest matron or the blushing maid,
> Forced from their homes, a melancholy train,
> To traverse climes beyond the western main;
> Where wild Oswego spreads her swamps around
> And Niagara[1] stuns with thundering sound.
> Even now, perhaps, as there some pilgrim strays
> Through tangled forests and through dangerous ways,
> Where beasts with man divided empire claim,
> And the brown Indian marks with murderous aim;
> There, while above the giddy tempest flies,
> And all around distressful yells arise,
> The pensive exile, bending with his woe,
> To stop too fearful and too faint to go,
> Casts a long look where England's glories shine,
> And bids his bosom sympathize with mine.[2]

Obviously, Oliver Goldsmith's "Traveller," in its American allusions, reflected the current literature of those years when Englishmen heard more of Oswego

---

[1] The pronunciation of "Niagara" here, the reader will remark, is necessarily with the primary accent on the third syllable; the correct pronunciation, as eminent authorities maintain; and, as I hold, the more musical. "Ni-ag'-a-ra" gives us one hard syllable; "Ni [or better, -nee] -a-ga'-ra" makes each syllable end in a vowel, and softens the word to the ear. "Ni-ag'-a-ra" would have been impossible to the Iroquois tongue. But the word is now too fixed in its perverted usage to make reform likely, and we may expect to hear the harsh "Ni-ag'-a-ra" to the end of the chapter.

[2] Dr. Samuel Johnson, as is well known, was responsible for a number of lines in "The Traveller." In the verses above quoted the line
  "To stop too fearful and too faint to go"
is attributed to him. Thus near does the mighty Johnson, the "Great Cham of Literature," come to legitimate inclusion among the poets of Niagara!

than they ever have since. Niagara and Oswego were uttermost points told of in the dispatches, during that long war, reached and held by England's "far-flung battle line"; but if Britain's poets found any inspiration in Niagara's mighty fount for a half century after Goldsmith, I know it not.

And this brings us again to our first visiting poet, Tom Moore, whose approach to Niagara by way of Buffalo in 1804 has been described. Penning an epistle in rhyme from "Buffalo, on Lake Erie," to the Hon. W. R. Spencer — writing, we are warranted in fancying, after a supper of poor bacon and tea, or an evening among the loutish Indians who hung about Crow's log-tavern — he recorded his emotions in no amiable mood:

> Even now, as wandering upon Erie's shore
> I hear Niagara's distant cataract roar,[1]
> I sigh for home — alas! these weary feet
> Have many a mile to journey, ere we meet.

Niagara in 1804 was most easily approached from the East by schooner on Lake Ontario from Oswego, though the overland trail through the woods was beginning to be used. Moore came by the land route. The record of the journey is to be found in the preface to his American Poems, and in his letters to his mother,

---

[1] This is not necessarily hyperbole, by any means. Before the Niagara region was much settled, filled with the din of towns, the roar of trains, screech of whistles and all manner of ear-offending sounds, Niagara's voice could be heard for many miles. Many early travelers testify to the same effect as Moore. An early resident of Buffalo, the late Hon. Lewis F. Allen, has told me that many a time, seated on the veranda of his house on Niagara Street near Ferry, in the calm of a summer evening, he has heard the roar of Niagara Falls.

Niagara and the Poets. 281

published for the first time in his "Memoirs, Journal and Correspondence," edited by Earl Russell and issued in London and Boston in 1853-'56. The letters narrating his adventures in the region are dated "Geneva, Genessee County, July 17, 1804"; "Chippewa, Upper Canada, July 22d"; "Niagara, July 24th"; — in which he copies a description of the falls from his journal, not elsewhere published — and "Chippewa, July 25th," signed "Tom." There is no mention in these letters of Buffalo, but in the prefatory narrative above alluded to we have this interesting account of the visit:

> It is but too true, of all grand objects, whether in nature or art, that facility of access to them much diminishes the feeling of reverence they ought to inspire. Of this fault, however, the route to Niagara, at this period — at least the portion of it which led through the Genesee country — could not justly be accused. The latter part of the journey, which lay chiefly through yet but half-cleared woods, we were obliged to perform on foot; and a slight accident I met with in the course of our rugged walk laid me up for some days at Buffalo.

And so laid up — perhaps with a blistered heel — he sought relief by driving his quill into the heart of democracy. His friend, he lamented, had often told him of happy hours passed amid the classic associations and art treasures of Italy:

> But here alas, by Erie's stormy lake,
> As far from such bright haunts my course I take,
> No proud remembrance o'er the fancy plays,
> No classic dream, no star of other days

> Hath left the visionary light behind,
> That lingering radiance of immortal mind,
> Which gilds and hallows even the rudest scene,
> The humblest shed where Genius once had been.

He views, not merely his immediate surroundings in the pioneer village by Lake Erie, but the general character of the whole land:

> All that creation's varying mass assumes,
> Of grand or lovely, here aspires and blooms.
> Bold rise the mountains, rich the gardens glow,
> Bright lakes expand and conquering rivers flow ;
> But mind, immortal mind, without whose ray
> This world's a wilderness and man but clay,
> Mind, mind alone, in barren still repose,
> Nor blooms, nor rises, nor expands, nor flows.
> Take Christians, Mohawks, democrats and all,
> From the rude wigwam to the Congress Hall,
> From man the savage, whether slaved or free,
> To man the civilized, less tame than he,
> 'Tis one dull chaos, one unfertile strife
> Betwixt half-polished and half-barbarous life ;
> Where every ill the ancient world could brew
> Is mixed with every grossness of the new ;
> Where all corrupts, though little can entice,
> And naught is known of luxury, but its vice !
> Is this the region then, is this the clime
> For soaring fancies? for those dreams sublime,
> Which all their miracles of light reveal
> To heads that meditate and hearts that feel?
> Alas! not so !

And after much more of proud protest against Columbia and "the mob mania that imbrutes her now," our disapproving poet turned in to make the best, let us hope, of Landlord Crow's poor quarters, and to prepare for Niagara. Years afterwards he admitted that there was some soul for song among the men of the Far West of that day. Very complacently he tells us that "Even then, on the shores of those far lakes, the title of 'Poet'— however in that instance unworthily bestowed — bespoke a kind and distinguished welcome for its wearer. The captain who commanded the packet in which I crossed Lake Ontario, in addition to other marks of courtesy, begged, on parting with me, to be allowed to decline payment for my passage." I cannot do better than to quote further from his account of the visit to the falls:

When we arrived at length at the inn, in the neighborhood of the Falls, it was too late to think of visiting them that evening; and I lay awake almost the whole night with the sound of the cataract in my ears. The day following I consider as a sort of era in my life; and the first glimpse I caught of that wonderful cataract gave me a feeling which nothing in this world can ever awaken again. It was through an opening among the trees, as we approached the spot where the full view of the Falls was to burst upon us, that I caught this glimpse of the mighty mass of waters falling smoothly over the edge of the precipice; and so overwhelming was the notion it gave me of the awful spectacle I was approaching, that during the short interval that followed, imagination had far outrun the reality — and vast and wonderful as was the scene that then opened upon me, my first feeling was that of disappointment. It would have been impossible, indeed, for anything real to come up to the vision I had, in these few seconds, formed of it, and those awful scriptural words, 'The fountains of the great deep were broken up,' can alone give any notion of the vague wonders for which I was prepared.

But, in spite of the start thus got by imagination, the triumph of reality was, in the end, but the greater; for the gradual glory of the scene that opened upon me soon took possession of my whole mind; presenting from day to day, some new beauty or wonder, and like all that is most sublime in nature or art, awakening sad as well as elevating thoughts. I retain in my memory but one other dream — for such do events so long past appear — which can by any respect be associated with the grand vision I have just been describing; and however different the nature of their appeals to the imagination, I should find it difficult to say on which occasion I felt most deeply affected, when looking at the Falls of Niagara, or when standing by moonlight among the ruins of the Coliseum.

It was the tranquillity and unapproachableness of the great fall, in the midst of so much turmoil, which most impressed him. He tried to express this in a Song of the Spirit of the region:

> There amid the island sedge,
> Just upon the cataract's edge,
> Where the foot of living man
> Never trod since time began,
> Lone I sit at close of day,[1] . . .

The poem as a whole, however, is not a strong one, even for Tom Moore.

As the Irish bard sailed back to England, another pedestrian poet was making ready for a tour to Niagara. This was the Paisley weaver, rhymster and roamer, Alexander Wilson, whose fame as an ornithologist outshines his reputation as a poet. Yet in him America has — by adoption — her Oliver Goldsmith. In 1794, being then twenty-eight years old, he arrived in Phila-

---

[1] Introduced in the Epistle to Lady Charlotte Rawdon. In Moore's day there was a tiny islet, called Gull Island, near the edge of the Horseshoe Fall. It long since disappeared.

delphia. For eight years he taught school, or botanized, roamed the woods with his gun, worked at the loom, and peddled his verses among the inhabitants of New Jersey. In October, 1804, accompanied by his nephew and another friend, he set out on a walking expedition to Niagara, which he satisfactorily accomplished. His companions left him, but he persevered, and reached home after an absence of fifty-nine days and a walk of 1,260 miles. It is very pleasant, especially for one who has himself toured afoot over a considerable part of this same route, to follow our naturalist poet and his friends on their long walk through the wilderness, in the pages of Wilson's descriptive poem, "'The Foresters." Its first edition, it is believed, is a quaint little volume of 106 pages, published at Newtown, Penn., in 1818.[1] The route led through Bucks and Northumberland counties, over the mountains and up the valley of the Susquehanna; past Newtown, N. Y., now Elmira, and so on to the Indian village of Catherine, near the head of Seneca Lake. Here, a quarter of a century before, Sullivan and his raiders had brought desolation, traces of which stirred our singer to some of his loftiest flights. In that romantic wilderness of rocky glen and marsh and lake, the region where Montour Falls and Watkins now are, Wilson lingered to shoot wild fowl. Thence the route lay through that interval of long ascents — so long that the trudging poet thought

To Heaven's own gates the mountain seemed to rise

---

[1] It had prior publication, serially, with illustrations, in the " Portfolio " of Philadelphia, 1809-'10.

— and equally long descents, from Seneca Lake to Cayuga. Here, after a night's rest, under a pioneer's roof:

> Our boat now ready and our baggage stored,
> Provisions, mast and oars and sails aboard,
> With three loud cheers that echoed from the steep,
> We launched our skiff "Niagara" to the deep.

Down to old Cayuga bridge they sailed and through the outlet, passed the salt marshes and so on to Fort Oswego. That post had been abandoned on the 28th of October, about a week before Wilson arrived there. A desolate, woebegone place he found it:

> Those struggling huts that on the left appear,
> Where fence, or field, or cultured garden green,
> Or blessèd plough, or spade were never seen,
> Is old Oswego; once renowned in trade,
> Where numerous tribes their annual visits paid.
> From distant wilds, the beaver's rich retreat,
> For one whole moon they trudged with weary feet;
> Piled their rich furs within the crowded store,
> Replaced their packs and plodded back for more.
> But time and war have banished all their trains
> And naught but potash, salt and rum remains.
> The boisterous boatman, drunk but twice a day,
> Begs of the landlord; but forgets to pay;
> Pledges his salt, a cask for every quart,
> Pleased thus for poison with his pay to part.
> From morn to night here noise and riot reign;
> From night to morn 'tis noise and roar again.

Not a flattering picture, truly, and yet no doubt a trustworthy one, of this period in Oswego's history.

But we must hurry along with the poet to his destination, although the temptation to linger with him in this part of the journey is great. Indeed, "The Foresters" is a historic chronicle of no slight value. There is no doubting the fidelity of its pictures of the state of nature and of man along this storied route as seen by its author at the beginning of the century; while his poetic philosophizing is now shrewd, now absurd, but always ardently American in tone.

Our foresters undertook to coast along the Ontario shore in their frail "Niagara"; narrowly escaped swamping, and were picked up by

> A friendly sloop for Queenstown Harbor bound,

where they arrived safely, after being gloriously seasick. It was the season of autumn gales. A few days before a British packet called the Speedy, with some twenty or thirty persons on board, including a judge advocate, other judges, witnesses and an Indian prisoner, had foundered and every soul perished. No part of the Speedy was afterwards found but the pump, which Wilson says his captain picked up and carried to Queenston.

Wilson had moralized, philosophized and rhapsodized all the way from the Schuylkill. His verse, as he approaches the Mecca of his wanderings, fairly palpitates with expectation and excitement. He was not a bard to sing in a majestic strain, but his description of the falls and their environment is vivid and of historic value. As they tramped through the forest, —

> Heavy and slow, increasing on the ear,
> Deep through the woods a rising storm we hear.

> Th' approaching gust still loud and louder grows,
> As when the strong northeast resistless blows,
> Or black tornado, rushing through the wood,
> Alarms th' affrighted swains with uproar rude.
> Yet the blue heavens displayed their clearest sky,
> And dead below the silent forests lie ;
> And not a breath the lightest leaf assailed ;
> But all around tranquillity prevailed.
> "What noise is that?" we ask with anxious mien,
> A dull salt-driver passing with his team.
> "Noise? noise? — why, nothing that I hear or see
> But Nagra Falls — Pray, whereabouts live ye?"

This touch of realism ushers in a long and over-wrought description of the whole scene. The "crashing roar," he says,

> —— bade us kneel and Time's great God adore.

Whatever may have been his emotions, his adjectives are sadly inadequate, and his verse devoid of true poetic fervor. More than one of his descriptive passages, however, give us those glimpses of conditions past and gone, which the historian values. For instance, this :

> High o'er the wat'ry uproar, silent seen,
> Sailing sedate, in majesty serene,
> Now midst the pillared spray sublimely lost,
> Swept the gray eagles, gazing calm and slow,
> On all the horrors of the gulf below ;
> Intent, alone, to sate themselves with blood,
> From the torn victims of the raging flood.

Wilson was not the man to mistake a bird ; and many other early travelers have testified to the former presence of eagles in considerable numbers, haunting the gorge below the falls in quest of the remains of animals that had been carried down stream.

Moore, as we have seen, denounced the country for its lack of

> That lingering radiance of immortal mind

which so inspires the poet in older lands. He was right in his fact, but absurd in his fault-finding. It has somewhere been said of him, that Niagara Falls was the only thing he found in America which overcame his self-importance; but we must remember his youth, the flatteries on which he had fed at home and the crudities of American life at that time. For a quarter of a century after Tom Moore's visit there was much in the crass assertiveness of American democracy which was as ridiculous in its way as the Old-World ideas of class and social distinctions were in their way — and vastly more vulgar and offensive. Read, in evidence, Mrs. Trollope and Capt. Basil Hall, two of America's severest and sincerest critics. It should be put down to Tom Moore's credit, too, that before he died he admitted to Washington Irving and to others that his writings on America were the greatest sin of his early life.[1]

---

[1] Tom Moore's infantile criticisms of American institutions have often been quoted with approbation by persons sharing his supposed hostile views. What his maturer judgment was may be gathered from the following extract from a letter which he wrote, July 12, 1818, to J. E. Hall, editor of the "Portfolio," Philadelphia. I am not aware that it ever has been published. I quote from the original manuscript, in my possession:

"You are mistaken in thinking that my present views of politics are a *change* from those I formerly entertained. They are but a *return* to those of my school & college days — to principles, of which I may say what Propertius said of his mistress: *Cynthia prima fuit, Cynthia finis erit.* The only thing that has ever made them *librate* in their *orbit* was that foolish disgust I took at what I thought the *consequences* of democratic principles in America — but I judged by the *abuse,* not the *use* — and the little information I took the trouble of seeking came to me through twisted

Like Moore, Alexander Wilson felt America's lack of a poet; and, like Barlow and Humphreys and Freneau and others of forgotten fame, he undertook — like them again, unsuccessfully — to supply the lack. There is something pathetic — or grotesque, as we look at it — in the patriotic efforts of these commonplace men to be great for their country's sake.

To Europe's shores renowned in deathless song,

asks Wilson,

> Must all the honors of the bard belong?
> And rural Poetry's enchanting strain
> Be only heard beyond th' Atlantic main?
> Yet Nature's charms that bloom so lovely here,
> Unhailed arrive, unheeded disappear;
> While bare black heaths and brooks of half a mile
> Can rouse the thousand bards of Britain's Isle.
> There, scarce a stream creeps down its narrow bed,
> There scarce a hillock lifts its little head,
> Or humble hamlet peeps their glades among
> But lives and murmurs in immortal song.
> Our Western world, with all its matchless floods,
> Our vast transparent lakes and boundless woods,
> Stamped with the traits of majesty sublime,
> Unhonored weep the silent lapse of time,
> Spread their wild grandeur to the unconscious sky,
> In sweetest seasons pass unheeded by;
> While scarce one Muse returns the songs they gave,
> Or seeks to snatch their glories from the grave.

---

and tainted channels — and, in short, I was a rash boy & made a fool of myself. But, thank Heaven, I soon righted again, and I trust it was the only deviation from the path of pure public feeling I ever shall have to reproach myself with. I mean to take some opportunity (most probably in the Life of Sheridan I am preparing) of telling the few to whom my opinions can be of any importance, how much I regret & how sincerely I retract every syllable, injurious to the great cause of Liberty, which my hasty view of America & her society provoked me into uttering. . . . .

"Always faithfully & cordially Yours,   "THOMAS MOORE."

Niagara and the Poets. 291

This solicitude by the early American writers, lest the poetic themes of their country should go unsung, contrasts amusingly, as does Moore's ill-natured complaining, with the prophetic assurance of Bishop Berkeley's famous lines, written half a century or so before, in allusion to America :

> The muse, disgusted at an age and clime
> Barren of every glorious theme,
> In distant lands now waits a better time,
> Producing subjects worthy fame.
>
> . . . .
> Westward the course of empire takes its way, . . .

I have found no other pilgrim poets making Niagara their theme, until the War of 1812 came to create heroes and leave ruin along the frontier, and stir a few patriotic singers to hurl back defiance to the British hordes. Iambic defiance, unless kindled by a grand genius, is a poor sort of fireworks, even when it undertakes to combine patriotism and natural grandeur. Certainly something might be expected of a poet who sandwiches Niagara Falls in between bloody battles, and gives us the magnificent in nature, the gallant in warfare and the loftiest patriotism in purpose, the three strains woven in a triple pæan of passion, ninety-four duodecimo pages in length. Such a work was offered to the world at Baltimore in 1818, with this title-page : "Battle of Niagara, a Poem Without Notes, and Goldau, or the Maniac Harper. Eagles and Stars and Rainbows. By Jehu O' Cataract, author of 'Keep Cool.'" I have never seen "Keep Cool," but it must be very different from the "Battle of Niagara," or it belies its name. The fiery Jehu O' Cataract was John Neal.[1]

The "Battle of Niagara," he informs the reader, was written when he was a prisoner; when he "felt the victories of his countrymen." "I have attempted," he says, "to do justice to American scenery and American character, not to versify minutiæ of battles." The poem has a metrical introduction and four cantos, in which is told, none too lucidly, the story of the battle of Niagara; with such flights of eagles, scintillation of stars and breaking of rainbows, that no brief quotation can do it justice. In style it is now Miltonic, now reminiscent of Walter Scott. The opening canto is mainly an apostrophe to the Bird, and a vision of glittering horsemen. Canto two is a dissertation on Lake Ontario, with word-pictures of the primitive Indian. The rest of the poem is devoted to the battle near the great cataract—and throughout all are sprinkled the eagles, stars and rainbows. Do not infer from this characterization that the production is wholly bad; it is merely a good specimen of that early Ameri-

---

[1] John Neal, or "Yankee Neal," as he was called, is a figure in early American letters which should not be forgotten. He was of Quaker descent, but was read out of the Society of Friends in his youth, as he says, "for knocking a man head over heels, for writing a tragedy, for paying a militia fine and for desiring to be turned out whether or no." He was a pioneer in American literature, and won success at home and abroad several years before Cooper became known. He was the first American contributor to English and Scotch quarterlies, and compelled attention to American topics at a time when English literature was regarded as the monopoly of Great Britain. His career was exceedingly varied and picturesque. He was an artist, lawyer, traveler, journalist and athlete. He is said to have established the first gymnasium in this country, on foreign models, and was the first to advocate, in 1838, in a Fourth-of-July oration, the right of woman suffrage. His writings are many, varied, and for the most part hard to find nowadays.

can poetry which was just bad enough to escape being good.

A brief passage or two will sufficiently illustrate the author's trait of painting in high colors. He is a word-impressionist whose brush, with indiscreet dashes, mars the composition. I select two passages descriptive of the battle :

> The drum is rolled again. The bugle sings
> And far upon the wind the cross flag flings
> A radiant challenge to its starry foe,
> That floats — a sheet of light ! — away below,
> Where troops are forming — slowly in the night
> Of mighty waters ; where an angry light
> Bounds from the cataract, and fills the skies
> With visions — rainbows — and the foamy dyes
> That one may see at morn in youthful poets' eyes.

> Niagara ! Niagara ! I hear
> Thy tumbling waters. And I see thee rear
> Thy thundering sceptre to the clouded skies :
> I see it wave — I hear the ocean rise,
> And roll obedient to thy call. I hear
> The tempest-hymning of thy floods in fear ;
> The quaking mountains and the nodding trees —
> The reeling birds and the careering breeze —
> The tottering hills, unsteadied in thy roar ;
> Niagara ! as thy dark waters pour
> One everlasting earthquake rocks thy lofty shore !
> . . . .
> The cavalcade went by. The day hath gone ;
> And yet the soldier lives ; his cheerful tone
> Rises in boisterous song ; while slowly calls
> The monarch spirit of the mighty falls :
> Soldier, be firm ! and mind your watchfires well ;
> Sleep not to-night !

The following picture of the camp at sunset, as the reveille rings over the field, and Niagara's muffled drums vibrate through the dusk, presents many of the elements of true poetry:

> Low stooping from his arch, the glorious sun
> Hath left the storm with which his course begun;
> And now in rolling clouds goes calmly home
> In heavenly pomp adown the far blue dome.
> In sweet-toned minstrelsy is heard the cry,
> All clear and smooth, along the echoing sky,
> Of many a fresh-blown bugle full and strong,
> The soldier's instrument! the soldier's song!
> Niagara, too, is heard; his thunder comes
> Like far-off battle — hosts of rolling drums.
> All o'er the western heaven the flaming clouds
> Detach themselves and float like hovering shrouds.
> Loosely unwoven, and afar unfurled,
> A sunset canopy enwraps the world.
> The Vesper hymn grows soft. In parting day
> Wings flit about. The warblings die away,
> The shores are dizzy and the hills look dim,
> The cataract falls deeper and the landscapes swim.

Jehu O'Cataract does not always hold his fancy with so steady a rein as this. He is prone to eccentric flights, to bathos and absurdities. His apostrophe to Lake Ontario, several hundred lines in length, has many fine fancies, but his luxuriant imagination continually wrecks itself on extravagancies which break down the effect. This I think the following lines illustrate:

> . . . He had fought with savages, whose breath
> He felt upon his cheek like mildew till his death.
> . . . .
> So stood the battle. Bravely it was fought,

> Lions and Eagles met. That hill was bought
> And sold in desperate combat. Wrapped in flame,
> Died these idolaters of bannered fame.
> Three times that meteor hill was bravely lost —
> Three times 'twas bravely won, while madly tost,
> Encountering red plumes in the dusky air ;
> While Slaughter shouted in her bloody lair,
> And spectres blew their horns and shook their whistling hair.
>
> . . . .

There are allusions to Niagara in some of the ballads of the War of 1812, one of the finest of which, "Sea and Land Victories," beginning

> With half the western world at stake
> See Perry on the midland lake, —

appeared in the Naval Songster of 1815, and was a great favorite half a century or more ago. So far, however, as the last War with Great Britain has added to our store of poetry by turning the attention of the poets to the Niagara region as a strikingly picturesque scene of war, there is little worthy of attention. One ambitious work is remembered, when remembered at all, as a curio of literature. This is "The Fredoniad, or Independence Preserved," an epic poem by Richard Emmons, a Kentuckian, afterwards a physician of Philadelphia. He worked on it for ten years, finally printed it in 1826, and in 1830 got it through a second edition, ostentatiously dedicated to Lafayette. "The Fredoniad" is a history in verse of the War of 1812 ; it was published in four volumes ; it has forty cantos, filling 1,404 duodecimo pages, or a total length of about 42,000 lines. The first and second cantos are devoted to Hell, the third to Heaven, and the fourth to Detroit. About one-third of the whole work is occupied with military operations on the Niagara frontier. Nothing from Fort Erie to Fort Niagara escapes this meter-machine. The Doctor's poetic feet stretch out to miles and leagues, but not a single verse do I find that prompts to quotation; though, I am free to confess, I have not read them all, and much doubt if any one save the infatuated author, and perhaps his proof-reader, ever did read the whole of "The Fredoniad."

No sooner was the frontier at peace, and the pathways of travel multiplied and smoothed, than there set in the first great era of tourist travel to Niagara. From 1825, when the opening of the Erie Canal first made the falls easily accessible to the East, the tide of visitors steadily swelled. In that year came one other poetizing pilgrim, from York, now Toronto, who, returning home, published in his own city a duodecimo of forty-six pages, entitled "Wonders of the West, or a Day at the Falls of Niagara in 1825. A Poem. By a Canadian." The author was J. S. Alexander, said to have been a Toronto school-teacher. It is a great curio, though of not the least value as poetry; in fact, as verse it is ridiculously bad. The author does not narrate his own adventures at Niagara, but makes his descriptive and historical passages incidental to the story of a hero named *St. Julian*. Never was the name of this beloved patron saint of travelers more unhappily bestowed, for this *St. Julian* is a lugubrious, crack-

Niagara and the Poets. 297

brained individual who mourns the supposed death of a lady-love, *Eleanor St. Fleur*. Other characters are introduced; all French except a remarkable driver named *Wogee*, who tells legends and historic incidents in as good verse, apparently, as the author was able to produce. *St. Julian* is twice on the point of committing suicide; once on Queenston Heights, and again at the falls. Just as he is about to throw himself into the river he hears his *Ellen's* voice — the lady, it seems, had come from France by a different route — all the mysteries are cleared up, and the reunited lovers and their friends decide to "hasten hence,"

> Again to our dear native France,
> Where we shall talk of all we saw,
> At thy dread falls, Niagara.[1]

From about this date the personal adventures of individuals bound for Niagara cease to be told in verse, and if they were they would cease to be of much historic interest. The relation of the poets to Niagara no longer concerns us because of its historic aspect.

There remains, however, an even more important division of the subject. The review must be less narrative than critical, to satisfy the natural inquiry, What impress upon the poetry of our literature has

---

[1] Those interested in scarce Americana may care to know that this "Wonders of the West" is said by some authorities to be the second book — certain almanacs and small prints excluded — that was published in Canada West, now Ontario. Of its only predecessor, "St. Ursula's Convent, or the Nuns of Canada," Kingston, 1824, no copy is believed to exist. Of the York school-master's Niagara poem, I know of but two copies, one owned by M. Phileas Gagnon, the Quebec bibliophile; the other in my own possession. It is at least of interest to observe that Ontario's native poetry began with a tribute to her greatest natural wonder, though it could be wished with a more creditable example.

this greatest of cataracts made during the three-quarters of a century that it has been easily accessible to the world? What of the supreme in poetry has been prompted by this mighty example of the supreme in nature? The proposition at once suggests subtleties of analysis which must not be entered upon in this brief survey. The answer to the question is attempted chiefly by the historical method. A few selected examples of the verse which relates to Niagara will, by their very nature, indicate the logical answer to the fundamental inquiry.

There is much significance in the fact, that what has been called the best poem on Niagara was written by one who never saw the falls. Chronologically, so far as I have ascertained, it is the work which should next be considered, for it appeared in the columns of a New-England newspaper, about the time when the newly-opened highway to the West robbed Niagara forever of her majestic solitude, and filled the world with her praise. They may have been travelers' tales that prompted, but it was the spiritual vision of the true poet that inspired the lines printed in the *Connecticut Mirror* at Hartford, about 1825, by the delicate, gentle youth, John G. C. Brainard. It is a poem much quoted, of a character fairly indicated by these lines:

> It would seem
> As if God formed thee from his "hollow hand"
> And hung his bow upon thine awful front;
> And spoke in that loud voice, which seemed to him

> Who dwelt in Patmos for his Savior's sake,
> "The sound of many waters"; and bade
> Thy flood to chronicle the ages back,
> And notch his centuries in the eternal rocks.

Measured by the strength of an Emerson or a Lowell, this is but feeble blank verse, approaching the bombastic; but as compared with what had gone before, and much that was to follow, on the Niagara theme, it is a not unwelcome variation.

The soul's vision, through imagination's magic glass, receives more of Poesy's divine light than is shed upon all the rapt gazers at the veritable cliff and falling flood.

During the formative years of what we now regard as an established literary taste, but which later generations will modify in turn, most American poetry was imitative of English models. Later, as has been shown, there was an assertively patriotic era; and later still, one of great laudation of America's newly-discovered wonders, which in the case of Niagara took the form of apostrophe and devotion. To the patriotic literature of Niagara, besides examples already cited, belongs Joseph Rodman Drake's "Niagara," printed with "The Culprit Fay, and Other Poems" in 1835.[1] It is a poem which would strike the critical ear of today, I think, as artificial; its sentiment, however, is not to be impeached. The poet sings of the love of freedom which distinguishes the Swiss mountaineer; of the sailor's daring and bravery; of the soldier's hero-

---

[1] It is a striking fact that "The Culprit Fay," which appeared in 1819, was the outgrowth of a conversation between Drake, Halleck and Cooper, concerning the unsung poetry of American rivers.— *See* Richardson's "American Literature," Vol. II., p. 24.

ism, even to death. Niagara, like the alp, the sea, and the battle, symbolizes freedom, triumph and glory:

> Then pour thy broad wave like a flood from the heavens,
>   Each son that thou rearest, in the battle's wild shock,
> When the death-speaking note of the trumpet is given,
>   Will charge like thy torrent or stand like thy rock.
>
> Let his roof be the cloud and the rock be his pillow,
>   Let him stride the rough mountain or toss on the foam,
> Let him strike fast and well on the field or the billow,
>   In triumph and glory for God and his home!

Nine years after Drake came Mrs. Sigourney, who, notwithstanding her genuine love of nature and of mankind, her sincerity and occasional genius, was hopelessly of the sentimental school. Like Frances S. Osgood, N. P. Willis and others now lost in even deeper oblivion, she found great favor with her day and generation. Few things from her ever-productive pen had a warmer welcome than the lines beginning:

> Up to the table-rock, where the great flood
>   Reveals its fullest glory,

and her "Farewell to Niagara," concluding

> . . . . it were sweet
> To linger here, and be thy worshipper,
> Until death's footstep broke this dream of life.

Supremely devout in tone, her Niagara poems are commonplace in imagination. Her fancy rarely reaches higher than the perfectly obvious. I confess that I cannot read her lines without a vision of the lady herself standing in rapt attitude on the edge of Table Rock, with note-book in hand and pencil uplifted to catch the purest inspiration from the scene before her. She is the type of a considerable train of writers whose Niagara effusions leave on the reader's mind little impression beyond an iterated "Oh, thou great Niagara, Oh!" Such a one was Richard Kelsey, whose "Niagara and Other Poems," printed in London in 1848, is likely to be encountered in old London bookshops. I have read Mr. Kelsey's "Niagara" several times. Once when I first secured the handsome giltedged volume; again, later on, to discover why I failed to remember any word or thought of it; and again, in the preparation of this paper, that I might justly characterize it. But I am free to confess that beyond a general impression of Parnassian attitudinizing and extravagant apostrophe I get nothing out of its pages. Decidedly better are the lines "On Visiting the Falls of Niagara," by Lord Morpeth, the Earl of Carlisle, who visited Niagara in 1841.[1] He, too, begins with the inevitable apostrophe:

> There's nothing great or bright, thou glorious fall!
> Thou mayst not to the fancy's sense recall —

but he saves himself with a fairly creditable sentiment:

> Oh! may the wars that madden in thy deeps
> There spend their rage nor climb the encircling steeps,
> And till the conflict of thy surges cease
> The nations on thy bank repose in peace.

A British poet who should perhaps have mention in

---

[1] Lord Morpeth made three visits to Niagara. He was the friend and guest, during his American travels, of Mr. Wadsworth at the Geneseo Homestead; and was also entertained by ex-President Van Buren and other distinguished men. His writings reveal a poetic, reflective temperament, but rarely rise above the commonplace in thought or expression.

this connection is Thomas Campbell, whose poem, "The Emigrant," contains an allusion to Niagara. It was published anonymously in 1823 in the *New Monthly Magazine*, which Campbell then edited.[1]

No poem on Niagara that I know of is more entitled to our respectful consideration than the elaborate work which was published in 1848 by the Rev. C. H. A. Bulkley of Mt. Morris, N. Y. It is a serious attempt to produce a great poem with Niagara Falls as its theme. Its length — about 3,600 lines — secures to Western New York the palm for elaborate treatment of the cataract in verse. "Much," says the author, "has been written hitherto upon Niagara in fugitive verse, but no attempt like this has been made to present its united wonders as the theme of a single poem. It seems a bold adventure and one too hazardous, because of the greatness of the subject and the obscurity of the bard; but his countrymen are called upon to judge it with impartiality, and pronounce its life or its death. The author would not shrink from criticism. . . . His object has been, not so much to describe at length the scenery of Niagara in order to excite emotions in the reader similar to those of the beholder, for this would be a vain endeavor, as to give a transcript of what passes through the mind of one who is supposed to witness so grand an achievement of nature. The difficulty," he adds, "with those who visit this wonderful cataract is to give utterance to those feelings and

---

[1] The lines are not included in ordinary editions of Campbell's poems. The original MS. is in the possession of the Buffalo Public Library.

Niagara and the Poets.

thoughts that crowd within and often, because thus pent up, produce what may be termed the pain of delight."

Of a poem which fills 132 duodecimo pages it is difficult to give a fair idea in a few words. There is an introductory apostrophe, followed by a specific apostrophe to the falls as a vast form of life. Farther on the cataract is apostrophized as a destroyer, as an historian, a warning prophet, an oracle of truth, a tireless laborer. There are many passages descriptive of the islands, the gorge, the whirlpool, etc. Then come more apostrophes to the fall respecting its origin and early life. It is viewed as the presence-chamber of God, and as a proof of Deity. Finally, we have the cataract's hymn to the Creator, and the flood's death-dirge.

No long poem is without its commonplace intervals. Mr. Bulkley's "Niagara" has them to excess, yet as a whole it is the work of a refined and scholarly mind, its imagination hampered by its religious habit, but now and than quickened to lofty flights, and strikingly sustained and noble in its diction. Only a true poet takes such cognizance of initial impulses and relations in nature as this:

> In thy hoarse strains is heard the desolate wail
> Of streams unnumbered wandering far away,
> From mountain homes where, 'neath the shady rocks
> Their parent springs gave them a peaceful birth.

It presents many of the elements of a great poem, reaching the climax in the cataract's hymn to the Creator, beginning

> Oh mighty Architect of Nature's home !

At about this period — to be exact, in 1848 — there was published in New York City, as a pamphlet or thin booklet, a poem entitled "Niagara," by "A Member of the Ohio Bar," of whose indentity I know nothing. It is a composition of some merit, chiefly interesting by reason of its concluding lines:

> . . . . Then so live,
> That when in the last fearful mortal hour,
> Thy wave, borne on at unexpected speed,
> O'erhangs the yawning chasm, soon to fall,
> Thou start not back affrighted, like a youth
> That wakes from sleep to find his feeble bark
> Suspended o'er Niagara, and with shrieks
> And unavailing cries alarms the air,
> Tossing his hands in frenzied fear a moment,
> Then borne away forever! But with gaze
> Calm and serene look through the eddying mists,
> On Faith's unclouded bow, and take thy plunge
> As one whose Father's arms are stretched beneath,
> Who falls into the bosom of his God!

The close parallelism of these lines with the exalted conclusion of "Thanatopsis" is of course obvious; but they embody a symbolism which is one of the best that has been suggested by Niagara.

From the sublime to the ridiculous was never a shorter descent than in this matter of Niagara poetry. At about the time Mr. Bulkley wrote, and for some years after, it was the pernicious custom to keep public albums at the Table Rock and other points at the falls, for the record of "impressions." Needless to

Niagara and the Poets. 305

say, these albums filled up with rubbish. To bad taste was added the iniquity of publication, so that future generations may be acquainted with one of the least creditable of native American literary whims. The editor of one of these albums, issued in 1856, lamented that "the innumerable host of visitors who have perpetrated composition in the volumes of manuscript now before us, should have added so little to the general stock of legitimate and permanent literature"; and he adds — by way seemingly of adequate excuse — that "the actual amount of frivolous nonsense which constitutes so large a portion of the contents . . . is not all to be calculated by the specimens now and then exhibited. We have given the best," he says, "always taking care that decency shall not be outraged, nor delicacy shocked; and in this respect, however improbable it may seem, precaution has been by no means unnecessary." What a commentary on the sublime in nature, as reflected on man in the mass!

These Table-Rock Albums contain some true poetry; much would-be fine verse which falls below mediocre; much of horse-play or puerility; and now and then a gleam of wit. Here first appeared the lines which I remember to have conned years ago in a school-rhetoric, and for which, I believe, N. P. Willis was responsible:

> To view Niagara Falls one day,
> A parson and a tailor took their way;
> The parson cried, whilst wrapped in wonder,
> And listening to the cataract's thunder,

> "Lord! how thy works amaze our eyes,
> And fill our hearts with vast surprise";—
> The tailor merely made his note:
> "Lord! what a place to sponge a coat!"

There has been many a visitor at Niagara Falls who shares the sentiments of one disciple of the realistic school:

> Loud roars the waters, O,
> Loud roars the waters, O,
> When I come to the Falls again
> I hope they will not spatter so.

Another writes:

> My thoughts are strange, sublime and deep,
> As I look up to thee —
> What a glorious place for washing sheep,
> Niagara would be!

Examples of such doggerel could be multiplied by scores, but without profit. There was sense if not poetry in the wight who wrote:

> I have been to "Termination Rock"
> Where many have been before;
> But as I can't describe the scene
> I wont say any more.

Infinitely better than this are the light but pleasing verses written in a child's album, years ago, by the late Col. Peter A. Porter of Niagara Falls. He pictured the discovery of the falls by La Salle and Hennepin and ponders upon the changes that have followed:

> What troops of tourists have encamped upon the river's brink;
> What poets shed from countless quills Niagaras of ink;

What artist armies tried to fix the evanescent bow
Of the waters falling as they fell two hundred years ago.
. . . .
And stately inns feed scores of guests from well-replenished larder,
And hackmen drive their horses hard, but drive a bargain harder,
And screaming locomotives rush in anger to and fro;
But the waters fall as once they fell two hundred years ago.

And brides of every age and clime frequent the islands' bower,
And gaze from off the stone-built perch — hence called the Bridal Tower —
And many a lunar belle goes forth to meet a lunar beau,
By the waters falling as they fell two hundred years ago.

Towards the close of the long poem the author takes a more serious tone, but throughout he keeps up a happy cleverness, agreeably in contrast to the prevailing high gush on one hand and balderdash on the other.

Among the writers of serious and sometimes creditable verse whose names appear in the Table-Rock Albums were Henry D. O'Reilly, C. R. Rowland, Sarah Pratt, Maria del Occidente, George Menzies, Henry Lindsay, the Rev. John Dowling, J. S. Buckingham, the Hon. C. N. Vivian, Douglas Stuart, A. S. Ridgely of Baltimore, H. W. Parker, and Josef Leopold Stiger. Several of these names are not unknown in literature. Prof. Buckingham is remembered as an earlier Bryce, whose elaborate three-volume work on America is still of value. Vivian was a distinguished traveler who wrote books; and Josef Leopold Stiger's stanzas beginning

Sei mir gegrüsst, des jungen Weltreichs Stolz und Zierde!

are by no means the worst of Niagara poems.

I cannot conceive of Niagara Falls as a scene promotive of humor, or suggestive of wit. Others may see both in John G. Saxe's verses, of which the first stanza will suffice to quote:

> See Niagara's torrent pour over the height,
>   How rapid the stream! how majestic the flood
> Rolls on, and descends in the strength of his might,
>   As a monstrous great frog leaps into the mud!

The "poem" contains six more stanzas of the same stamp.

The writing of jingles and doggerel having Niagara as a theme did not cease when the Albums were no longer kept up. If there is no humor or grotesqueness in Niagara, there is much of both in the human accessories with which the spot is constantly supplied, and these will never cease to stimulate the wits. I believe that a study of this field — not in a restricted, but a general survey — would discover a decided improvement, in taste if not in native wit, as compared with the compositions which found favor half a century ago. Without entering that field, however, it will suffice to submit in evidence one "poem" from a recent publication, which shows that the making of these American *genre* sketches, with Niagara in the background, is not yet a lost art:

> Before Niagara Falls they stood,
>   He raised aloft his head,
> For he was in poetic mood,
>   And this is what he said:

Niagara and the Poets.   309

"Oh, work sublime! Oh, wondrous law
   That rules thy presence here!
How filled I am with boundless awe
   To view thy waters clear!

"What myriad rainbow colors float
   About thee like a veil,
And in what countless streams remote
   Thy life has left its trail!"

"Yes, George," the maiden cried in haste,
   " Such shades I've never seen,
I'm going to have my next new waist
   The color of that green."

From about 1850 down to the present hour there is a striking dearth of verse, worthy to be called poetry, with Niagara for its theme. Newspapers and magazines would no doubt yield a store if they could be gleaned; perchance the one Niagara pearl of poetry is thus overlooked; but it is reasonably safe to assume that few really great poems sink utterly from sight. There is, or was, a self-styled Bard of Niagara, whose verses, printed at Montreal in 1872, need not detain us. The only long work on the subject of real merit that I know of, which has appeared in recent years, is George Houghton's " Niagara," published in 1882. Like Mr. Bulkley, he has a true poet's grasp of the material aspect of his subject:

Formed when the oceans were fashioned, when all the world was
     a workshop;
Loud roared the furnace fires and tall leapt the smoke from
     volcanoes,

Scooped were round bowls for lakes and grooves for the sliding
    of rivers,
Whilst with a cunning hand, the mountains were linkèd together.
Then through the day-dawn, lurid with cloud, and rent by forked
    lightning,
Stricken by earthquake beneath, above by the rattle of thunder,
Sudden the clamor was pierced by a voice, deep-lunged and
    portentous —
Thine, O Niagara, crying, "Now is creation completed!"

He sees in imagination the million sources of the streams in forest and prairie, which ultimately pour their gathered "tribute of silver" from the rich Western land into the lap of Niagara. He makes skillful use of the Indian legendry associated with the river; he listens to Niagara's "dolorous fugue," and resolves it into many contributory cries. In exquisite fancy he listens to the incantation of the siren rapids:

Thus, in some midnight obscure, bent down by the storm of
    temptation
(So hath the wind, in the beechen wood, confided the story),
Pine trees, thrusting their way and trampling down one another,
Curious, lean and listen, replying in sobs and in whispers;
Till of the secret possessed, which brings sure blight to the hearer
(So hath the wind, in the beechen wood, confided the story),
Faltering, they stagger brinkward — clutch at the roots of the
    grasses,
Cry — a pitiful cry of remorse — and plunge down in the darkness.

The cataract in its varied aspects is considered with a thought for those who

Sin, and with wine-cup deadened, scoff at the dread of hereafter, —
And, because all seems lost, besiege Death's door-way with
    gladness.

The master-stroke of the poem is in two lines:

That alone is august which is gazed upon by the noble,
That alone is gladsome which eyes full of gladness discover.

Herein lies the rebuking judgment upon Niagara's detractors, not all of whom have perpetrated album rhymes.

Mr. Houghton, as the reader will note, recognizes the tragic aspect of Niagara. Considering the insistence with which accident and suicide attend, making here an unappeased altar to the weaknesses and woes of mankind, this aspect of Niagara has been singularly neglected by the poets. We have it, however, exquisitely expressed, in the best of all recent Niagara verse — a sonnet entitled "At Niagara," by Richard Watson Gilder.[1] The following lines illustrate our point:

There at the chasm's edge behold her lean
Trembling, as, 'neath the charm,
A wild bird lifts no wing to 'scape from harm;
Her very soul drawn to the glittering, green,
Smooth, lustrous, awful, lovely curve of peril;
While far below the bending sea of beryl
Thunder and tumult — whence a billowy spray
Enclouds the day.

. . . .

There is a considerable amount of recent verse commonly called "fugitive" that has Niagara for its theme, but I find little that calls for special attention. A few Buffalo writers, the Rev. John C. Lord, Judge Jesse Walker, David Gray, Jas. W. Ward, Henry Chandler, and the Rev. Benjamin Copeland among them, have

---

[1] See "Five Books of Song," by R. W. Gilder, 1894.

found inspiration in the lake and river for some of the best lines that adorn the purely local literature of the Niagara region. Indeed, I know of no allusion to Niagara more exquisitely poetical than the lines in David Gray's historical poem, "The Last of the Kah-Kwahs," in which he compares the Indian villages sleeping in ever-threatened peace to

> . . . . . the isle
> That, locked in wild Niagara's fierce embrace,
> Still wears a smile of summer on its face —
> Love in the clasp of Madness.

With this beautiful imagery in mind, recall the lines of Byron:

> On the verge
> . . . .
> An Iris sits amidst the infernal surge
> . . . .
> Resembling, 'mid the tortures of the scene,
> Love watching Madness with unalterable mien.

Byron did not write of Niagara, but these stanzas beginning

> The roar of waters . . .

often have been applied to our cataract. Mr. Gray may or may not have been familiar with them. In any event he improved on the earlier poet's figure.

Merely as a matter of chronicle, it is well to record here the names of several writers, some of them of considerable reputation, who have contributed to the poetry of Niagara. Alfred B. Street's well-known narrative poem, "Frontenac," contains Niagara passages. So does Levi Bishop's metrical volume

Niagara and the Poets. 313

"Teuchsa Grondie" ("Whip-poor-will"), the Niagara portion dedicated to the Hon. Augustus S. Porter. Ever since Chateaubriand wrote "Atala," authors have been prompted to associate Indian legends with Niagara, but none has done this more happily than William Trumbull, whose poem, "The Legend of the White Canoe," illustrated by F. V. Du Mond, is one of the most artistic works in all the literature of Niagara.

The Rev. William Ellery Channing, the Rev. Joseph H. Clinch, the Rev. Joseph Cook, Christopher P. Cranch, Oliver I. Taylor, Grenville Mellen, Prof. Moffat, John Savage, Augustus N. Lowry, Claude James Baxley of Virginia, Abraham Coles, M. D., Henry Howard Brownell, the Rev. Roswell Park, Willis Gaylord Clark, Mary J. Wines, M. E. Wood, E. H. Dewart, G. W. Cutter, J. N. McJilton, and the Chicago writer, Harriet Monroe, are, most of them, minor poets (some, perhaps, but poets by courtesy), whose tributes to our cataract are contained in their collected volumes of verse. In E. G. Holland's "Niagara and Other Poems" (1861), is a poem on Niagara thirty-one pages long, with several pages of notes, "composed for the most part by the Drachenfels, one of the Seven Mountains of the Rhine, in the vicinity of Bonn, September, 1856, and delivered as a part of an address on American Scenery the day following." Among the Canadian poets who have attempted the theme, besides several already named, may be recorded John Breakenridge, a volume of whose verse was printed at Kingston in 1846 ; Charles

Sangster, James Breckenridge, John Imrie, and William Rice, the last three of Toronto. The French-Canadian poet, Louis Fréchette, has written an excellent poem, "Le Niagara." Wm. Sharpe, M. D., "of Ireland," wrote at length in verse on "Niagara and Nature Worship." Charles Pelham Mulvaney touches the region in his poem, "South Africa Remembered at Niagara." One of the most striking effusions on the subject comes from the successful Australian writer, Douglas Sladen. It is entitled "To the American Fall at Niagara," and is dated "Niagara, Oct. 18, 1899":

> Niagara, national emblem ! Cataract
>   Born of the maddened rapids, sweeping down
>   Direct, resistless from the abyss's crown
> Into the deep, fierce pool with vast impact
> Scarce broken by the giant boulders, stacked
>   To meet thine onslaught, threatening to drown
>   Each tillaged plain, each level-loving town
> 'Twixt thee and ocean. Lo! the type exact!
>
> America Niagarized the world.
>   Europe, a hundred years agone, beheld
> An avalanche, like pent-up Erie, hurled
>   Through barriers, to which the rocks of eld
> Seemed toy things — leaping into godlike space
> A sign and wonder to the human race.[1]

Friedrich Bodenstedt and Wilhelm Meister of Germany, J. B. Scandella and the Rev. Santo Santelli of Italy ("Cascada di Niagara," 1841), have place

---

[1] Dedicatory sonnet in "Younger American Poets, 1830–1890," edited by Douglas Sladen and G. B. Roberts.

among our Niagara poets. So, conspicuously, has Juan Antonio Perez Bonalde, whose illustrated volume, "El Poema del Niagara," dedicated to Emilio Castelar, with a prose introduction of twenty-five pages by the Cuban martyr José Martí, was published in New York, reaching at least a second edition, in 1883. Several Mexican poets have addressed themselves to Niagara. "Á la Catarata del Niágara" is a sonnet by Don Manuel Carpio, whose collected works have been issued at Vera Cruz, Paris, and perhaps elsewhere. In the dramatic works of Don Vincente Riva Palacio and Don Juan A. Mateos is found "La Catarata del Niágara," a three-act drama in verse; the first two acts occur in Mexico, in the house of *Dona Rosa*, the third act is at Niagara Falls, the time being 1847.[1] The Spanish poet Antonio Vinageras, nearly fifty years ago, wrote a long ode on Niagara, dedicating it to "la célebre poetisa, Doña Gertrudis Gomez de Avellaneda." In no language is there a nobler poem on Niagara than the familiar work by María José Heredosia, translated from the Spanish by William Cullen Bryant. The Comte de Fleury, who visited Niagara a few years ago, left a somewhat poetical souvenir in French verse. Fredrika Bremer, whose prose is often unmetered poetry even after translation, wrote of Niagara in a brief poem. The following is a close paraphrase of the Swedish original:

> Niagara is the betrothal of Earth's life
> With the Heavenly life.

---
[1] The only edition I have seen was printed in the City of Mexico in 1871.

> That has Niagara told me to-day.
> And now can I leave Niagara. She has
> Told me her word of primeval being.

Another Scandinavian poet, John Nyborn, has written a meritorious poem on Niagara Falls, an adaptation of which, in English, was published some years since by Dr. Albin Bernays.

It is a striking fact that Niagara's stimulus to the poetic mind has been quite as often through the ear as through the eye. The best passages of the best poems are prompted by the sound of the falling waters, rather than by the expanse of the flood, the height of cliffs, or the play of light. In Mr. Bulkley's work, which indeed exhausts the whole store of simile and comparison, we perpetually hear the voice of the falls, the myriad voices of nature, the awful voice of God. "Minstrel of the Floods," he cries:

> What pæans full of triumph dost thou hymn!
> . . . .
> However varied is the rhythm sweet
> Of thine unceasing song! The ripple oft
> Astray along thy banks a lyric is
> Of love; the cool drops trickling down thy sides
> Are gentle sonnets; and thy lesser falls
> Are strains elegiac, that sadly sound
> A monody of grief; thy whirlpool fierce,
> A shrill-toned battle-song; thy river's rush
> A strain heroic with its couplet rhymes;
> . . . .
> While the full sweep of thy close-crowded tide
> Resounds supreme o'er all, an epic grand.

Of this class, too, is the "Apostrophe to Niagara," by one B. Frank Palmer, in 1855. It is said to have been "written with the pencil in a few minutes, the author seated on the bank, drenched, from the mighty bath at Termination Rock, and still listening to the roar and feeling the eternal jar of the cataract." The Rev. T. Starr King, upon reading it in 1855, said: "The apostrophe has the music of Niagara in it." As a typical example of the devotional apostrophe it is perhaps well to give it in full:

> This is Jehovah's fullest organ strain!
>   I hear the liquid music rolling, breaking.
> From the gigantic pipes the great refrain
>   Bursts on my ravished ear, high thoughts awaking!
>
> The low sub-bass, uprising from the deep,
>   Swells the great pæan as it rolls supernal —
> Anon, I hear, at one majestic sweep
>   The diapason of the keys eternal!
>
> Standing beneath Niagara's angry flood —
>   The thundering cataract above me bounding —
> I hear the echo: "Man, there is a God!"
>   From the great arches of the gorge resounding!
>
> Behold, O man! nor shrink aghast in fear!
>   Survey the vortex boiling deep before thee!
> The Hand that ope'd the liquid gateway here
>   Hath set the beauteous bow of promise o'er thee!
>
> Here, in the hollow of that Mighty Hand,
>   Which holds the basin of the tidal ocean,
> Let not the jarring of the spray-washed strand
>   Disturb the orisons of pure devotion.
>
> Roll on, Niagara! great River King!
>   Beneath thy sceptre all earth's rulers, mortal,

> Bow reverently; and bards shall ever sing
>   The matchless grandeur of thy peerless portal!
>
> I hear, Niagara, in this grand strain,
>   His voice, who speaks in flood, in flame and thunder —
> Forever mayst thou, singing, roll and reign —
>   Earth's grand, sublime, supreme, supernal wonder.

Such lines as these — which might be many times multiplied — recall Eugene Thayer's ingenious and highly poetic paper on "The Music of Niagara."[1] Indeed, many of the prose writers, as well as the versifiers, have found their best tribute to Niagara inspired by the mere sound of falling waters.

That Niagara's supreme appeal to the emotions is not through the eye but through the ear, finds a striking illustration in "Thoughts on Niagara," a poem of about eighty lines written prior to 1854 by Michael McGuire, a blind man.[2] Here was one whose only impressions of the cataract came through senses other than that of sight. As is usual with the blind, he uses phrases that imply consciousness of light; yet to him, as to other poets whose devotional natures respond to this exhibition of natural laws, all the phenomena merge in "the voice of God":

> I stood where swift Niagara pours its flood
> Into the darksome caverns where it falls,
> And heard its voice, as voice of God, proclaim
> The power of Him, who let it on its course
> Commence, with the green earth's first creation;

---

[1] *See* Scribner's Monthly, Feb., 1881.
[2] *See* "Beauties and Achievements of the Blind," by Wm. Artman and L. V. Hall, Dansville, N. Y., 1854.

> And I was where the atmosphere shed tears,
> As giving back the drops the waters wept,
> On reaching that great sepulchre of floods, —
> Or bringing from above the bow of God,
> To plant its beauties in the pearly spray.
>
> And as I stood and heard, *though seeing nought*,
> Sad thoughts took deep possession of my mind,
> And rude imagination venturing forth,
> Did toil to pencil, though in vain, that scene,
> Which, in its every feature, spoke of God.

The poem, which as a whole is far above commonplace, develops a pathetic prayer for sight; and employs much exalted imagery attuned to the central idea that here Omnipotence speaks without ceasing; here is

> A temple, where Jehovah is felt most.

But for the most part, the world's strong singers have passed Niagara by; nor has Niagara's newest aspect, that of a vast engine of energy to be used for the good of man, yet found worthy recognition by any poet of potentials.

This survey, though incomplete, is yet sufficiently comprehensive to warrant a few conclusions. More than half of all the verse on the subject which I have examined was written during the second quarter of this century. The first quarter, as has been shown, was the age of Niagara's literary discovery, and produced a few chronicles of curious interest. During the last half of the century — the time in which practically the whole brilliant and substantial fabric of American literature has been created — Niagara well-nigh has been ignored by the poets. In all our list, Goldsmith and Moore are the British writers of chief eminence who have touched the subject in verse, though many British poets, from Edwin Arnold to Oscar Wilde, have written poetic prose about Niagara. Of native Americans, I have found no names in the list of Niagara singers greater than those of Drake and Mrs. Sigourney. Emerson nor Lowell, Whittier nor Longfellow, Holmes nor Stedman, has given our Niagara wonder the dowry of a single line. Whitman, indeed, alludes to Niagara in his poem "By Blue Ontario's Shore," but his poetic vision makes no pause at the falls; nor does that of Joseph O'Connor, who in his stirring and exalted Columbian poem, "The Philosophy of America," finds a touch of color for his continental cosmorama by letting his sweeping glance fall for a moment,

> To where, 'twixt Erie and Ontario,
> Leaps green Niagara with a giant roar.

But in such a symphony as his, Niagara is a subservient element, not the dominating theme. Most of the Niagara poets have been of local repute, unknown to fame.

What, then, must we conclude? Shall we say with Martin Farquhar Tupper — who has contributed to the alleged poetry of the place — that there is nothing sublime about Niagara? The many poetic and impassioned passages in prose descriptions are against such a view. If dimensions, volume, exhibition of power, are elements of sublimity, Niagara Falls are sublime. But it cannot be said that superlative exhibitions of nature, some essentially universal phenomena, like those ot the sea and sky, excepted, have been made the specific subject of verse, with a high degree of success. The reason is not far to seek, and lies in the inherent nature of poetry. It is a chief essential of poetry that it express, in imaginative form, the insight of the human soul. The feeble poets who have addressed themselves to Niagara have stopped, for the most part, with purely objective utterance. In some few instances, as we have seen, a truly subjective regard has given us noble lines.

The poetic in nature is essentially independent of the detail of natural phenomena. A waterfall 150 feet high is not intrinsically any more poetic than one but half that height; or a thunder-peal than the tinkle of a rill. True poetry must be self-expression, as well as interpretive of truths which are manifested through physical phenomena. Hence it is in the nature of things that a nameless brook shall have its Tennyson, or a Niagara flow unsung.

www.ingramcontent.com/pod-product-compliance
Lightning Source LLC
Chambersburg PA
CBHW021156230426
43667CB00006B/429